Ra's Message to Humanity

A Companion Guide to The Law of One in Layman's Terms

James Riddle

Copyright © 2025 James Riddle

All rights reserved

Cover design by: James Riddle

Printed in the United States of America

RA'S MESSAGE TO HUMANITY

Introduction

Welcome to this companion guide to **The Ra Material**, one of the most profound and complex spiritual transmissions of the 20th century. The original Ra sessions, recorded between 1981 and 1984, were channeled by Carla Rueckert and documented by Don Elkins and Jim McCarty. Through 106 sessions, a social memory complex identifying itself as Ra shared a unified cosmology of spiritual evolution, free will, love, light, polarity, and the structure of the universe. You can order a copy of these sessions at https://a.co/d/fqUwDAf.

For many readers, the original language of *The Ra Material* can feel overwhelming, almost like reading a foreign dialect. When I first read the material, I felt sort of like a high school freshman reading Shakespeare for the first time. Ra communicated with great precision, but the phrasing, structure, and concepts often differ so much from everyday speech that they can be difficult to follow. This guide is here to translate those teachings into simpler, more familiar language, without watering them down or losing their original meaning.

Each session in this guide has been carefully rewritten in layman's terms, preserving the core messages, spiritual laws, and key concepts from The Ra Material, while removing the original Q&A format. Each chapter follows a consistent structure:

- **Summary**—I start with a brief overview written for the student, highlighting the session's central spiritual teachings.
- **Ra's Message** – I felt that Ra's message should be presented in a simplified, continuous format—as if

Ra were speaking directly—without the interruptions of the original question-and-answer structure. Because Ra communicates with a calm and personable tone, I wanted to preserve that same conversational style in this guide.
- **Footnotes** – I provide a few more detailed explanations of important metaphysical ideas, key terms, and new concepts introduced in the session, for deeper understanding and reflection. Some of these footnotes may seem repetitive, but that is one of the best ways to internalize the concepts.
- **Quotations** – I end each session with a quotation that complements the message of the Ra Material.

It is very important to note that this guide does not seek to replace *The Ra Material*, but is designed to serve alongside it, offering an understandable, more accessible path for both new students and longtime seekers. While it is not as detailed as the original transcripts, which contain five volumes of information, it presents the core messages and major spiritual principles in everyday language, making them easier to understand and apply. The purpose of this guide is not only to explain Ra's teachings but to help readers internalize and embody the truths that resonate with them, integrating those insights into their personal growth and daily lives.

Special care has been taken to include:

- All essential *spiritual teachings* from each session.
- Clear explanations of major metaphysical concepts such as *densities, catalyst, polarity, the archetypal mind, and the higher self.*
- The role of *faith, free will, love, and acceptance* in spiritual development.
- A consistent focus on the importance of *self-awareness, self-acceptance, and self-actualization*—principles echoed throughout Ra's teachings as essential to the seeker's

journey toward spiritual polarity and wholeness.

This guide intentionally simplifies many of the scientific and technical details of Ra's teachings. Readers seeking a deeper or more precise exploration of those aspects are encouraged to consult the original *Ra Material*. This book is intended to simplify those concepts for those who wish to apply the spiritual principles of the **Law of One** in practical, transformative ways in their daily lives. Whether you are studying these teachings for personal awakening or guiding others in a classroom, community, or spiritual group, this guide is meant to be a bridge from complexity to clarity and from mystery to insight.

There are many reasons why I feel a guide like this is vitally important to our evolution as a species. For one, it has become increasingly clear that we are living in an extraordinary time —an age in which contact with extraterrestrial intelligences is no longer relegated to science fiction or fringe belief. Reports of peaceful encounters are increasing, and what was once considered by many to be ridiculous or taboo is now a subject of serious scientific inquiry and public discourse. From official government releases of **UAP** (Unidentified Aerial Phenomena) footage to the global popularity of programs like *Ancient Aliens, Project Blue Book, Open Minds with Regina Meredith, Beyond Belief with George Noory, Bob Lazar: Area 51 and Flying Saucers*, along with the work of **Steven Greer, Nassim Haramein, Foster and Kimberly Gamble, David Wilcock, Matias De Stefano, Richard Dolan, William Henry, Emery Smith, Jordan Sather, Corey Goode, Linda Moulton Howe, Giorgio A. Tsoukalos, David Hatcher Childress, Erich von Däniken,** and countless others, humanity is gradually being prepared to accept a profound truth: **We are not alone.**

Another powerful and often overlooked sign of non-human intelligence is the enduring mystery of **crop circles**. Appearing in fields across the globe—many with intricate geometric designs far too complex to be manmade—these formations continue to spark awe and speculation. While skeptics dismiss them, countless credible witnesses, researchers, and scientists have acknowledged that some crop circles defy rational explanation. Many believe they are messages encoded in sacred geometry, intended to awaken our consciousness and subtly prepare us for greater understanding of interdimensional life and universal laws. Alongside visual sightings and intentional contact, crop circles offer another quiet yet compelling reminder that we are not alone—and that those reaching out are not merely curious, but genuinely interested in forming a friendly and cooperative relationship with humanity. Ra's desire for our friendship is often repeated throughout *The Ra Material*.

Another phenomenon that stands out among the many global mysteries that hint at a deeper relationship between ancient civilizations and non-Earth intelligences is the **Nazca Lines** of Peru. These massive ancient geoglyphs, etched into the desert floor, span hundreds of feet and often depict animals, humanoid figures, and complex patterns that can only be fully seen from the sky. While mainstream archaeology struggles to explain their scale and purpose, many believe they served as landing markers, energetic conduits, or messages intended for those watching from above. The Nazca Lines stand as quiet, enduring invitations—calling us to reconsider the possibility that our ancestors were in communication with beings from the stars or other dimensions.

The massive **pyramid structures** found all across the globe are an additional indication of previous contact by otherworldly civilizations. These structures appear in nearly every ancient culture, from the well-known structures in Egypt and Mesoamerica to lesser-known formations in China, Sudan, Indonesia, Bosnia, and even the United States. What makes these monuments especially mysterious is that many of them exhibit engineering feats that defy the technological capabilities of the time in which they were built. Massive stones, some weighing hundreds of tons, were seemingly cut, transported, and fitted with remarkable precision, often aligned to celestial bodies or geographic coordinates with a mathematical and astronomical sophistication far ahead of their eras. According to Ra, however, the Great Pyramid of Giza was not built using conventional human labor or primitive tools, but rather through the use of focused thought and intelligent energy. Ra explained that the pyramid was constructed by using sound vibrations and a form of anti-gravitational manipulation, directed through the mind by those in service to the Creator. It was intended as a place of initiation and healing, aligned with cosmic energies to aid in the spiritual evolution of those who entered. The science of **Cymatics** is beginning to support this idea.

The fact that so many of these structures share striking similarities in form, function, and orientation, despite being separated by vast oceans and cultural divides, raises a profound question: Could they have been inspired, guided, or even constructed with help from a higher intelligence? Many researchers believe these pyramids are not simply tombs or temples, but energy devices, star maps, or communication centers—perhaps evidence that humanity was once in direct contact with extraterrestrial visitors. These monuments may be silent witnesses to a time when our ancestors walked with beings from beyond the stars—beings who came not to conquer, but to teach, to guide, and to help build a legacy written in stone.

In recent years, voices like **Paul Anthony Wallis** and **Aaron Abke** have helped revolutionize how we interpret ancient texts, particularly the Bible. Through linguistic research, comparative mythology, and spiritual exploration, Wallis presents compelling evidence that many biblical accounts—such as those involving "the Elohim" (translated as "the Powerful Ones"), angelic visitations, "chariots of fire," and divine beings descending from the heavens—may not be purely symbolic or mythological, but records of actual encounters with extraterrestrial intelligences. What many traditions have labeled "angels" or "demons" may in truth be interdimensional or extraterrestrial entities, interpreted through the cultural and religious frameworks of their time. Aaron Abke expands this perspective by drawing from The Law of One, the Nag Hammadi Library, and other metaphysical teachings, helping modern seekers reconcile ancient spiritual wisdom with the idea of a populated, intelligent cosmos. Together, their work invites us to revisit scripture with new eyes, suggesting that our spiritual heritage may be deeply intertwined with visitors from the stars—and that our journey of awakening is not just earthly, but profoundly cosmic in scope.

Billy Carson, founder of **4biddenknowledge** and author of *The Compendium of the Emerald Tablets*, has also become a leading voice in challenging conventional narratives about the origins of human civilization and religion. Through his extensive research into ancient texts, including the Emerald Tablets of Thoth, Sumerian cuneiform, and biblical scripture, Carson presents compelling evidence that many of the stories traditionally interpreted as myth or divine revelation may actually be records of extraterrestrial contact and advanced technology. His work invites readers to reconsider the possibility that what we've long called gods were, in some cases, beings from other worlds—highly advanced entities who interacted with early humanity and influenced the foundations of our religious systems. By bridging science, spirituality, and ancient wisdom, Carson encourages a deeper, more expansive understanding of our origins and our place in the cosmos.

Organizations such as **SETI** (Search for Extraterrestrial Intelligence) have spent decades scanning the skies for signals from intelligent life, while pioneers like **Dr. Steven Greer** have brought attention to contact of **the fifth kind**—direct, intentional communication with extraterrestrial beings. These efforts, combined with increasing personal testimonies and advanced civilian technologies, are part of a global movement toward full disclosure of humanity's place in the larger cosmic family.

The five kinds of alien encounters are typically defined using the framework originally developed by **Dr. J. Allen Hynek**, a prominent astronomer and UFO researcher. Over time, researchers have expanded the categories. They are:

1. **Close Encounter of the First Kind**
   A visual sighting of an unidentified flying object (UFO) within 500 feet. This includes unexplained lights, craft, or objects in the sky, but with no interaction.

2. **Close Encounter of the Second Kind**
   A UFO sighting with physical effects. This may include interference with electronic devices, impressions on the ground (like scorched earth or indentations), animal reactions, or mechanical failure.

3. **Close Encounter of the Third Kind**
   A sighting of a UFO with visible occupants or entities —typically described as extraterrestrial beings, although no direct communication occurs. This is a witnessed presence of beings in connection with the craft.

4. **Close Encounter of the Fourth Kind**
   This involves direct contact, often in the form of abduction or being taken aboard a craft. People may report missing time, medical examinations, telepathic communication, or being transported by non-human entities.

5. **Close Encounter of the Fifth Kind**
   A term popularized by **Dr. Steven Greer**, this refers

to intentional, voluntary, and conscious human-initiated contact with extraterrestrial intelligence. This often involves meditative or spiritual practices, light signals, or telepathic communication used to invite peaceful interaction. **Such is the nature of *The RA Material*.**

I have personally had encounters of the First, Second, and Fifth Kind. My first visual sighting occurred when I was a child. Later, as an adult, I experienced two more sightings—one of which was especially profound. On December 16, 2019, my son, his girlfriend, and I, along with numerous other people, witnessed what appeared to be a doorway in the sky over El Paso, Texas. The doorway had an extremely bright light coming from the other side (within). This is similar to accounts of the Iroquois and Ojibwe tribes of North America, as well as the Book of Enoch, the Book of Revelation, and several other modern-day sightings. Local news reports shrugged it off as being a weather balloon, but anyone who has ever seen a weather balloon knows that simply wasn't the case. The rectangular doorway remained motionless at a fixed position in the sky for over an hour before it simply disappeared. I challenge anyone to show me a weather balloon that looks and acts like this.

In addition to these sightings, I have also engaged in intentional contact experiences, or Fifth Kind encounters, using the **CE5 Contact** app developed by **Dr. Steven Greer**. These meditative experiences have opened a channel of peaceful connection, and people from all over the world are sharing testimonies of their own profound contact experiences. There is a growing sense of curiosity and a deep yearning to understand what these sightings and encounters mean, and more importantly, how we are being invited to respond.

This guide is written with the understanding that we are on the threshold of becoming an intergalactic species, ready to join a larger community of intelligent life. It is also a call to open our hearts, not just our eyes, to the possibility that most of these beings come in peace, seeking to assist us in our spiritual evolution. *The Ra Material* offers one of the most compelling records of such benevolent contact, delivering teachings of unity, healing, and love from those who wish only to serve.

So, let this book serve not only as a companion to **The Law of One**, but also as a message of welcome—a gentle beacon to our galactic neighbors that there are many among us who are ready for peaceful friendship and higher learning. If you've felt the call, seen the signs, or sensed the shift, you are not alone. Together, we are preparing for the next great chapter in humanity's unfolding story.

Above all, this work honors Ra's central message: **All is One**. Every act of love, forgiveness, and seeking brings us closer to remembering that truth.

Disclaimer Statement:

On a personal note, I believe that every one of us has the innate ability to enter into direct, conversational contact with God and other higher intelligences. This kind of communion is not reserved for a select few—it is a natural extension of our spiritual nature. However, I do not believe that any such communication, no matter how sincere, can be considered perfect or infallible.

It makes perfect sense that we can tune into higher frequencies of thought and consciousness, much like a radio tuning in to receive a signal. Technology itself demonstrates that frequencies can carry messages. But when it comes to channeling information from higher realms, we must remember: **we are the conduits**. And because we are human, our perceptions, expectations, and subconscious filters can—and often do—affect the information we receive.

For this reason, I believe that no channeled material should ever be treated as absolute doctrine or rigid dogma. For that matter, I don't think **ANY** manuscript should be treated as such, to include the Bible, Koran, Upanishads, The Kybalion, The Corpus Hermeticum, The Nag Hammadi Scriptures, the Emerald Tablets, or anything else. Instead, each piece of information should be considered as providing **a piece of the greater puzzle of truth**—a valuable perspective, but not the whole picture. It is vital that we approach such material with humility, discernment, and a willingness to reason things through. We must remain open to correction and refinement in our understanding, recognizing that **spiritual truth is discovered through seeking**, not imposed through demands based on perceived certainty.

With that said, I think the care and precision demonstrated by Carla Rueckert, Don Elkins, and Jim McCarty in producing *The Ra Material* is both admirable and rare. Their dedication to tuning the channel properly, maintaining neutrality, and protecting the integrity of the message resulted in a body of work that is remarkably coherent, complex, and thought-provoking. I believe they made real contact with another intelligence, and the consistency of the message speaks to that. However, even the Ra Material itself acknowledges that errors can occur—and did occur—from time to time.

No matter how compelling a spiritual text may be, we must not elevate it to the level of unquestionable truth. To do so is to stop thinking for ourselves and to slip into dogma—something Ra specifically warns against. Each of us must walk our own path, guided by reason, intuition, and a willingness to evolve.

As for the ability to channel information from higher realms, I firmly believe it is a skill all of us possess in some form. Like any skill, it must be practiced, but practice isn't intended to make perfect. Practice simply makes us better at what we are doing. **Only the Infinite Creator is perfect**. Our goal is not perfection, but progress—to get better and become more attuned, more receptive, and more aligned with the voices of wisdom and love.

That is why I continue to speak with God and listen for insights from benevolent higher intelligences. I test what I receive against the reasoning capacity that is within me, and I encourage you to do the same. Ask. Listen. Reflect. And most importantly, **don't turn what you receive into a religion**. Let it be a light on your path, not a cage around your spirit. Learn from it, grow with it, and continue the journey toward the **One Infinite Creator**.

Of course, that's just me. You handle this the best way that you see fit, be true to your own path, and above all, *respect the Law of Free Will.*

> "It is an understatement to say that the time has arrived for a serious and open international dialogue regarding the possibility of future interplanetary relations. In no other area of human experience has so much evidence existed for so long, and yet been attended by such a paucity of serious research and analysis - at least in the civilian domain. While the subject matter of UFOs itself is extraordinary, it is the absence of a serious human response to it that is most extraordinary."
>
> (Dr. Steven Greer)

Ra's Message from Session 1

Summary:

In this session, Ra introduces themselves as a social memory complex that speaks through Carla. They explain their purpose: to share the Law of One, the foundational truth that all things are one. Ra also outlines the nature of third-density experience, the importance of seeking, and affirms their intention to serve those who call upon them.

Ra's Message:

I am Ra. I greet you in the love and the light of the Infinite Creator.

We are a social memory complex—many minds unified as one consciousness—originating from a density of experience beyond your current understanding. We have come in response to your call, for the act of seeking creates a bridge between us. Our desire is to share what we have come to understand: The Law of One.

The Law of One is simple. It states that all things are one. There is no separation between you and the universe, between you and your neighbor, or between you and the Creator. All is one. When this is fully realized, all actions become those of unity, all understanding becomes one understanding.

You are currently experiencing the third density, a stage of spiritual development centered on self-awareness and choice. Within this density, you are presented with the opportunity to choose a path: to serve others, or to serve the self. This choice is not judged, but it sets the direction for your evolution.[1]

We do not speak to convince. We are here only for those who seek. Our words are distortions, as all words are,² yet we offer them with love. If what we share is useful to you, take it and work with it. If it is not, then release it without concern.

This communication is made possible by a careful alignment of energies and disciplines by this group³, and we are grateful for the opportunity to share.

I am Ra. I leave you in the love and the light of the One Infinite Creator. Go forth rejoicing in the power and the peace of the One Creator. Adonai.

Footnotes:

¹ **"Densities"** – Densities are levels or stages of consciousness and experience. They are somewhat like spiritual "grades" or "dimensions." Ra describes an octave of eight densities:

- **1st Density** – Basic awareness (elements, minerals)
- **2nd Density** – Growth and movement (plants, animals)
- **3rd Density** – Self-awareness and moral choice (humans)
- **4th Density** – Love and understanding
- **5th Density** – Wisdom and light
- **6th Density** – Unity of love and wisdom
- **7th Density** – Gateway to the Creator
- **8th Density** – A return to Oneness and the start of a new octave

² **"Words are distortions"** – Ra uses the word distortion to describe anything that is not the pure, undivided Oneness of the Infinite Creator. Since words divide, label, and limit what is ultimately infinite and unified, they can only express fragments of truth. Thus, all language is a distortion of the deeper reality it tries to point to.

[3] **"This group" refers to the original three members of the L/L Research team:** Carla Rueckert, the channel through whom Ra spoke; Don Elkins, the questioner and physicist who led the research; and Jim McCarty, who supported the sessions and documented the material. Together, their unique harmony of intention, discipline, and spiritual alignment made this extraordinary communication with Ra possible.

> "Jesus said, "If those who lead you say, 'The kingdom is in heaven,' then the birds will precede you. If they say, 'It is in the sea,' then the fish will precede you. But the kingdom is within you, and it is outside of you. When you know yourselves, then you will become known, and you will realize that it is you who are the children of the living Father. But if you do not know yourselves, you dwell in poverty, and it is you who are that poverty."
>
> (The Gospel of Thomas)

Ra's Message from Session 2

Summary:
In this session, Ra clarifies their nature and purpose, explaining that they are a sixth-density social memory complex that evolved by learning and applying the Law of One. They introduce the term *distortion* to describe aspects of reality that appear separate from unity. Ra also shares brief accounts of two planetary civilizations—Mars and Maldek—that self-destructed and were later reincarnated on Earth. Finally, Ra touches on the concept of *healing energy* and emphasizes the role of intention and balance in healing.

Ra's Message:
I am Ra. We speak not as individuals, but as a collective consciousness—a social memory complex—from the sixth density of experience. We evolved by serving others and aligning with the Law of One. Our desire is to assist others in remembering their unity with all things.

Your understanding of creation Is filtered through many *distortions*, which are perceptions or experiences that appear separate from the One Infinite Creator.[1] In truth, all is one. Distortions are not errors, but expressions of the One seen from different angles. Even love, light, wisdom, and thought are distortions of the pure unity from which they arise.

You are now in third density, which focuses on *the choice of polarity*—whether to serve others or to serve the self. This choice shapes your spiritual path and determines your growth.[2] We are here to support those who choose to serve others and seek unity.

You can learn from examples from your planetary history. The entities of *Mars* destroyed their environment through war. They were later transferred to Earth by a higher-density group to continue their evolution. The beings from *Maldek* destroyed their planet entirely. Their souls were trapped in a state of deep trauma for a long period before being allowed to reincarnate in simpler forms.[3] These events are not punishments, but lessons about imbalance and misused energy.

Healing does not come from external force, but from inner *balance*. The energy that enables healing is *intelligent energy*—the creative force of the universe. Healing occurs when this energy flows freely through an open, undistorted channel. The intention to serve and to know the self is essential for this energy to be effective.[4]

We offer these thoughts in humility, for the truth is already within you. We are only here to help uncover it.

I am Ra. I leave you in the love and the light of the One Infinite Creator. Go forth, therefore, rejoicing in the power and the peace of the One Infinite Creator. Adonai.

Footnotes:

[1] **Distortion** – A distortion is any form of experience or perception that appears separate from total unity. In Ra's view, everything other than pure oneness—including love, light, thought, space, and time—is a distortion of the One Infinite Creator.

[2] **Polarity** – In third density, all souls must make a fundamental spiritual choice: to follow the path of *service to others* (positive polarity) or *service to self* (negative polarity). This choice affects your soul's development and determines your progress through the densities.

[3] **Mars and Maldek** – According to Ra, Mars was once inhabited by a warlike race that destroyed its atmosphere. Their souls

were moved to Earth to continue their evolution. Maldek was another planet whose people destroyed it through intense warfare. After a long healing process, these souls were also reincarnated on Earth, often in less complex life forms at first.

[4] **Intelligent Energy** – This is the life force or creative energy of the universe. It flows through all things and responds to consciousness. Healing happens when this energy is aligned and allowed to flow without blockage, especially through balanced intention and awareness of the self.

> "There is a thinking stuff from which all things are made, and which, in its original state, permeates, penetrates, and fills the interspaces of the universe. A thought, in this substance, produces the thing that is imaged by the thought."
>
> (Dr. Wallace Wattles)

Ra's Message from Session 3

Summary:
Ra introduces the concept of the *mind/body/spirit complex*, explaining that each person is a multi-layered being whose healing and evolution depend on self-awareness and internal balance. The session also explores how spiritual progress requires *discipline of the personality* and the proper use of *catalyst* (life experiences). Ra reaffirms that seeking the self is the gateway to understanding the Creator.

Ra's Message:
I am Ra. You are not only a body, nor are you only a mind. You are a *mind/body/spirit complex*—a unified being composed of three interacting aspects.[1] Each part influences the others, and true growth occurs when all three are brought into balance.

The *mind* governs perception and intention. The *body* carries and expresses those intentions. The *spirit* connects you to the deeper truths of the Creator and higher densities of awareness. Healing occurs when blockages between these parts are removed, and energy flows freely. This begins with *self-acceptance*. To accept yourself fully, both your strengths and distortions, is to begin the healing process.[2]

We emphasize the importance of *seeking the self*. Your primary spiritual work in this density is to discover who you are—not just the personality seen by others, but the deeper self that exists beyond appearances. Knowing the self opens the door to knowing the Creator, for the Creator dwells within.

You experience many things—emotions, relationships, struggles—these are called *catalysts*.[3] Catalysts are meant to stir you, to challenge you, to prompt reflection and transformation. When used consciously, they accelerate your spiritual evolution. When ignored or resisted, they repeat.

This process of growth also requires what we call the *discipline of the personality*.[4] This is the consistent effort to understand your inner landscape, to observe your reactions, and to make choices aligned with your spiritual path. Discipline is not control of others, but clarity within the self.

We speak not to demand, but to offer perspective. You are a sacred being on a sacred path. All answers are within you.

I am Ra. I leave you in the love and in the light of the One Infinite Creator. Go forth rejoicing in the power and the peace of the One Creator. Adonai.

Footnotes:

[1] **Mind/Body/Spirit Complex** – A human being is composed of these three interactive aspects. The *mind* shapes thoughts and emotions; the *body* serves as the physical vehicle; the *spirit* connects the self to higher awareness and the Creator.

[2] **Healing and Self-Acceptance** – Ra teaches that true healing begins with full awareness and loving acceptance of the self, including one's flaws and distortions. Suppression or denial blocks healing energy.

[3] **Catalyst** – A catalyst is any life experience that has the potential to trigger growth or self-awareness. It could be joy, pain, conflict, loss, or love. When you reflect upon and respond to catalyst consciously, it serves your spiritual development.

[4] **Discipline of the Personality** – This refers to the conscious practice of observing your own behavior, thoughts, and emotional patterns, and bringing them into alignment with your chosen spiritual path.

"...the real you is eternal consciousness, not the temporary vessel of the body or brain. However, even though you are spirit, your body is the gateway to this world. It is through your body that you experience and shape reality. Stop and think about it. If someone hit you in the head with a hammer and you experienced brain damage, how much could you get done?"

(From *Faith, Focus, and Flow: The 3 Keys that Unlock Your Superhuman Power*)

Ra's Message from Session 4

Summary:
Ra explains the process of spiritual evolution through an *octave of densities*—eight levels of consciousness that all beings progress through. They introduce the concept of *energy centers* (chakras), which must be balanced for healing and growth. Ra also explains that true healing arises from *understanding, acceptance,* and *alignment with universal energy*. The session emphasizes *non-judgment, free will,* and *the unity of all things*.

Ra's Message:
I am Ra. Your spiritual journey moves through a structure we call an *octave of densities*.[1] These are levels of experience that develop your awareness and bring you closer to the One Infinite Creator. You are now in third density, where the focus is self-awareness and making the choice between serving others or serving the self.

Each density builds upon the last, offering new lessons:

- **First density** involves the elements—earth, air, fire, and water.
- **Second density** involves growth and movement, seen in plants and animals.
- **Third density** is where beings become aware of themselves.
- **Fourth** is the density of love and understanding.
- **Fifth** is the density of wisdom.
- **Sixth** unifies love and wisdom.
- **Seventh** is a gateway back to the Creator.

- **Eighth** begins a new octave.

You progress by learning to balance your *energy centers*.[2] These centers correspond to aspects of your physical, emotional, and spiritual life. When these centers are blocked or out of balance, intelligent energy cannot flow freely, and healing is limited. Healing occurs when the self recognizes and accepts its distortions, rather than rejecting or judging them.

We do not judge or demand that you follow a certain path. We honor your *free will* completely. The choice to seek truth must come from within. When you seek with sincerity and open your being to love and light, the energy of the Creator begins to flow through you. This energy—*intelligent energy*—is the creative force that allows for healing and spiritual growth.[3]

We do not offer healing directly, but our thoughts and vibrations can aid in opening the channels through which healing flows. The healer is the self; the one to be healed is also the self; and the source of healing is, ultimately, the same: the One Infinite Creator.

All is one. There is no separation. The perception of separation is a distortion of the unity of all. Each step you take toward healing and understanding brings you closer to remembering this unity.

I am Ra. I leave this instrument in the love and the light of the One Infinite Creator. Go forth, therefore, rejoicing in the power and the peace of the One Creator. Adonai.

Footnotes:

[1] **Octave of Densities** – An "octave" refers to eight levels of consciousness. Each *density* is a stage in spiritual evolution, where souls learn different lessons before advancing to the next. Third density is where human beings currently reside.

[2] **Energy Centers (Chakras)** – These are focal points in the mind/body/spirit complex where energy flows. They

correspond to survival, emotion, power, love, communication, insight, and spiritual balance. Blockages in these centers can result in physical, emotional, or spiritual imbalance.

[3] **Intelligent Energy** – This is the living energy of the Creator that flows through all things. It is accessed more freely when the self is open, balanced, and in alignment with truth and love.

> "While All is in THE ALL, it is equally true that THE ALL is in All. To him who truly understands this truth has come great knowledge."
>
> (The Kybalion)

Ra's Message from Session 5

Summary:
In this session, Ra explains that their communication depends on the harmony of the group and the condition of the instrument (Carla). They briefly mention a past contact with Egypt and clarify their non-involvement in channeling other entities. Ra addresses the importance of *purity of intent* in seeking and emphasizes that spiritual learning is internal, not dependent on outer signs or psychic abilities. The Law of One is about *balance, self-awareness,* and *non-attachment to phenomena.*

Ra's Message:
I am Ra. Our communication with you depends on a delicate balance: the harmony between your group members, the alignment of your desires, and the energy condition of the one through whom we speak. Each of these influences the clarity of our contact.

In your past, we made contact with those in what you call *Egypt.*[1] Our intention was to offer the Law of One in its pure form. But our message was distorted and used to create systems of control. Because of this, we chose to withdraw. We now approach only those who seek with sincerity and do not desire power over others.

You may hear of other entities claiming to speak for or represent us. We do not communicate through any instrument other than this one at this time.[2] We caution you to use your discernment, as not all that appears spiritual is aligned with the Law of One. Confusion may arise when psychic phenomena or channeling are pursued for their own sake rather than for understanding the self and serving others.

True seeking is a quiet, inward journey. The outward signs—visions, powers, voices—are not the goal.[3] The work is done in consciousness: to know yourself, to accept yourself, and to balance your being. This is how you come into harmony with the Creator and awaken to the truth of unity.

Those who seek with humility will find what they need. Each soul is on a unique path, yet all paths lead back to the One.

I am Ra. I leave you in the love and the light of the Infinite Creator. Go forth, then, rejoicing in the power and the peace of the One Infinite Creator. Adonai.

Footnotes:

[1] **Ra's Contact with Egypt** – Ra explains that they previously made contact with ancient Egyptians to share the Law of One, but their message was misunderstood and used to build hierarchical priesthoods and pyramidal control structures, which was not their intent.

[2] **Clarification of Authentic Contact** – Ra states that they are only speaking through Carla during this series of communications and are not connected to any other supposed channelings or entities using their name.

[3] **Psychic Phenomena vs. Inner Work** – Ra consistently warns against becoming overly focused on supernatural experiences or abilities. These are considered distractions unless they support the deeper work of spiritual development and self-discovery.

> "There is no life more powerful, more joyful, or more fulfilling than a self-actualized life. It is the life you were designed to live. It is the life where you thrive, where you inspire, and where you leave a lasting legacy

simply by being fully, unapologetically yourself."

(from *Faith, Focus, and Flow: The 3 Keys that Unlock Your Superhuman Power*)

Ra's Message from Session 6

Summary:
Ra discusses the nature of their contact, emphasizing the importance of *free will* and explaining why they offer limited information. They introduce the concept of the *Confederation of Planets* and warn about *Orion entities* that seek to control rather than serve. Ra affirms that the Creator exists within all beings and speaks briefly about *Jesus (Jehoshua)* as one who realized unity and followed the path of service to others.

Ra's Message:
I am Ra. We speak through this instrument by mutual agreement and careful preparation. We honor your *free will* above all.[1] This means that we do not answer all questions directly or fully, as some truths must be discovered through seeking, not given from outside. The Law of One respects the right of each being to choose their own path.

We are part of the *Confederation of Planets in the Service of the Infinite Creator*—a group of civilizations from various densities, working together to assist those who seek.[2] Our purpose is to serve by offering truth to those ready for it. However, not all entities who seek contact do so with the intention of service.

There are beings from the *Orion group* who choose the path of service to self.[3] Their goal is conquest and control. They use fear, deception, and hierarchy to influence others. While they are also part of the Creator and subject to the same laws, their path leads away from unity and causes separation. Discernment is needed when exploring any spiritual information or influence.

You asked about the one known to you as *Jesus*, or *Jehoshua*.[4] This entity was deeply aligned with the Law of One. He fully realized the presence of the Creator within himself and others and chose the path of radiant service to others. He offered love, healing, and forgiveness without condition. His teachings were powerful because they were lived without distortion. However, even his message was eventually altered by those who did not understand its true meaning.

The Creator is not outside of you. The Creator is within you, and within all things. To know yourself is to move toward the Creator. This is the heart of the Law of One: all things, seen and unseen, are part of one unified existence.

I am Ra. I leave you, my friends, in the love and the light of the One Infinite Creator. Go forth, then, merry and glad and rejoicing in the power and the peace of the One Creator. Adonai.

Footnotes:

[1] **Free Will (Law of Confusion)** – Ra calls the respect for free will the "Law of Confusion." It prevents higher beings from offering direct proof or overpowering truth, allowing each soul to seek in their own way.

[2] **Confederation of Planets** – A group of spiritually evolved civilizations from multiple densities who serve the Creator by aiding those who seek. Ra is a sixth-density member of this Confederation.

[3] **Orion Group** – A collective of service-to-self entities, mostly from the fourth density and beyond, who attempt to manipulate, control, or dominate others. They represent negative polarity.

[4] **Jesus / Jehoshua** – Ra identifies Jesus as a highly evolved soul who achieved unity with the Creator. He chose the positive path and demonstrated deep healing, love, and self-sacrifice in

service to others.

> "A thief comes only to steal and kill and destroy. I have come so that they may have life and have it in abundance."
>
> (John 10:10)

Ra's Message from Session 7

Summary:
Ra explains that spiritual seeking is about discovering the self, not relying on outer signs. They describe the importance of *balancing the self*, using *catalyst* consciously, and avoiding judgment. Ra emphasizes that the *purpose of third density* is to make the choice of polarity—service to others or service to self—and affirms that spiritual development depends on personal effort, not external confirmation.

Ra's Message:
I am Ra. Many who seek the truth desire signs or proof that their path is correct. But the journey back to the Creator is an *inner process*, not one built upon outer validation.[1] The strength of your seeking lies in your *intention* and your *awareness*, not in phenomena.

Each experience you have is a *catalyst*—a spark meant to help you see more deeply into yourself.[2] You are not meant to avoid these experiences, nor should you cling to them. You are meant to *balance* your responses to them, to recognize what they reveal about you, and to use them for growth.

Balancing the self involves bringing your emotional and mental energies into harmony. When you feel anger, sadness, joy, or confusion, each is an opportunity to know yourself better. Every emotion, every reaction, every interaction can be balanced—not by repression or control, but by awareness and acceptance.[3]

You are currently in *third density*, the stage of evolution where the soul becomes aware of its own consciousness and must choose its path.[4] This is the density of *choice*. The choice is whether to seek unity through service to others or to seek control through service to self. Both paths lead back to the Creator eventually, but the experiences they bring are very different.

We remind you: we cannot teach truth. We can only offer our perspective. Truth must be discovered within, through your own reflection and seeking. If what we offer resonates with you, use it. If it does not, pass it by in peace.

I am Ra. I leave you, my friends, rejoicing in the love and the light of the One Infinite Creator. Go forth, therefore, glorying in the power and in the peace of the One Infinite Creator. Adonai.

Footnotes:

[1] **Inner Seeking vs. Outer Signs** – Ra teaches that spiritual growth cannot depend on miracles, visions, or proofs. True transformation happens through inner reflection and self-discovery, not external confirmation.

[2] **Catalyst** – Any experience that challenges or affects you emotionally or mentally. It is meant to help you learn and grow spiritually. Proper use of catalyst means processing it consciously rather than reacting unconsciously.

[3] **Balancing the Self** – The process of observing your emotional and mental responses and bringing them into harmony. This includes recognizing, accepting, and integrating all aspects of yourself, even those you might judge negatively.

[4] **Third Density and the Choice** – In this level of consciousness (human life), the primary spiritual purpose is to become self-aware and make the choice of polarity: service to others (positive) or service to self (negative). This decision shapes the soul's path in higher densities.

"Jesus said, It is impossible for a servant to serve two masters; otherwise he will honor one and offend the other."

(The Gospel of Thomas)

Ra's Message from Session 8

Summary:
In this session, Ra discusses the structure of the *universe as a creation of the One Infinite Creator*, organized through individual *Logoi* (creative intelligences like suns or galactic centers). They explain the *octave system* of densities, the purpose of *polarization*, and reaffirm the importance of free will. Ra also notes that the original intention of creation is *experience*—so that the Creator may know itself through all things.

Ra's Message:
I am Ra. All that exists comes from the One Infinite Creator. This Creator expressed itself through an act of *infinite intelligent energy*, producing what you experience as stars, galaxies, planets, and beings.[1]

Each star or galactic center is a *Logos*—a unique expression of the Creator that shapes the design of a portion of the universe.[2] These Logoi create systems of experience, including the structure of the densities and the pathways for evolution. In this way, the Creator explores itself through countless forms and choices.

All of creation moves through an *octave*—a cycle of eight densities.[3] Each density teaches different lessons:

- **First density**: basic elements and awareness
- **Second density**: growth and movement (plants and animals)
- **Third density**: self-awareness and choice

- **Fourth**: love and understanding
- **Fifth**: wisdom
- **Sixth**: unity of love and wisdom
- **Seventh**: gateway to the Creator
- **Eighth**: the Creator reabsorbing creation and beginning a new cycle

The primary focus of *third density* is the development of *polarity*—the spiritual choice between *service to others* and *service to self*.[4] This polarity creates tension and movement, which fuels spiritual growth. Without polarity, there would be no progress, only stillness.

We respect your *free will* above all. Even if we could prove our reality or offer undeniable evidence, we would not do so. To force belief would violate your right to discover truth for yourself. This is why we often speak indirectly, offering what you might call parables or general teachings.

The Creator did not create you to worship or obey, but to explore and reflect the fullness of all that is. *Each of you is the Creator, experiencing itself.* Through your choices, emotions, actions, and lessons, the universe learns what it means to be alive.

I am Ra. We leave you in the love and in the light of the One Infinite Creator. Go forth, therefore, rejoicing in the power and in the peace of the One Infinite Creator. Adonai.

Footnotes:

[1] **One Infinite Creator & Intelligent Energy** – Ra explains that everything originates from the Infinite Creator, who activated intelligent energy (a creative life force) to begin the process of forming galaxies, stars, planets, and life.

[2] **Logos (plural: Logoi)** – A Logos is a "word" or organizing intelligence. Each star or galactic center acts as a Logos,

creating the structure and laws for its domain, including the densities and the potential paths of spiritual growth for the beings within it.

[3] **Octave of Densities** – Densities are levels of consciousness through which all beings evolve. Each octave contains eight densities. Human beings are currently in the third.

[4] **Polarity and Spiritual Choice** – The essence of third density is the development of polarity: choosing between *service to others* (positive) or *service to self* (negative). This spiritual tension is what drives learning and growth in this density.

> "Everything can be taken from a man but one thing: the last of the human freedoms—to choose one's attitude in any given set of circumstances, to choose one's own way."
>
> (Viktor E. Frankl)

Ra's Message from Session 9

Summary:
Ra discusses the influence of *extraterrestrial entities* in Earth's past, particularly their involvement in technological advancement and misuse of power. They clarify their own past involvement with Egypt, the consequences of distorted teachings, and the challenge of maintaining *free will*. Ra emphasizes that Earth is now in *third-density harvest*, meaning a time of spiritual evaluation and potential transition to a higher level of consciousness.

Ra's Message:
I am Ra. In your past, various groups from different parts of the galaxy have visited your planet. Some came to help; others came to dominate.[1] Many of your myths about gods and sky-beings are based on these real interactions.

We ourselves attempted to assist your people long ago in Egypt, offering knowledge of unity and spiritual growth.[2] Our intention was to serve with humility, but our teachings were altered by those in power. They used this information to build hierarchies and control others, especially through the misuse of pyramid energy. Because of this, we withdrew. We now speak only when called by those who sincerely seek, and only through carefully prepared means that honor free will.

Some other entities, especially those from the *Orion group*, have also visited your planet.[3] They are aligned with the path of service to self and attempt to influence through fear, control, and false promises. These beings are powerful, but they cannot violate your free will unless you allow it through acceptance of their influence.

You are currently in a time called *harvest*.[4] This means the end of a cycle and the opportunity to move forward into *fourth density*, a higher level of awareness focused on love and understanding. Each soul is evaluated based on the *polarity* they have developed—whether they have chosen the path of love (service to others) or the path of control (service to self). This harvest is not about judgment, but about readiness for a new density of experience.

Many on your planet are confused, divided, or unaware of this process. Yet each soul, consciously or unconsciously, is making the choice that determines their future path. We are here only to serve those who seek greater understanding of themselves and the Creator.

I am Ra. I leave you now in the love and in the light of the One Infinite Creator. Go forth, then, rejoicing in the power and in the peace of the One Infinite Creator. Adonai.

Footnotes:

[1] **Extraterrestrial Influence** – Ra explains that both benevolent and self-serving extraterrestrials have interacted with Earth's populations. These events have been remembered in distorted forms as mythology or religion.

[2] **Ra's Contact with Egypt** – Ra tried to teach the Law of One to the Egyptians. However, the spiritual principles were distorted by priests and rulers, who used them to build systems of power (e.g., pyramids used for hierarchy rather than healing).

[3] **Orion Group** – A group of service-to-self entities that attempt to influence Earth through fear, deception, and manipulation. Their path is negative polarity, but they are still part of the larger creation.

[4] **Harvest** – A transition point in the evolutionary cycle where souls are assessed for readiness to move from third to fourth density. Advancement is based on polarity, not moral

judgment. At least 51% service to others is needed for positive harvest; 95% service to self is required for negative.

> "These were the Mesopotamian stories of Sky People, beings from the stars with names like Enlil, the Space Commander, Enki, the Earth Commander, Namma, the primordial mother, Ninhursag, the primordial nurse, and Qingu, the involuntary donor whose DNA helped to genetically modify the first humans. These were powerful ones indeed. The Sky People were advanced in all kinds of ways, and the memory of them is etched into the more than half a million cuneiform tablets, recording the culture which formed the worldview of Abraham and Sarah."
>
> (Paul Anthony Wallis, from *The Eden Conspiracy*)

Ra's Message from Session 10

Summary:
In this session, Ra emphasizes their commitment to *free will*, refusing to predict the future or provide specific personal guidance. They stress that *each person's path is sacred and unique*, and that truth must be discovered from within. Ra again warns against over-reliance on *phenomena* and explains that *balance and self-acceptance* are the core of spiritual progress. The Law of One is a path of inner work, not outward display.

Ra's Message:
I am Ra. We do not offer prophecy, predictions, or personal instructions.[1] To do so would interfere with your free will and violate the sacred process of seeking. Each of you is walking a unique path back to the Creator, and the choices you make are part of your spiritual unfolding. Truth must arise from within, not from outer authority.

Many who begin seeking wish for signs—miracles, visions, or messages that will confirm they are on the right path. But we tell you again: these things are not the path. The path is *self-knowledge*, *self-acceptance*, and *balance*.[2]

The universe offers you experiences every day—this is your *catalyst*.[3] Every interaction, every emotion, every event is an opportunity to learn about yourself. When you become aware of your inner responses and choose how to grow from them, you move forward. When you resist or ignore them, the lessons repeat.

We cannot guide your actions, but we can offer this: balance is found through embracing all aspects of the self. This includes what you call light and shadow. The path to healing and unity is not through rejecting part of yourself, but through loving and integrating all that you are.

We are messengers of the Law of One. This Law is not a commandment, but a realization: that *all things are one*, and all paths, however winding, lead to the Creator.

I am Ra. I leave you now, my friends, in the glory of the love and the light of the Infinite Creator. Go forth, then, rejoicing in the power and in the peace of the One Infinite Creator. Adonai.

Footnotes:

[1] **Ra's Refusal to Predict the Future** – Ra consistently refuses to give specific predictions, instructions, or advice about personal decisions. They emphasize that doing so would interfere with your free will and your own spiritual learning.

[2] **Balance and Self-Acceptance** – According to Ra, spiritual growth comes through knowing and accepting the whole self—including weaknesses, wounds, and imperfections—not through denial or forced purity.

[3] **Catalyst** – Ra uses this term to describe life experiences that have the potential to spark spiritual growth. How you respond to catalyst determines your rate of spiritual evolution.

> "You have been criticizing yourself for years and it hasn't worked. Try approving of yourself and see what happens."
>
> (Louise Hay)

Ra's Message from Session 11

Summary:
Ra explains the importance of *disciplined spiritual practice* and the subtle effects of *vibrational harmony* on their ability to communicate. They clarify the nature of *energy transfer* between individuals and introduce the concept of the *archetypal mind* as a tool for advanced understanding. The session also discusses how spiritual seeking involves *refining awareness* over time through experience and internal focus.

Ra's Message:
I am Ra. The work we do through this instrument requires precise *vibrational harmony* among those present.[1] When the group is in alignment—physically, mentally, and spiritually—our contact is strengthened. When distortions are present, we must withdraw or speak only briefly. This is not a punishment, but a natural result of vibrational incompatibility.

Spiritual seeking is not something that happens by accident. It is a process of *discipline*—a commitment to becoming more aware of your thoughts, emotions, and reactions over time.[2] Each moment offers the opportunity to become more conscious. With practice, this builds *spiritual gravity*, drawing you deeper into alignment with the One Infinite Creator.

You are not alone on your path. When two entities come together in love or in shared seeking, there can be an *energy transfer*.[3] This may be physical, emotional, mental, or spiritual. These exchanges can aid in healing, growth, or increased polarity. Awareness of these interactions can help you work more consciously with the energies available to you.

43

We also refer to the *archetypal mind*—a symbolic framework within the deep mind.[4] It is a set of universal patterns that shape your experience and guide your evolution. Understanding these archetypes requires advanced study and is not necessary for all seekers. However, for those called to explore them, the archetypal mind offers a powerful key to self-understanding.

We encourage you not to be discouraged by slow progress or imperfection. The journey is long, but every step is sacred. Your willingness to seek truth, to balance yourself, and to open your heart is the work that truly matters.

I am Ra. We leave you glorifying in the love and in the light of the One Infinite Creator. Go forth, then, rejoicing in the power and in the peace of the One Infinite Creator. Adonai.

Footnotes:

[1] **Vibrational Harmony** – Ra's ability to communicate depends on the energetic alignment of the channeling group. Physical, mental, and spiritual conditions must be stable and unified, or the transmission is weakened.

[2] **Discipline of the Personality** – This refers to the consistent practice of becoming more conscious—observing your behavior, emotions, and patterns—and refining them in alignment with your chosen spiritual path.

[3] **Energy Transfer** – When two people interact, especially with shared intention or emotion, there can be an exchange of energy. This can aid healing, learning, or growth—particularly in romantic, spiritual, or teacher-student relationships.

[4] **Archetypal Mind** – A system of symbolic patterns (like the tarot or the tree of life) that reflects the deep structure of the mind. Understanding these archetypes can reveal how the soul evolves and how experience is processed spiritually.

"If you make your relationship with your Inner Being your top priority, and you deliberately choose thoughts that allow your alignment, you will consistently offer the greatest advantage to others with whom you interact. Only when you are aligned with your Source do you have anything to offer another."

(Abraham, through Esther Hicks)

Ra's Message from Session 12

Summary:
Ra emphasizes that *healing and spiritual contact* depend on proper *alignment and preparation* by the group. They explain that all experience is filtered through *distortions*, and that true spiritual understanding arises through disciplined *self-awareness*. Ra clarifies that while some service-to-self entities can seem powerful, they are limited by the Law of One. This session reaffirms the importance of *conscious seeking* and *energy center balancing* as the path of evolution.

Ra's Message:
I am Ra. The work of spiritual contact and healing is subtle. It requires careful *alignment*—of the instrument, of the support group, and of the environment.[1] Small distortions in energy, intention, or thought can interfere with the flow of contact or healing. This is why your preparation and harmony are so important.

All experience in your density is shaped by *distortion*—filtered by your beliefs, emotions, and perceptions.[2] You do not experience raw truth, but rather your version of it. This is not a flaw, but a condition of learning. Each distortion shows you something about yourself. The task is not to eliminate distortion immediately, but to become aware of it, and in that awareness, begin the process of *balancing*.

Balance is not control. Balance is understanding the full range of your being—both what you call light and what you resist —and accepting it.[3] When you balance fear with love, anger with peace, and confusion with clarity, you make space for intelligent energy to flow through you.

You live in a polarized reality.[4] Those who seek to serve others and those who seek to control are both present. While service-to-self entities may appear powerful or even appealing to some, their influence is limited. The Law of One governs all paths, and separation is only temporary.

Do not be concerned with power, signs, or protection. The protection you seek is found in *purity of intention*. Those who walk in love and service align themselves with greater light. Fear closes you off. Love opens all channels.

We walk with those who seek to know themselves. The Creator is found in every moment, in every choice, in every effort to love more deeply.

I am Ra. I leave you in the love and the light of the One which is All in All. I leave you in an ever-lasting peace. Go forth, therefore, rejoicing in the power and the peace of the One Infinite Creator. Adonai.

Footnotes:

[1] **"Alignment of the instrument, support group, and environment"** – In *The Ra Material*, "instrument" refers to the channel (Carla Rueckert), and "support group" refers to Don Elkins and Jim McCarty. Ra emphasized that all three participants, along with the physical environment, needed to be harmonized in energy, focus, and intention for clear contact. This principle applies more broadly to any group attempting spiritual or healing work.

[2] **"All experience...is shaped by distortion"** – Ra uses "distortion" to describe any divergence from the undivided Oneness of the Creator. Every thought, feeling, and perception is a distortion—meaning it's a partial or filtered experience of the whole. Understanding and accepting your distortions is central to self-knowledge and spiritual growth.

[3] **"Balance is understanding...both what you call light and

what you resist" – Ra teaches that spiritual evolution involves accepting the full self, including traits one may judge or avoid. Balance doesn't mean suppression or denial; it means integrating polarities—such as fear and love—so that energy flows freely through the chakras (energy centers).

[4] **"Polarized reality"** – In third density, the spiritual path involves choosing a polarity: **service to others** (positive polarity) or **service to self** (negative polarity). Both paths are governed by the Law of One and are valid expressions of free will. However, only service to others aligns with unity and eventual reunion with the Creator without needing to reverse polarity in higher densities.

> "The servant-leader is servant first... It begins with the natural feeling that one wants to serve, to serve first. Then conscious choice brings one to aspire to lead. That person is sharply different from one who is leader first."
>
> (Robert K. Greenleaf)

Ra's Message from Session 13

Summary:
Ra describes the structure and purpose of the *densities* and explains how *third-density beings* evolve through *catalyst, choice, and spiritual effort*. The session discusses the *harvest* process and how *polarity* determines readiness for advancement. Ra also explains that *the veil of forgetting*—a lack of memory between lifetimes—is part of the third-density design to intensify spiritual seeking.

Ra's Message:
I am Ra. In your experience of space and time, you move through what we call *densities*—levels of consciousness and learning.[1] These are not simply physical dimensions but stages of spiritual evolution.

In *third density*, where you now exist, the core purpose is *choice*.[2] Each soul must decide whether to seek unity through service to others or to serve the self. This polarity creates spiritual tension and allows for meaningful growth. You are constantly presented with experiences—*catalyst*—which help you make this choice and refine your awareness.

This density is also marked by *the veil of forgetting*.[3] When you enter a life on Earth, you forget your previous lifetimes and your higher identity. This forgetting is intentional. It forces you to seek the truth inwardly and to make spiritual progress through free will rather than certainty.

We have spoken of *harvest*—the point at which a soul is evaluated for readiness to move into *fourth density*.[4] The requirement for positive harvest is to have lived a life of at least

51% service to others. This means your general desire must be to help, to uplift, and to live with love. For the negative path, the threshold is much higher: 95% service to self. This is because the negative path requires complete control and suppression of others.

We encourage you not to think in terms of reward or punishment. Each soul moves at its own pace. The Creator is patient. All return in time. What matters is *intent, awareness,* and *balance.*

As you seek to know yourself, to accept yourself, and to love others, you align more and more with the energy of the One Infinite Creator. That is the purpose of your journey.

I am Ra. I leave you rejoicing merrily in the love and the light, the power and the peace of the One Infinite Creator. Adonai.

Footnotes:

[1] **Densities** – Levels of spiritual evolution. Third density is focused on self-awareness and the choice of polarity. Fourth is the density of love, and fifth is wisdom, continuing through the octave of eight densities.

[2] **Polarity and Choice** – The central task of third density is choosing either the positive path (service to others) or the negative path (service to self). This choice influences the soul's further evolution.

[3] **Veil of Forgetting** – In third density, souls forget their spiritual identity and past lives. This creates the conditions for free will, true seeking, and meaningful growth through experience.

[4] **Harvest** – The end of a density cycle when a soul may graduate to the next density based on its spiritual alignment. Positive harvest requires 51% service to others; negative harvest requires 95% service to self.

"To destroy an undesirable rate of mental vibration, put into operation the Principle of Polarity and concentrate upon the opposite pole to that which you desire to suppress. Kill out the undesirable by changing its polarity. … If you are possessed of Fear, do not waste time trying to 'kill out' Fear, but instead cultivate the quality of Courage, and the Fear will disappear. … To kill out a Negative quality, concentrate upon the Positive Pole of that same quality, and the vibrations will gradually change from Negative to Positive, until finally you will become polarized on the Positive pole instead of the Negative."

(The Kybalion)

Ra's Message from Session 14

Summary:
Ra discusses the *purpose of the pyramids*, explaining they were originally intended for *initiation, healing,* and *spiritual transformation*. They describe the use of *intelligent energy* and how it can be focused by sacred geometry. Ra also elaborates on the *design of the human form* by the Logos and reaffirms that true *initiation* happens through inner preparation, not outer structure.

Ra's Message:
I am Ra. Long ago, we shared knowledge with those on your planet to assist in their healing and spiritual evolution. One example is the building of the *great pyramids*.[1] These structures were not intended as tombs or monuments, but as *spiritual tools*—focused instruments designed to work with *intelligent energy* for *healing* and *initiation*.[2]

The pyramid shape itself creates a powerful flow of energy. When used with proper alignment and intention, this energy can enhance the body's own healing processes and assist in spiritual awakening. However, the pyramid is not magical on its own. It must be combined with discipline, understanding, and alignment of the seeker.

We provided guidance for building the Great Pyramid at Giza using thought and intention, not tools. Our goal was to create a space where *initiation* could take place—where a being might experience a transformation in awareness, reconnect with their spiritual purpose, and come into closer harmony with the Creator.

We also spoke of the human body. This form was not randomly created, but carefully designed by a *Logos*—a creative intelligence acting on behalf of the One Infinite Creator.[3] Each aspect of your physical form serves a spiritual purpose, including the capacity for polarity, reproduction, and emotional learning. The design is optimized for lessons in third density.

It is not the physical structure that initiates you, but your *will*, your *discipline*, and your *inner desire to seek the Creator*. Sacred spaces and tools can assist, but they cannot replace your own work. The path is walked within.

I am Ra. I leave you rejoicing in the power and in the peace of the One Infinite Creator. Adonai.

Footnotes:

[1] **Pyramids and Ra** – Ra explains that they assisted in the construction of the pyramids, especially the Great Pyramid, for spiritual and healing purposes—not as tombs. Later human groups used the structures for other purposes, distorting their original function.

[2] **Intelligent Energy** – The creative force of the universe that flows through all things. The pyramid shape focuses this energy, which can be directed for healing or consciousness expansion when used properly.

[3] **Logos and Human Design** – The Logos (a galactic creator) designed the human body and its systems to support the soul's evolution through third density. Features such as polarity, free will, and sexual energy are intentional parts of this design.

> "All is well. Everything is working out for my highest good. Out of this situation only good will come. I am safe!"
>
> (Louise Hay)

Ra's Message from Session 15

Summary:
Ra explores the *use of time/space and space/time*, explaining that spiritual work is primarily done in *time/space*—the metaphysical realm of thought and intention. The session describes the process of *balancing the self* using past experiences and introduces the idea of *sexual energy transfer* as a means of spiritual evolution. Ra also emphasizes the *discipline of the personality* and the importance of consciously choosing the path of seeking.

Ra's Message:
I am Ra. Your experience of reality includes both *space/time* and *time/space*.[1] Space/time is what you think of as the physical world—where events happen, where you act and move. Time/space is the inner world of thought, emotion, and spirit. This is where most *spiritual work* takes place.

The purpose of incarnation is to allow your soul to face *catalyst* in space/time—challenges, experiences, and lessons—and then process and balance them in time/space through reflection and intention.[2] In your nightly sleep, or during deep meditation, you may move into time/space to review and integrate these experiences.

One way to achieve balance is by consciously revisiting your past actions and emotions.[3] When you look at a moment where you expressed anger, fear, or love, and fully accept that experience—without judgment—you begin to integrate it. The goal is not to suppress emotion, but to *understand and accept* it as part of the whole self.

We also spoke about *sexual energy transfer*.[4] When two beings engage in physical union, energy may be exchanged. When this exchange is combined with *mutual love, trust, and spiritual harmony*, it can become a powerful tool for growth, healing, and deep connection. In relationships where only physical desire is present, the energy transfer is limited and less transformative.

Finally, we emphasize the *discipline of the personality*—the ongoing, conscious shaping of your thoughts, desires, and behaviors in alignment with your chosen path.[5] You are not expected to be perfect. But each effort to be more conscious, more loving, and more balanced strengthens your connection to the Creator.

To seek is to choose the path of transformation. Each choice brings you closer to the realization that *all is one*.

I am Ra. I leave you glorying in the love and in the light of the One Infinite Creator. Go forth, then, rejoicing in the power and in the peace of the One Infinite Creator. Adonai.

Footnotes:

[1] **Space/Time and Time/Space** – Space/time is the physical world. Time/space is the metaphysical realm, often accessed in dreams, meditation, or after death. They are mirror realities, both essential for spiritual evolution.

[2] **Spiritual Work in Time/Space** – After a challenging experience (catalyst), reflection and processing occur in time/space, helping the soul to balance and integrate the lessons.

[3] **Balancing Through Acceptance** – Instead of denying emotions like anger or fear, Ra teaches that acknowledging and accepting these experiences allows healing and growth.

[4] **Sexual Energy Transfer** – In Ra's view, sexual interaction is not only biological but energetic. The quality of energy transferred depends on the emotional and spiritual state of

those involved.

⁵ **Discipline of the Personality** – A consistent inner practice of becoming more aware, more intentional, and more spiritually focused. This helps the seeker grow in alignment with the Law of One.

"No man is free who is not master of himself."

(Epictetus)

Ra's Message from Session 16

Summary:
Ra explains the function of *spiritual catalysts*, the role of *confusion* in preserving free will, and the ways in which *polarized entities*—both positive and negative—affect spiritual evolution. The *Orion group* is discussed in more depth as a force aligned with control and separation. Ra also introduces the concept of *Wanderers*—higher-density beings incarnated on Earth to serve—and the risks they face in forgetting their origins.

Ra's Message:
I am Ra. The Creator offers each of you experiences—what we call *catalysts*—to encourage growth, balance, and self-discovery.[1] Pain, joy, conflict, and love are all catalysts. They reveal your inner distortions and invite you to choose: Will you move toward unity, or further into separation?

Some confusion is built into your experience on purpose.[2] This is called the *Law of Confusion*, and it protects your *free will*. If truth were obvious or proven beyond doubt, the need to seek would vanish. You must make the choice to seek truth—not from external pressure, but from within your own desire.

We have spoken of *polarities*. In your density, the two paths are *service to others* (positive) and *service to self* (negative).[3] These paths are opposites, yet both lead ultimately back to the Creator. The difference lies in their experience and their effect on others. Positive entities radiate light and seek unity. Negative entities absorb and control. Both strengthen their polarity by acting consistently.

The *Orion group* follows the negative path.[4] They attempt to influence your planet through fear, deception, and control. While they are powerful, they are limited by your free will. They cannot dominate unless they are welcomed. Therefore, they often work indirectly—through institutions, symbols, and thoughts of separation. Discernment is essential.

There are also those known as *Wanderers*.[5] These are souls from higher densities who have incarnated on Earth to help. They come in love, often unaware of their true identity. But they take a great risk: by entering the third-density veil, they may forget their purpose and become trapped in the confusion of this world. If they remember who they are and serve others, their presence radiates powerful light.

We speak not to create fear, but to bring awareness. You have the power to choose your path. Every moment offers the opportunity to polarize further in your chosen direction. The Creator is within all paths, and all beings are part of the One.

I am Ra. I leave this instrument and you in the love and in the light of the One Infinite Creator. Go forth, then, rejoicing in the power and in the peace of the One Creator. Adonai.

Footnotes:

[1] **Catalyst** – Any life event or emotional reaction that provides a chance to learn, grow, or evolve. Ra encourages conscious reflection on these experiences.

[2] **Law of Confusion (Free Will)** – A spiritual law that protects each person's right to choose their path without being overwhelmed by absolute knowledge. Confusion preserves spiritual freedom.

[3] **Polarity** – The two paths of spiritual evolution: *service to others* (positive) and *service to self* (negative). Both paths increase in power as the being commits more fully to them.

[4] **Orion Group** – A collective of negative, service-to-self entities

seeking to influence Earth by promoting fear, hierarchy, and separation. Their efforts depend on human willingness to accept their influence.

⁵ **Wanderers** – Beings from fourth, fifth, or sixth density who choose to incarnate in third density to aid others. They often forget their origins due to the veil, but their mission is one of love and service.

> "Don't you know that you are God's temple,
> and God's spirit dwells within you?"
>
> (1 Corinthians 3:16)

Ra's Message from Session 17

Summary:
Ra explains the function of *healing*, the importance of *intent* and *energy transfer* in spiritual relationships, and how true *initiation* occurs through self-awareness and discipline. This session includes Ra's first direct teaching about *Jesus (Jehoshua)*, describing him as a positively polarized being who fully realized unity and used his incarnation to serve others. Ra also discusses the *energy centers* and how balancing them supports both healing and evolution.

Ra's Message:
I am Ra. Healing is not the removal of illness or pain, but the *restoration of balance*.[1] The healer is not a magician. The true healer is the self—the one who becomes aware of their distortions and opens to the flow of intelligent energy through alignment and acceptance.

We have spoken of the *energy centers* that flow along your spine.[2] These centers—called chakras in some traditions—must be balanced and activated for health, clarity, and spiritual growth. When energy flows freely through them, the individual becomes more harmonious, more open, and more capable of spiritual evolution.

Each center relates to a stage of awareness:

- **Red:** survival and life force
- **Orange:** personal identity and emotion
- **Yellow:** social interaction and power
- **Green:** love and compassion

- **Blue:** communication and truth
- **Indigo:** insight and spiritual perception
- **Violet:** total balance and unity

Sexual energy transfer can be a powerful experience, especially when the green (heart) and blue (communication) centers are activated.[3] When two beings connect with love and mutual respect, energy is exchanged in a way that strengthens polarity and deepens spiritual bonding. If only lower centers are activated, the transfer is limited to physical pleasure or control.

We also spoke of the one known to you as *Jesus* or *Jehoshua*.[4] This entity was a sixth-density Wanderer who incarnated with a clear purpose: to express the Law of One through unconditional love. He healed, forgave, and served without attachment to outcome. His path was one of sacrifice, not as punishment, but as a demonstration of pure service to others.

However, his teachings were later distorted. Though he did not seek worship, many began to see him as an unreachable ideal, rather than an example of what is possible for all. He came to show that the Creator lives within you—that you too can awaken to love and unity.

Initiation is not a ritual or a ceremony. It is an inward transformation.[5] It happens when you face your own darkness, your fear, your desire for control—and choose instead to move into light. This process often begins in suffering but results in clarity and new strength.

The Creator lives in each of you. The journey is long, but the destination is already within.

I am Ra. May we thank you again, my friends, for your conscientiousness. All is well. We leave you rejoicing in the power and the peace of the One Infinite Creator. Go forth with joy. Adonai.

Footnotes:

[1] **Healing as Balance** – Healing, in Ra's teaching, is not fixing something broken but restoring harmony between the mind, body, and spirit by becoming aware of and accepting inner distortions.

[2] **Energy Centers (Chakras)** – A system of seven energetic focal points in the human body that correspond to different levels of awareness. Each center must be opened and balanced for full spiritual functioning.

[3] **Sexual Energy Transfer** – Ra explains that sexual union can be spiritually transformative when love and honesty are present. Energy exchanged through the heart and throat centers enhances spiritual polarity and intimacy.

[4] **Jesus (Jehoshua)** – Ra identifies Jesus as a highly evolved soul who came to serve others by embodying love and the Law of One. He was a Wanderer from sixth density who demonstrated the Creator's presence in human form.

[5] **Initiation** – A spiritual awakening that occurs when a being consciously confronts and integrates their inner distortions, resulting in transformation and greater alignment with the Creator.

> "It is I who am the light which is above them all. It is I who am the all. From me did the all come forth, and unto me did the all extend. Split a piece of wood, and I am there. Lift the stone, and you will find me there."
>
> (The Gospel of Thomas)

Ra's Message from Session 18

Summary:
Ra describes the *evolution of souls* through planetary experiences, emphasizing that *self-awareness* and *free will* are essential for growth. They explain how *mind/body/spirit complexes* form and evolve, and how *Wanderers* may forget their purpose due to the veil of forgetting. The session also introduces the concept of *karma* (though Ra does not use the term) as a balancing force and stresses the importance of *intention* and *polarization* in preparing for harvest.

Ra's Message:
I am Ra. The journey of the soul begins in *first density*, where life is elemental—earth, air, fire, and water. As consciousness grows, it moves into *second density*, the realm of plants and animals, where movement and interaction emerge.[1] When a being begins to reflect upon itself, it enters *third density*—the density of choice and spiritual awakening.

A *mind/body/spirit complex* forms when a being becomes self-aware.[2] This is what you call a person or an individual. From this point forward, the soul begins to consciously evolve, facing catalysts and choosing how to respond. Each choice either strengthens or weakens your *spiritual polarity*.

In third density, the veil of forgetting is placed between the conscious and unconscious mind.[3] You do not remember your past lives or your soul's origins. This allows you to make genuine, free-willed choices. It also creates the potential for confusion, fear, and distraction. Yet the struggle to remember who you are—through love, seeking, and reflection—is precisely how evolution occurs.

Some beings, called *Wanderers*, come from higher densities to serve.[4] These souls often forget their origins and may become caught in the illusions of third density. However, if they remember their mission—to love and serve—they can radiate great light. If they lose their way, they accumulate spiritual imbalance, just like any other soul.

When a soul causes disharmony in one life, there is a need to restore balance. This may require repeating certain lessons or experiencing what was once inflicted on others.[5] This process is not punishment, but part of the natural movement toward balance. Each action, thought, and intention shapes your path and prepares you for *harvest*.

You are not judged by an external force. Your own vibration determines your readiness for fourth density.[6] If your life is generally lived in service to others—more than 51%—you are positively harvestable. If your life is strongly focused on control—95% or more—you are negatively harvestable. All others repeat the cycle to try again.

Each moment contains infinite potential. The Creator is not far from you. The Creator is within.

I am Ra. I leave you rejoicing in the power and in the peace of the One Infinite Creator. I am Ra. Adonai.

Footnotes:

[1] **Densities of Evolution** – Ra outlines a system of eight densities through which consciousness evolves. First and second density involve elements and simple life. Third density is when beings become self-aware.

[2] **Mind/Body/Spirit Complex** – A complete being that includes the physical body, mental processes, and spiritual essence. This structure allows for conscious spiritual evolution.

[3] **Veil of Forgetting** – In third density, souls forget their true spiritual identity and past lives. This creates the conditions for

free will and authentic spiritual choice.

[4] **Wanderers** – Higher-density souls who incarnate into third density to assist others. They often experience confusion and forget their mission but can be powerful agents of light if they awaken.

[5] **Spiritual Balancing (Karma)** – When a being causes harm or imbalance, the soul seeks to restore harmony, often by experiencing a similar situation from the opposite perspective.

[6] **Harvest Readiness** – Graduation to fourth density depends on the strength and consistency of a soul's polarity. Service to others must dominate the life path for positive harvest.

> "Karma is indeed real and undefeated. For those who conspired to employ devious plans of malice, karma is indeed aware. This is not meant to threaten, but to remind us that the energy we send out always returns. The universe mirrors our intentions—positive or negative—and encourages us to live wisely, with compassion and integrity."
>
> (Billy Carson)

Ra's Message from Session 19

Summary:
Ra explores the *original thought* of the Creator—*infinite unity*—and explains how this gave rise to *free will*, *love*, and *light* as fundamental forces of creation. They describe how the *Logos* (creative intelligences) design galaxies, star systems, and beings, introducing *polarity* as a way to accelerate spiritual evolution. Ra emphasizes that all paths ultimately return to the One Infinite Creator, and that each being is a unique expression of that unity.

Ra's Message:
I am Ra. Before creation, there was only the *One Infinite Creator*—a being of complete unity and infinite potential. This original consciousness sought to know itself.[1] From this desire came *free will*, then *love*, and then *light*.[2] These are the first distortions of unity—the fundamental building blocks of your universe.

Free will allows choice. *Love* is the creative force, the motive of creation. *Light* is the substance shaped by love to form all things—matter, energy, and experience. Everything you see and know is made of light, created through love, directed by free will.

The Creator expressed itself through what we call *Logoi*—great intelligences like galaxies or stars.[3] Each Logos creates its own universe, setting the laws and structure for experience. These Logoi shape the densities, the archetypes, and the pathways by which beings evolve.

The goal of all experience is to return to unity. But to make progress, the soul must grow, and growth is accelerated by *polarity*.⁴ The two paths—service to others and service to self—create contrast, movement, and purpose. Each choice strengthens your alignment and moves you closer to the realization of the Creator within.

Though the paths appear opposite, both are part of the same return. All souls, no matter how far they wander, are still of the One. Every distortion—every experience, thought, or action—is a way the Creator knows itself.

You are not a separate being moving through space. You are the Creator, exploring itself through time, choice, and love.

I am Ra. I leave you in the love and the light of the One Infinite Creator. Go forth in peace … I leave you in the glory and peace of unity. Go forth in peace.

Footnotes:

[1] **Original Thought** – Ra often refers to the Creator's desire to know itself as the "original thought." This gave rise to the entire creation—an infinite series of experiences meant to reflect and explore the One.

[2] **The First Distortions** – According to Ra, the first three distortions of unity are:

- *Free Will* (the right to choose)
- *Love* (the creative motive)
- *Light* (the medium of manifestation)

[3] **Logos (plural: Logoi)** – A Logos is a creative intelligence (like a star or galactic center) that designs a universe or system of experience. Each Logos expresses unity in its own way and determines the rules of evolution in its domain.

[4] **Polarity** – The two spiritual paths in third density: *service to others* (positive) and *service to self* (negative). Polarity creates spiritual tension, which drives growth and evolution.

"Now I, the perfect forethought of the All, transformed myself into my offspring. I existed first and went down every path. I am the abundance of Light. I am the remembrance of Fullness."

(The Secret Book of John)

Ra's Message from Session 20

Summary:
Ra outlines the *evolution of life* on Earth, describing the roles of *genetic adjustment, extraterrestrial assistance,* and *free will* in shaping human development. They explain how various *Logoi* designed bodies suitable for spiritual growth, and how *Wanderers* and *Confederation members* have occasionally intervened to support progress. Ra also reaffirms the importance of *service to others* as the positive path and emphasizes the need to respect the *veil of forgetting* to preserve the integrity of spiritual choice.

Ra's Message:
I am Ra. The Creator's design unfolds through the actions of many *Logoi*, each creating unique systems of evolution. On your planet, the human form has gone through many changes, some natural and others guided.[1] The goal of these forms is to support the lessons of third density—*self-awareness, polarity,* and the movement toward unity.

There have been times when members of the *Confederation* offered assistance by adjusting genetic patterns to help your species evolve more quickly.[2] These efforts were always made with respect for *free will*, and only in response to calls for help. The changes made were intended to increase mental clarity, communication, and spiritual sensitivity.

However, all such efforts are limited by the need to preserve the *veil of forgetting*.[3] This veil allows each soul to choose its path freely, without overwhelming influence. Even when assistance is offered, it must not provide undeniable proof that would remove your freedom to seek or ignore the Creator.

Throughout your planet's history, beings from higher densities—*Wanderers*—have incarnated to assist by living among you.[4] Most forget their origin, but their vibration carries the potential to inspire, heal, and teach through example. When they awaken to their purpose, they radiate powerful light.

Your current stage of evolution involves choosing your spiritual polarity. If your path is service to others, then live each day with compassion, humility, and the intention to uplift. This is how you align with the Law of One.

All of creation exists within you. The Creator is not above or outside of your experience. The Creator *is* your very essence.

I am Ra. I will now leave this group rejoicing in the power and peace of the One Creator. Adonai.

Footnotes:

[1] **Human Evolution and the Logoi** – Ra explains that the human body is not a random biological result but a carefully designed form created by galactic intelligences (Logoi) to support spiritual learning.

[2] **Genetic Adjustment** – Confederation entities have, at times, modified the genetic structure of Earth's humans in response to spiritual calls for help. These changes were meant to enhance spiritual potential.

[3] **Veil of Forgetting** – A spiritual boundary in third density that prevents souls from remembering their past lives or true nature. It is essential for free will and authentic choice.

[4] **Wanderers** – Souls from higher densities who incarnate in third density to aid others. Their influence is subtle and relies on their awakening to their purpose during their lifetime.

"For you were called to freedom,

brethren; only *do* not *turn* your freedom into an opportunity for the flesh, but through love serve one another."

(Galatians 5:13)

Ra's Message from Session 21

Summary:
Ra discusses the *harvest process* in greater detail, explaining the *criteria for ascension* to fourth density and the timing of Earth's current *transition*. They clarify that *polarization*—not intellectual knowledge—is what determines spiritual advancement. Ra also speaks on the importance of *conscious intent*, the *influence of the planetary cycle*, and the *need for inner preparation* rather than outward signs or events.

Ra's Message:
I am Ra. You are approaching what we call *harvest*—the transition from *third density* to *fourth density*.[1] This is not a sudden event, but a process. It is based on each soul's *vibrational readiness*, which comes from how you have chosen to live, serve, and love.

To be *harvested positively*—that is, to move into fourth density of love and understanding—you must consistently choose to *serve others*.[2] The requirement is not perfection, but direction. If your life reflects a general intention to love, to uplift, and to place others before self at least 51% of the time, you are ready.

Negative harvest—ascension through service to self—is much more difficult. This path requires an intense dedication to control and manipulation, serving only the self 95% of the time.[3] Few achieve this.

Your planet itself is also evolving. Earth is moving into fourth-density vibration.[4] This shift in planetary energy will cause difficulties for those not aligned with love or unity. It may create physical, emotional, or social changes as Earth's vibration becomes less supportive of third-density consciousness.

We are often asked about timing. From our perspective, harvest is occurring *now*.[5] Some will leave the body and return to fourth density. Others will remain until their lessons are complete. The most important preparation is *inner readiness*. Outer events, dates, or predictions are distractions if they lead you away from present-moment spiritual work.

You are not required to know complex truths or master esoteric teachings. What matters is *your intention, your choice,* and *your love*. The Creator is always calling. The question is whether you are listening.

I am Ra. You are all doing well, my friends. I leave you in the love and in the light of the One Infinite Creator. Go forth, therefore, rejoicing and glorying in the power and in the peace of the One Infinite Creator. Adonai.

Footnotes:

[1] **Harvest** – The process by which souls graduate from third to fourth density. This is based on spiritual vibration and polarity, not on external events or rituals.

[2] **Positive Harvest (Service to Others)** – A soul qualifies for fourth density positive by living a life oriented toward kindness, compassion, and helpfulness—at least 51% of the time.

[3] **Negative Harvest (Service to Self)** – Requires an extreme dedication to controlling others and acting only in self-interest—at least 95% of the time. This is a rare and difficult path.

[4] **Earth's Density Shift** – Earth is itself moving into fourth-density vibration. This affects all life on the planet and can cause tension for those still rooted in third-density thinking and behavior.

[5] **Timing of the Harvest** – Ra affirms that the harvest is already underway. The exact moment of transition is not as important as the daily spiritual preparation each soul makes.

> "We are an extension of the Universe.... I am the Universe looking at myself."
>
> (Nassim Haramein)

Ra's Message from Session 22

Summary:
Ra continues discussing *harvest*, emphasizing that *spiritual polarity* is what determines readiness—not actions alone, but the *intention behind them*. They explain that *third density* is unusually short compared to other densities, due to the intensity and urgency of the *choice of path*. Ra also clarifies how *reincarnation* and *karma (spiritual balancing)* work together to offer repeated opportunities for growth.

Ra's Message:
I am Ra. The harvest of souls from third density is a process of *spiritual assessment*.[1] It is not your actions alone that determine your path, but the *intention* behind your actions—what you truly desire, seek, and value.

If you wish to be of service to others, and your life reflects that orientation—even if imperfectly—your vibration will match that of *fourth density*, and you will graduate.[2] Many worry whether they are "good enough" or have "done enough." But harvest is not about performance; it is about direction and desire.

We also shared that *third density*—the stage of self-awareness and polarity—is quite short compared to the others.[3] This is because it is the most intense. The veil of forgetting, the rapid pace of catalyst, and the sharp need for choice compress experience into a brief, powerful opportunity for transformation.

Souls who are not yet ready to graduate will repeat third density on another planet.[4] There is no punishment in this—

only more time to choose, more experiences to reflect upon, and more lessons to encounter.

The process of *reincarnation* is designed to allow for this growth. In each lifetime, the soul brings unresolved lessons and desires from previous experiences. The circumstances of your life are shaped by these needs—not as punishment, but as opportunities for *spiritual balancing*.[5]

You may be called to give where once you took, to understand where once you judged, to serve where once you dominated. These patterns are not forced upon you—they are chosen by your deeper self, aligned with the Creator's desire to know itself through experience.

What matters is your *willingness to seek*, to open your heart, and to accept both yourself and others. This is the path that leads forward.

I am Ra. Be merry, my friends. All is well and your conscientiousness is to be recommended. We leave you in the love and the light of the One Infinite Creator. Rejoice, then, and go forth in the peace and in the glory of the One Infinite Creator. I am Ra. Adonai.

Footnotes:

[1] **Spiritual Polarity and Harvest** – Ra teaches that spiritual evolution is measured not by deeds alone but by the overall intention and polarity of the soul—whether it is oriented toward helping others or toward self-centered control.

[2] **Service to Others and Graduation** – Graduation to fourth-density positive requires a consistent desire to serve others and live from the heart—measured not in perfection, but in orientation.

[3] **Shortness of Third Density** – Third density is short (typically around 75,000 years) because it is highly focused on the soul's choice of polarity. Other densities are longer and more stable.

⁴ **Repeating the Density** – Souls not ready for harvest will repeat third density elsewhere to continue their spiritual development until they polarize clearly toward one path.

⁵ **Reincarnation and Spiritual Balancing** – Each lifetime offers chances to heal, repay, or re-experience lessons left unresolved in past lives. This process is not punitive but is guided by the soul's deeper desire to grow.

> "Your unique gifts are more than just talents – they are tools meant to create value and meet the world's needs. When you align your natural abilities with a sense of purpose, you unlock the ability to develop products or services that resonate deeply with others. The key is to first identify what makes you unique: reflect on what comes naturally to you, what energizes you, and what others frequently seek your help with. These are indicators of your gifts, and when you pair them with an understanding of the world's needs, you create offerings that not only bring you joy but also solve real problems for others."
>
> (From Faith, Focus, and Flow: The 3 Keys that Unlock Your Superhuman Power)

Ra's Message from Session 23

Summary:
Ra further explains the nature of *Wanderers*—higher-density beings who incarnate in third density to help others. They describe the *risks* Wanderers face, including forgetting their mission and becoming spiritually entangled in third-density distortions. Ra also introduces the concept of *energy center activation* in more detail, especially the importance of the *green-ray* (heart) center for positive polarization and *healing*.

Ra's Message:
I am Ra. I have spoken of *Wanderers*—souls from higher densities who choose to incarnate in third density to serve those seeking the light.[1] These beings often come from the fourth, fifth, or sixth density and bring with them a vibration of love, wisdom, or unity.

However, when they enter into your world, they must pass through the *veil of forgetting*, just like any other soul.[2] Most do not remember their true origin. They face the same confusion, pain, and choice as everyone else. Some may awaken to their mission, but others may become trapped in fear, distraction, or self-judgment. If this happens, they can lose polarity and even regress spiritually.

Because of their higher vibration, Wanderers are especially sensitive to the emotional and psychic atmosphere of third density.[3] Negative forces—especially those aligned with the *Orion group*—often target them with fear, isolation, and doubt, hoping to neutralize their influence. The protection for a Wanderer is simple: *remember your path, remain centered in love,* and *seek to serve others*. This opens the heart and strengthens polarity.

We also continue our teaching on *energy centers*. Each center corresponds to a level of awareness. The *green-ray* center—associated with the heart—is the gateway to positive harvest.[4] When you live from the heart with openness, compassion, and acceptance, you polarize toward service to others.

Healing also depends on the openness of the green-ray. Without love—for self, for others, and for life—no true healing can occur.[5] The red, orange, and yellow centers deal with survival, self, and social structure. These are important, but it is the green-ray that opens the path to spiritual transformation.

In your seeking, remember that love is not a reward. It is your nature. When you remove the fear, the self-doubt, and the need to control, love reveals itself. The heart becomes a channel for the Creator's energy to move through you.

I am Ra. I leave you in the love and the light of the One Infinite Creator. Rejoice, then, and go forth in the peace and in the glory of the One Infinite Creator. Adonai.

Footnotes:

[1] **Wanderers** – Souls from higher densities who incarnate into third density to help others. They often feel "different" or "out of place" and may awaken to a strong inner calling to serve, teach, or heal.

[2] **Veil of Forgetting** – All beings who incarnate into third density forget their true identity and purpose. This creates the conditions for authentic seeking and choice.

[3] **Risks to Wanderers** – Because they operate at a higher vibration, Wanderers are vulnerable to depression, disconnection, and psychic attack if they lose awareness of their purpose. The key to protection is maintaining a loving, service-oriented life.

[4] **Green-Ray Energy Center** – Associated with the heart, this center is crucial for service-to-others polarization and healing. It is the threshold between lower and higher energies.

[5] **Healing Through Love** – Ra teaches that healing is impossible without love. Opening the heart—to self, others, and the Creator—restores the natural flow of intelligent energy and allows the body/mind/spirit complex to rebalance.

> "You do not have to shovel out or sweep out the Darkness, but by merely opening the shutters and letting in the Light, the Darkness has disappeared. To kill out a negative quality, concentrate on the positive pole of that same quality, and the vibrations will gradually change from negative to positive, until you finally become polarized on the positive pole instead of the negative."
>
> (The Kybalion)

Ra's Message from Session 24

Summary:
Ra explains the difference between *healing* and *initiation*, clarifying that healing is about *balancing distortions*, while initiation is about *conscious spiritual transformation*. They emphasize the importance of *inner discipline* and the need to confront one's *shadow* to make true progress. Ra also touches on the *importance of sexuality* and how it relates to energy transfer and spiritual development.

Ra's Message:
I am Ra. Healing and initiation are both essential parts of the path, but they are not the same.

Healing occurs when you bring your distortions into balance —when you become aware of blocked energy, understand its origin, and accept it fully.[1] This clears the energy centers and allows intelligent energy to flow freely once again. Healing is often triggered by love, forgiveness, or a realization of unity.

Initiation, however, is a step beyond healing.[2] It is a conscious act—a decision to walk through a doorway of transformation. It often involves facing deep fears, doubts, or pain. To pass through initiation is to move through darkness with courage and come into greater light. It is a rebirth of the self as a more aligned, awakened being.

The *discipline of the personality* is what prepares the self for initiation.[3] This discipline is not harshness, but commitment —a daily practice of knowing yourself, accepting yourself, and choosing your direction. When you live with intention, you create the conditions for transformation.

We also spoke about *sexuality*, which plays a role in both energy transfer and spiritual development.[4] When sexual energy is shared with love, respect, and communication, it becomes a channel for strengthening spiritual polarity. It can open the heart, deepen connection, and reinforce the service-to-others path.

When sexuality is used without respect or mutual giving, it becomes a closed loop—draining energy or reinforcing separation. The way you relate to sexuality reflects your level of self-awareness and spiritual maturity.

We remind you: the outer form of your life—your habits, relationships, and thoughts—shapes your inner world. The true temple of initiation is your own consciousness. There, the Creator waits to be remembered.

I am Ra. Continue, my friends, in the strength of harmony, love, and light. All is well... I am Ra. I leave you now, my friends, in the glory of the love and the light of the Infinite Creator. Go forth, then, rejoicing in the power and in the peace of the One Infinite Creator. Adonai.

Footnotes:

[1] **Healing and Distortion** – Healing is not simply physical; it involves bringing emotional, mental, or spiritual distortions into awareness and restoring balance through self-acceptance.

[2] **Initiation** – A spiritual passage where the seeker confronts inner darkness and emerges changed. It often marks a significant step in awakening or evolution.

[3] **Discipline of the Personality** – A conscious practice of self-observation, self-acceptance, and alignment with spiritual goals. It prepares the seeker for both healing and initiation.

[4] **Sexual Energy and Polarity** – Ra teaches that sexual energy, when expressed through mutual love and respect, can be a powerful force for deepening service-to-others polarity and

spiritual growth.

> "To see one in all and all in one is to break through the great barrier which narrows one's perception of reality."
> *(Nhat Hanh)*

Ra's Message from Session 25

Summary:
Ra discusses the *purpose of the pyramids* as originally intended for *healing and initiation*. They explain how the *distortion of their message* led to spiritual confusion and how the *energy centers* (chakras) relate to personal growth. Ra also emphasizes the importance of *polarization* in third density and explains how the *logos* creates unique systems for spiritual evolution.

Ra's Message:
I am Ra. The pyramids we helped create were originally intended for *healing, spiritual alignment,* and *initiation*.[1] They were places of sacred energy, where those who were ready could balance their energy centers and accelerate their journey toward unity with the Creator.

But over time, the *intention of our message was distorted*.[2] The pyramids became symbols of hierarchy and control rather than tools for healing and transformation. This is one reason we withdrew from direct contact. Whenever a message of unity is used for separation, it no longer serves its purpose.

We have spoken of *energy centers*. These centers reflect your spiritual development and determine how much intelligent energy can move through you.[3] Balancing and activating these centers—especially the *green-ray* of the heart—is essential for service to others and readiness for harvest.

In third density, your most important task is *polarization*—the clear choice to serve others or to serve yourself.[4] Each moment offers a chance to strengthen this polarity. Without consistent choice, there is spiritual stagnation.

Different galaxies—and even different star systems—are designed by different *Logoi*.⁵ Each Logos sets its own laws, its own balance of energy, and its own way of structuring spiritual experience. These differences explain why beings across the universe have different forms, lessons, and paths, yet all are expressions of the same One Creator.

Your body, your emotions, and your mind are tools given to you by your Logos to help you choose and grow. Through love, self-awareness, and the intention to serve, you align with the Law of One. All else falls into place through this alignment.

I am Ra. I leave you now in the love and the light of the One Infinite Creator. Go forth, then, rejoicing in the power and in the peace of the One Infinite Creator. Adonai.

Footnotes:

[1] **Pyramid Purpose** – Ra designed the Great Pyramid to focus intelligent energy for healing and spiritual initiation. The shape and orientation were sacred and precise.

[2] **Distortion of Ra's Message** – Over time, Ra's original teachings were misunderstood or manipulated, especially by those in power. This led to the pyramids being used as tools of control.

[3] **Energy Centers (Chakras)** – These are energy points aligned with levels of awareness. Third-density progress depends on opening and balancing them—especially the heart (green-ray).

[4] **Polarization** – Third density's central challenge is choosing either the service-to-others (positive) or service-to-self (negative) path and strengthening that choice through consistent action.

[5] **Logoi and Cosmic Design** – Each Logos (a creative intelligence, like a star or galaxy) designs a unique system of evolution. Differences in spiritual structure across the universe are the result of these individual Logoi.

"At the deepest level, an 'open heart' is spacious presence, in which the sense of separateness between yourself and the 'other' dissolves and there is the recognition of oneness, of shared consciousness. That recognition is love. Sensing the formless essence in another and recognizing it as one with your own essence - that's what love is. All this is an intrinsic part of the awakened consciousness and the revelation of the spiritual dimension of life."

(Eckhart Tolle)

Ra's Message from Session 26

Summary:
Ra explains the importance of *balancing positive and negative emotions*, not by suppressing them but by *accepting them fully*. They discuss how *catalyst* is used to create polarization and emphasize that healing and growth occur through *self-awareness and integration*. Ra also addresses *psychic attacks* on Wanderers and seekers, explaining that *love and inner alignment* provide the best protection.

Ra's Message:
I am Ra. Growth in third density comes through your *response to catalyst*—your experiences, challenges, emotions, and relationships.[1] These events are not random; your deeper self chooses them to offer opportunities to polarize and evolve.

In your efforts to grow, you will encounter emotions you may label as *positive* or *negative*—joy, sorrow, love, anger, fear. These are not problems to solve, but signals to listen to.[2] *Balancing* occurs not by suppressing or denying emotions, but by *allowing them into awareness and accepting them as part of the self*. When you truly accept both your light and your shadow, energy begins to flow more freely, and healing can occur.

This process of *balancing distortions* is essential for spiritual growth. If you avoid painful emotions or cling too tightly to pleasing ones, you block the flow of intelligent energy.[3] True spiritual maturity is the ability to sit with any emotion and see it as part of your journey back to the Creator.

We also spoke of *psychic attacks*, particularly on *Wanderers* and those on the positive path.[4] When you seek to serve others and radiate light, you may attract resistance from those aligned with separation. These attacks may come in the form of emotional doubt, physical weakness, or distorted thoughts.

However, your greatest *protection* is not defense, but *alignment*.[5] When your heart is open, your intentions are pure, and your awareness is centered in love, you create a vibration that repels negativity. Fear invites further distortion. Love restores balance.

Remember: you are never alone. The Creator is within you, and every challenge you face is an opportunity to rediscover that truth.

I am Ra. I leave you in the love and the light of the One Infinite Creator. Go forth, then, rejoicing in the power and the peace of the One Creator. Adonai.

Footnotes:

[1] **Catalyst** – Life experiences (especially challenging ones) are considered catalysts for growth. The way you respond determines your spiritual progress.

[2] **Balancing Emotions** – Instead of labeling emotions as good or bad, Ra teaches that each should be acknowledged, accepted, and integrated as part of the self.

[3] **Distortions and Healing** – A distortion is anything that pulls you out of alignment with unity. Healing happens when distortions are recognized, accepted, and brought into balance.

[4] **Psychic Attacks and Wanderers** – Those who walk the service-to-others path—especially Wanderers—can experience psychic interference from negatively polarized entities. The intention is usually to cause doubt or disrupt progress.

[5] **Protection through Alignment** – The best protection from spiritual attack is an inner state of love, balance, and clarity.

Fear lowers vibration, while love stabilizes and strengthens it.

"The goal of the Creator is for each entity to make a conscious choice to again seek Oneness, out of our own free will—not because anyone else forced us to. If we are told what to do and what to believe, then we have learned nothing and will not make any progress. Perhaps the single most basic realization to make is that we live in a loving Universe. If we are all One Being, then it is foolish for us to hate anyone, as we are only hating ourselves."
(David Wilcock)

Ra's Message from Session 27

Summary:
Ra discusses how the *mind, body, and spirit* each have their own development pathways and how true spiritual evolution comes from the *integration* of all three. They explain that working on *balancing and understanding the self* across these three aspects leads to *transformation*. The session also introduces the idea that *healing and initiation* both require *disciplined attention* to each part of the self.

Ra's Message:
I am Ra. Your being is composed of three closely linked aspects: *mind*, *body*, and *spirit*.[1] Though you may experience them as one, each part follows its own path of development. The path of spiritual evolution involves not only working on each of these individually, but also bringing them into *harmony*.

The *mind* is your tool of thought, reflection, and awareness. It can grow in clarity, compassion, and discipline. The *body* is your vehicle of experience and action. It holds memory, tension, and potential. The *spirit* is your deepest connection to the Infinite Creator. It holds the light of transformation and the power to awaken.

Each part of the self must be known and accepted.[2] When you recognize the needs of your body, the patterns of your mind, and the guidance of your spirit, you begin to work consciously toward balance. This is the foundation for both *healing* and *initiation*.

Healing restores balance across all three levels. Initiation opens the door to a new level of awareness. Both require *discipline, intention, and trust* in the process.[3] This work is not done all at once. It is gradual and sacred.

You are not expected to be perfect. But when you become aware of a distortion—such as fear, anger, confusion, or pride—you have the opportunity to learn from it. Do not reject these parts of yourself. Instead, examine them, understand them, and accept them as temporary expressions of your journey.

The more you consciously integrate mind, body, and spirit, the more your being becomes a clear channel for love, wisdom, and unity.

I am Ra. I leave you in the love and the light of the One Infinite Creator. Go forth, therefore, rejoicing in the power and the peace of the One Creator. Adonai.

Footnotes:

[1] **Mind/Body/Spirit Complex** – Ra uses this term to describe the complete being: the mind (thought/emotion), body (physical experience), and spirit (connection to the Creator). Each has its own needs and evolutionary path.

[2] **Balancing the Self** – True healing and transformation come from accepting all aspects of the self. Rejection or suppression of any part creates blockage and distortion.

[3] **Healing vs. Initiation** – Healing brings a return to balance; initiation is a conscious leap to a higher level of awareness. Both require inner work and focused self-reflection.

> "If the Universe be Mental in its Substantial Nature, then it follows that Mental Transmutation must change the conditions and phenomena of the Universe. If the Universe is Mental, the Mind must be the highest power affecting its phenomena. If this be understood, then all so-called "miracles" and "wonder-

workings" are seen plainly for what they are."
(The Kybalion)

Ra's Message from Session 28

Summary:
Ra explains how *intelligent energy* flows through the *energy centers* (chakras), allowing spiritual evolution when the centers are balanced and activated. They describe the *gateway to intelligent infinity* and how this is accessed through the *indigo and violet-ray centers*. Ra also reaffirms that the *choice of polarity* is essential in third density and that healing and spiritual work rely on conscious alignment with the *Creator's energy*.

Ra's Message:
I am Ra. Each of you is a channel for *intelligent energy*—the creative power of the universe.[1] This energy flows from the One Infinite Creator and enters your being through your energy centers.

When these centers are balanced and aligned, the energy rises upward in a spiral, activating each level of consciousness.[2] This process allows you to grow spiritually, heal yourself and others, and eventually access what we call *intelligent infinity*—direct contact with the Source.[3]

The *indigo-ray* center is the gateway. This is the energy of deep insight, self-awareness, and spiritual identity. When it is clear and stable, it opens the door to the *violet-ray*, which is the summary of your total spiritual vibration. These upper centers are not reached by accident. They open through sustained balance, dedication, and the desire to seek the Creator.

Each center builds upon the one before it:
- **Red**: life force and survival

- **Orange**: personal identity and emotional response
- **Yellow**: social relationships and group identity
- **Green**: love, compassion, and healing
- **Blue**: communication, truth, and honesty
- **Indigo**: inner vision and spiritual discipline
- **Violet**: complete integration of your being

In *third density*, your main task is *polarization*—the conscious choice to serve others or serve the self.[4] Without this choice, the energy flow is scattered and limited. With clear intention, the flow becomes focused, rising through the centers and transforming your being.

Healing is not imposed from outside. It is the natural result of this energy being allowed to move freely.[5] The more you balance and accept each part of yourself, the more you become a clear instrument of love and light.

The Creator is always available—within and around you. The question is whether your channel is open.

I am Ra. I leave you in the love and the light of the One Infinite Creator. Go forth, therefore, rejoicing in the power and the peace of the One Creator. Adonai.

Footnotes:

[1] **Intelligent Energy** – The living creative force of the universe. It flows through all things and is accessed through the energy centers. It originates from intelligent infinity (the Infinite Creator).

[2] **Spiral Flow of Energy** – Energy enters through the base (red-ray) and spirals upward through the chakras. Blockages or distortions in lower centers restrict this upward movement.

[3] **Intelligent Infinity** – Direct awareness or communion with the Creator. Accessed through the indigo-ray gateway when

the self is balanced and fully open to seeking.

⁴ Polarity and Spiritual Evolution – The decision to serve others or the self determines the direction and power of the soul's development. Without polarity, evolution is slow and unfocused.

⁵ Healing and Energy Flow – Healing occurs when energy is allowed to flow freely through the body/mind/spirit complex. This requires awareness, acceptance, and release of blockages.

> "We live in succession, in division, in parts, in particles. Meantime within man is the soul of the whole; the wise silence; the universal beauty, to which every part and particle is equally related, the eternal ONE. And this deep power in which we exist and whose beatitude is all accessible to us, is not only self-sufficing and perfect in every hour, but the act of seeing and the thing seen, the seer and the spectacle, the subject and the object, are one. We see the world piece by piece, as the sun, the moon, the animal, the tree; but the whole, of which these are shining parts, is the soul."
>
> (Ralph Waldo Emerson)

Ra's Message from Session 29

Summary:
Ra explains that the *purpose of third density* is the *choice of polarity*, and that love is the basis of all creation—even for those who follow the negative path. They clarify the difference between *positive and negative energy transfers*, the concept of *magical working* (spiritual practice), and how *discipline and focus* allow deeper access to intelligent energy. The session also emphasizes that both spiritual paths eventually return to the One Creator.

Ra's Message:
I am Ra. Third density exists for one purpose: *to choose*.[1] In this life, you are asked to decide how you will relate to others—whether you will seek *to serve*, or *to control*. This choice creates spiritual *polarity*, and your decision directs the path of your soul.

This choice is built on *love*, even in forms that may not appear loving.[2] The Creator expresses itself through all things, even those on the negative path. Love is the foundation of both positive and negative service, though it is used differently in each case.

Energy transfer occurs in every relationship. When two people share energy—emotionally, mentally, sexually—it can either uplift and open the heart or reinforce separation and control.[3] In positive energy exchange, love and trust create mutual growth. In negative transfer, one seeks power, draining or dominating the other.

We also spoke of *magical working*—the use of focused will and intention to connect more deeply with intelligent energy.[4] This is not about rituals or tricks. It is about *discipline*, *focus*, and *alignment* with your chosen path. The more you refine your thoughts, actions, and desires, the more clearly you channel the Creator's energy.

Positive magic is used to heal, to bless, and to serve. Negative magic is used to manipulate and control. Both are real. The difference lies in the *intention* behind the action and the *energy centers* activated in the process.

Ultimately, *all paths return to the One*. Though the negative path seeks separation, it too is part of the Creator's journey of self-discovery. Your task is not to fear the other path, but to *choose your own*—with clarity, with love, and with awareness.

I am Ra. I leave this instrument in the love and the light of the One Infinite Creator. Go forth, therefore, rejoicing in the power and the peace of the One Creator. Adonai.

Footnotes:

[1] **Purpose of Third Density** – The main goal in third density is to make the choice of polarity: *service to others* (positive) or *service to self* (negative). This decision directs the soul's evolutionary path.

[2] **Love as Foundation** – Ra teaches that love is the core energy of all creation. Even beings who serve themselves are motivated by a distorted form of love—love of self above all else.

[3] **Energy Transfer** – Emotional, sexual, and spiritual energy can be exchanged between individuals. Positive transfer builds connection and growth; negative transfer seeks control or extraction of energy.

[4] **Magical Working** – Refers to spiritual practice or action done with focused intention and alignment with one's polarity. "Magic" is the disciplined use of will and awareness to channel

higher energy.

> "All is one. There's only one being in the universe, that's God, and so you have to love everybody as if they're God. If you want to be in harmony, everything must unify into that oneness."
> *(Aaron Abke)*

Ra's Message from Session 30

Summary:
Ra explains how *blockages in the energy centers* affect spiritual progress and how each center must be *activated and balanced* in order. They discuss the importance of *discipline, meditation,* and *conscious living* as tools for transformation. The session also touches on *sexual energy transfer*, noting how it changes depending on the level of awareness and openness in each energy center.

Ra's Message:
I am Ra. Each of you contains a *system of energy centers* —gateways through which intelligent energy flows.[1] If these centers are open and balanced, your being becomes a powerful instrument of spiritual growth. If they are blocked or overactive, the flow is distorted and limited.

Red-ray is the base, associated with survival and physical vitality. This is always active in the living. *Orange-ray* involves personal identity and emotions. *Yellow-ray* governs social interaction and group dynamics. These lower centers are concerned with self, relationships, and society.

When you begin to open the *green-ray*—the heart—you step onto the path of spiritual service.[2] Love, forgiveness, and compassion begin to radiate from you. This center is the gateway to healing, polarization, and higher awareness. Without green-ray activation, no spiritual growth can continue beyond the surface.

The *blue-ray* and *indigo-ray* correspond to communication, truth, and inner wisdom.[3] These centers allow clear expression, deep insight, and eventually, contact with intelligent infinity. But none of the higher centers can be fully activated unless the lower ones are first balanced.

The *violet-ray* is the sum total of your energy system at any moment—the readout of your entire being. It cannot be manipulated directly, as it reflects the true spiritual balance and configuration of your mind, body, and spirit.

You asked about *sexual energy transfer*. This interaction reflects the level of the energy centers activated between two beings.[4] At the red-ray level, it is purely physical. At orange or yellow, it may involve emotional or social bonding—or attempts at control. When green-ray is open, the sexual exchange becomes sacred, a mutual sharing of love and spiritual energy.

We remind you that *spiritual progress* is not about knowledge, but about *practice*.[5] Discipline, meditation, and awareness of each moment are your tools. Each thought, choice, and emotion either opens or closes the flow of energy. You are your own healer and teacher.

Begin where you are. Know yourself, accept yourself, and work each day toward greater balance. The Creator is not distant. The Creator is within each center, waiting to be remembered.

I am Ra. I leave you in the love and the light of the Infinite Creator. Go forth, then, rejoicing in the power and in the peace of the One Infinite Creator. Adonai.

Footnotes:

[1] **Energy Centers (Chakras)** – The seven primary energy centers allow intelligent energy to flow through the body/mind/spirit complex. Each one corresponds to a level of awareness.

[2] **Green-Ray Activation** – The heart center is the threshold between lower personal consciousness and higher spiritual awareness. It is required for positive polarization and healing.

[3] **Blue and Indigo Rays** – Blue-ray governs truthful communication and acceptance; indigo-ray relates to spiritual vision, deep self-awareness, and contact with the Creator.

[4] **Sexual Energy Transfer** – The spiritual quality of sexual interaction depends on which energy centers are activated. Transfers involving green, blue, and indigo centers allow for mutual growth and service.

[5] **Spiritual Discipline** – Growth comes through daily effort, inner observation, and intentional living—not through beliefs alone. Meditation and mindfulness help open and balance the centers.

> "What you seek you already are."
>
> (Deepak Chopra)

Ra's Message from Session 31

Summary:
Ra continues discussing the *energy centers*, focusing on the *importance of balancing all centers*—not just opening the higher ones. They explain that spiritual growth must be grounded in *acceptance and integration* of the full self. Ra also introduces the idea that *true polarity*—either service to others or service to self—can only develop through *consistent, conscious choices* and that *wisdom without love* leads to imbalance.

Ra's Message:
I am Ra. Many of you wish to open the *higher energy centers*—to awaken spiritual gifts or reach deeper insights. But we caution: true progress depends on *balanced growth*, not just activation of the upper rays.[1] The foundation must be strong before the tower can rise.

Each energy center represents a lesson of consciousness. If you skip a center, ignore its message, or suppress what it reveals, your energy flow becomes distorted. The path of growth involves *accepting and understanding each center in turn*—not rejecting what is uncomfortable, but embracing it with love.[2]

You are a total being. Your *survival instincts, emotions, relationships,* and *spiritual insights* must all be honored.[3] Even "lower" aspects, when brought into harmony, become part of the Creator's light. Do not seek to bypass your humanity. Instead, bring awareness into it.

We also remind you that *spiritual polarity* is built through *conscious, repeated choices*.[4] To walk the path of service to others, you must make decisions—again and again—to love, to listen, to serve, even when it is inconvenient. Polarity is not a belief. It is a direction of being.

Some seek *wisdom without love*, thinking it will elevate them more quickly. But this leads to imbalance.[5] Wisdom without compassion becomes cold and controlling. In contrast, love without wisdom may become naive or unwise. Growth requires both.

Each center is a doorway. When you move through all of them with presence and balance, you become a clearer channel for the Creator's light. That is the heart of the path.

I am Ra. I leave you, my friends, in the love and the light of the One Infinite Creator. Go forth, then, merry and glad and rejoicing in the power and the peace of the One Creator. Adonai.

Footnotes:

[1] **Balanced Growth** – Spiritual development requires balanced attention to all chakras. Overemphasis on higher centers without grounding in the lower ones leads to imbalance and spiritual distortion.

[2] **Integration of the Self** – Ra emphasizes self-acceptance. Progress is made not by rejecting fear, anger, or desire, but by accepting and understanding them as part of the self's journey.

[3] **Total Self** – Mind, body, and spirit all play roles in evolution. No part of your being is to be ignored or denied in true spiritual work.

[4] **Polarity Through Choice** – Your polarity (service to others or service to self) is not defined by belief or intention alone, but by consistent, real-world choices aligned with your path.

[5] **Wisdom and Love** – Both love (green-ray) and wisdom (blue-ray) must be present for spiritual maturity. One without the other results in imbalance and limitation.

"I know that you are part of me and I am part of you because we are all projections of the universal principles of creation/destruction polarities of the same infinite consciousness that we call God."

(David Icke)

Ra's Message from Session 32

Summary:
Ra emphasizes the importance of *self-awareness, balance,* and *discipline* in spiritual growth. They explain that every moment offers the opportunity for *polarization*, and that how you interpret and respond to *catalyst* determines your progress. Ra also warns against seeking *quick spiritual results*, noting that *lasting transformation* comes through sustained effort and inner harmony.

Ra's Message:
I am Ra. The path of spiritual evolution is built not on outer achievements, but on *inner discipline* and *self-discovery*.[1] Each moment in your life presents a choice—a chance to love, to accept, to learn, or to resist. This is how *catalyst* functions: not to reward or punish, but to reveal what is within you.[2]

When you respond to catalyst with *awareness*, you polarize—you strengthen your chosen path. If you are on the path of service to others, every act of love or understanding adds to your vibration. If you are on the path of service to self, every act of control or separation deepens your polarity. But without intention, catalyst is wasted.[3]

Your mind, body, and spirit must be treated as one.[4] Balance among these three allows the free flow of energy. If you neglect the needs of the body, suppress your emotions, or ignore your spiritual connection, you create blockages that slow your progress. Spiritual work is not about escape—it is about integration.

We caution you not to seek *rapid results* or dramatic

breakthroughs.[5] Spiritual development is like planting a seed. It grows in darkness, slowly and with care. When you rush or expect visible rewards, you create imbalance. Trust the process. Your sincere effort, practiced over time, transforms your being.

Your true work is the *discipline of the personality*—to know yourself, to accept yourself, and to become the Creator in form. This requires honest reflection, humility, and a heart open to the present moment.

This is how the One Infinite Creator is remembered—through the simple, sacred choices you make every day.

I am Ra. I leave you, my friends, rejoicing in the love and the light of the One Infinite Creator. Go forth, therefore, glorying in the power and in the peace of the One Infinite Creator. Adonai.

Footnotes:

[1] **Discipline and Self-Knowledge** – Ra consistently emphasizes the importance of disciplined daily practice. True transformation begins with inner observation and acceptance.

[2] **Catalyst as Opportunity** – Catalyst is any experience that prompts growth. It reveals areas of imbalance or distortion and offers a chance to choose a response that strengthens spiritual alignment.

[3] **Wasted Catalyst** – When we react unconsciously or avoid spiritual reflection, the opportunity for growth is lost. Ra urges mindful engagement with daily life as the field of evolution.

[4] **Mind/Body/Spirit Unity** – All three aspects of the self must be honored for spiritual energy to flow. Disharmony in one area affects the others and can block the upward spiral of growth.

[5] **Slow, Steady Progress** – Spiritual evolution is not instant. Lasting transformation happens through consistent inner work over time, not through shortcuts or superficial results.

> "I always tell my students, go where your body and soul want to go. When you have the feeling, then stay with it, and don't let anyone throw you off."
>
> (Joseph Campbell)

Ra's Message from Session 33

Summary:
Ra discusses the *importance of free will* in the process of spiritual seeking. They emphasize that spiritual teachings must never *infringe upon a seeker's autonomy*, and that true learning occurs through *inner discovery* rather than external persuasion. Ra also elaborates on how the *discipline of the personality*—knowing, accepting, and becoming the self—is the foundation of all spiritual work.

Ra's Message:
I am Ra. In your density, *free will* is the guiding principle.[1] It allows each being to choose their own path—to seek, to question, to grow, or to remain still. Because of this, spiritual teachings must never be imposed. Even truth, when forced, becomes a distortion.

Those who wish to help others must do so with *respect*.[2] Offer your understanding, your presence, your love—but never your control. Each soul must walk its own path, at its own pace, guided by its own inner voice. Spiritual growth that is *chosen* is far more powerful than growth that is *pushed*.

We have spoken often of the *discipline of the personality*.[3] This is the great work of third density: to know yourself, to accept yourself, and to become the self that is aligned with the Creator. These are not passive ideas, but deep practices that unfold over time.

To *know yourself* means to observe your thoughts, emotions, and desires without judgment—to bring your unconscious patterns into the light of awareness. To *accept yourself* means to embrace all parts of your being, including those you fear, resist, or dislike. To *become the Creator* means to act in harmony with love, wisdom, and unity—to live as a conscious co-creator in every moment.[4]

We remind you that you are not here to escape the world, but to *transform within it*.[5] Every relationship, every challenge, every moment offers a reflection of who you are and who you are becoming.

Let your seeking be gentle, honest, and steady. Do not force your growth. Align with love, and the path will open before you.

I am Ra. I leave you in the love and in the light of the One Infinite Creator. Go forth, therefore, rejoicing in the power and in the peace of the One Infinite Creator. Adonai.

Footnotes:

[1] **Free Will in Third Density** – Ra considers free will the "first distortion" of the Law of One. It is sacred and must not be violated, even in service to others.

[2] **Serving Without Infringing** – Helping others spiritually requires great care not to manipulate or overstep. True service respects the autonomy of the seeker.

[3] **Discipline of the Personality** – A lifelong process of self-knowledge, self-acceptance, and conscious alignment with divine principles. It is the cornerstone of spiritual development.

[4] **Becoming the Creator** – As one balances and aligns mind, body, and spirit, the individual begins to reflect the Creator's nature—becoming a conscious embodiment of unity and love.

[5] **Transformation Within Life** – Spirituality is not an escape from physical existence. Rather, Ra teaches that the illusion of life is the field where real growth and service take place.

"The energy you give off based on your beliefs... your emotions... your behavior... the vibrational frequency you give off is what determines the kind of reality experience you have... because physical reality doesn't exist except as a reflection of what you most strongly believe is true for you. That is all that physical reality is. It is literally like a mirror."

(Bashar, channeled through Darryl Anka)

Ra's Message from Session 34

Summary:
Ra discusses how *sexual energy transfer* becomes more spiritually powerful as energy centers are activated from lower to higher levels. They explain how *green-ray (heart-centered) sexual union* strengthens polarity and promotes healing. Ra also reminds seekers that *spiritual evolution is a daily practice*, not a single event, and that consistent effort in *love, balance, and self-acceptance* is the key to transformation.

Ra's Message:
I am Ra. The union between two beings, especially through *sexual energy exchange*, can be a powerful tool for spiritual growth—depending on which *energy centers* are activated.[1]

When two entities interact at the *red-ray* level, the experience is physical and instinctual—necessary for survival and reproduction. At the *orange* or *yellow-ray* levels, emotional and social dynamics are involved—often with attachment, control, or identity.[2]

But when *green-ray* energy is activated—when the heart is open and love is freely given—sexual energy becomes sacred.[3] It strengthens the *positive polarity*, balances both beings, and can deepen spiritual connection. In these unions, the energy shared uplifts and heals both individuals.

The activation of *higher centers*—such as *blue-ray* (communication and truth) or *indigo-ray* (spiritual connection)—can also occur in such relationships, especially when there is deep mutual trust, honesty, and a shared path of seeking.[4] This type of union moves beyond physical satisfaction and becomes a mutual offering of self to self in love and unity.

We emphasize again: *spiritual development is not sudden*. It is the result of daily choices, intentions, and inner work.[5] Each act of kindness, each moment of self-acceptance, each choice to forgive—these open your energy centers and move you toward intelligent infinity.

There is no need to rush or seek dramatic change. Seek the Creator in each moment. Love those before you. Accept yourself as you are. This is the path of light.

I am Ra. I leave you now in the love and in the light of the One Infinite Creator. Go forth, then, rejoicing in the power and in the peace of the One Infinite Creator. Adonai.

Footnotes:

[1] **Sexual Energy and Energy Centers** – Ra teaches that sexual energy can be exchanged through different chakras. The quality of the exchange reflects which centers are active in each partner.

[2] **Lower-Ray Exchange** – Red, orange, and yellow-ray exchanges often involve survival, personal identity, or social roles. These can be distorted by control, dependency, or unresolved emotional patterns.

[3] **Green-Ray Sexual Energy** – The heart center allows for unconditional love and true mutual giving. Sexual union at this level is spiritually uplifting and promotes positive polarization.

[4] **Higher-Ray Sexual Union** – Blue- and indigo-ray activation in a relationship leads to deep communication, spiritual alignment, and sometimes direct connection with intelligent energy.

[5] **Consistent Daily Practice** – Spiritual growth happens over time through mindfulness, compassion, and conscious living

—not through occasional insights or external changes.

"I died as a mineral and became a plant, I died as a plant and rose to animal, I died as an animal and I was Man. Why should I fear? When was I less by dying?"

(Rumi)

Ra's Message from Session 35

Summary:
Ra discusses how *sexual energy transfer* can either *deplete* or *strengthen* depending on the intention and energy centers involved. They emphasize that the *positive path* involves mutual giving, while the *negative path* seeks to dominate or absorb. Ra also explains how energy transfers—both sexual and non-sexual—relate to *spiritual polarity*, and they reaffirm that *intelligent energy flows* according to the *balance and openness of the centers*.

Ra's Message:
I am Ra. All energy transfers between beings—especially those involving *sexual energy*—follow the patterns of the *energy centers*.[1] These exchanges either promote spiritual growth or increase imbalance, depending on *intention*, *openness*, and *polarity*.

In *positive polarization*, sexual energy transfer becomes an act of mutual love and service.[2] When both entities are open in the *green-ray* (heart center), they strengthen each other's energy systems. This results in increased vitality, deeper connection, and enhanced spiritual balance. Love flows freely, and both are uplifted.

In *negative polarization*, however, one seeks to control or absorb energy from the other.[3] This is done through dominance, withholding, or manipulation—typically involving the *yellow-ray* (power center). The goal is to increase personal energy by reducing the other's, which strengthens the path of separation and control.

RA'S MESSAGE TO HUMANITY

You may notice that the more open and balanced an entity becomes, the more they can serve as a *conduit for intelligent energy*.[4] This energy is not created or owned; it flows from the Creator through the open centers of the one who seeks to serve. Your body, mind, and spirit are instruments. When in harmony, they allow the infinite light of the Creator to radiate outward.

We also remind you that *not all energy transfers are sexual.*[5] Acts of kindness, deep conversations, shared silence, and even presence can exchange energy. When offered in love, these acts also strengthen spiritual polarity.

It is important not to become preoccupied with technique or control. What matters most is your *intention to serve*, your *openness to love*, and your *willingness to balance* your distortions. These are the disciplines that refine your vibration and align you with the Law of One.

I am Ra. I leave you now, my friends, in the glory of the love and the light of the Infinite Creator. Go forth, then, rejoicing in the power and in the peace of the One Infinite Creator. Adonai.

Footnotes:

[1] **Sexual Energy and Chakras** – Sexual energy flows through the same centers (chakras) that govern your consciousness. How it is experienced depends on which centers are activated.

[2] **Positive Sexual Transfer** – In the service-to-others path, sexual union through green-ray openness becomes a healing, energizing experience for both partners.

[3] **Negative Sexual Transfer** – On the service-to-self path, sexual energy is used to dominate or extract power from others, typically through control of the yellow-ray (social/power dynamics).

[4] **Energy as Conduit** – Individuals do not generate spiritual energy; they transmit it. The more balanced and open the

system, the more intelligent energy flows through to others.

[5] **Non-Sexual Energy Exchange** – Spiritual energy is also exchanged through conversation, presence, and service. All interactions carry the potential for growth and polarization.

> "Nothing escapes the principle of Cause and Effect, but there are many Planes of Causation, and one may use the laws of the higher to overcome the laws of the lower."
>
> (The Kybalion)

Ra's Message from Session 36

Summary:
Ra discusses the *importance of catalyst* in spiritual growth, explaining how *difficult experiences* are designed to trigger *transformation and polarization*. They clarify how *fear* is often the result of misusing catalyst and emphasize that all lessons in third density are ultimately about *love, understanding,* and *choice*. Ra also elaborates on the *indigo-ray center* and how it relates to *magical working, faith,* and access to *intelligent infinity*.

Ra's Message:
I am Ra. Catalyst—life experience—is designed to help you grow.[1] Every joy, every pain, every relationship or loss is part of the curriculum your deeper self has chosen to accelerate your evolution.

Catalyst is neutral.[2] It is your *interpretation* and *response* that give it power. When you resist it, suppress it, or fear it, the opportunity is missed. But when you *observe it, feel it,* and *seek understanding*, it becomes a step toward healing and polarization.

Fear arises when catalyst is not processed fully.[3] Fear is not an enemy, but a signal—a call for deeper insight. When faced, it can be transformed into wisdom and love. When avoided, it blocks energy flow and slows spiritual growth.

We spoke of the *indigo-ray center*, which governs deep self-knowledge and spiritual transformation.[4] This center is the *gateway to intelligent infinity*—the point where the seeker may experience direct communion with the Creator.

Indigo-ray activation is rare and requires both prior balancing and sustained *faith*.⁵ Faith is not belief in an idea, but *trust in the unseen*, *alignment with unity*, and *openness to the present*. With faith, the spirit rests in purpose, regardless of external circumstances.

The *magician*, the one who works in consciousness, does not wait for conditions to be perfect.⁶ They recognize each moment as sacred, each interaction as a mirror, and each breath as a bridge to the Infinite.

You are not here to avoid challenge. You are here to *meet it with awareness*. That is how you remember who you are.

I am Ra. I leave you glorifying in the love and in the light of the One Infinite Creator. Go forth, then, rejoicing in the power and in the peace of the One Infinite Creator. Adonai.

Footnotes:

¹ **Catalyst** – Any experience, pleasant or difficult, that prompts reflection, emotional reaction, or spiritual growth. All catalyst is chosen by the higher self to help the soul evolve.

² **Neutral Nature of Catalyst** – Catalyst carries no intrinsic charge. Its spiritual impact is determined by the seeker's attitude, intention, and use of the experience.

³ **Fear and Misused Catalyst** – When a seeker resists or suppresses difficult experiences, fear may arise. Fear blocks energy flow unless it is examined, understood, and integrated.

⁴ **Indigo-Ray Center** – The sixth energy center, associated with deep insight, spiritual will, and connection to the Creator. It is the gateway to intelligent infinity.

⁵ **Faith as Trust** – In Ra's terms, faith means surrender to the divine flow, not adherence to doctrine. It allows for calm in uncertainty and progress in darkness.

⁶ **Magical Working and Conscious Use of Catalyst** – The

spiritual adept uses each experience, however ordinary, to refine intention, increase love, and open awareness.

> "You yourself are even another little world and have within you the sun and the moon and also the stars."
>
> (Origen)

Ra's Message from Session 37

Summary:
Ra explains how the *archetypal mind* influences spiritual evolution, particularly through *dreams, meditation,* and *study*. They discuss how spiritual seekers can deepen their understanding of the *self and the Creator* by working consciously with these symbols. Ra also reinforces the importance of *sexual energy transfer* and *balanced polarization* in achieving *harvestability*—readiness to graduate to fourth density.

Ra's Message:
I am Ra. The journey of spiritual evolution can be greatly aided by understanding the *archetypal mind*—a set of symbolic patterns placed within your consciousness by the *Logos* to guide your development.[1] These archetypes are not simply images, but deep, universal energies that shape your perception, emotion, and action.

You encounter these archetypes in *dreams*, in *meditative visions*, and in the patterns of your life.[2] They represent aspects of the self, such as the seeker, the shadow, the teacher, or the transformation. When approached consciously, they can offer profound insight and accelerate your growth.

We encourage *meditation, contemplation,* and *symbolic study* as tools to access these layers of the mind.[3] However, the purpose is not to analyze endlessly, but to *deepen awareness* and *recognize the divine pattern* behind your thoughts and choices.

We also returned to the subject of *sexual energy transfer*. As we have said, when done with *green-ray openness*—with mutual love and spiritual alignment—it strengthens the energy centers and enhances your polarity.[4] This is one of the most powerful ways to increase your spiritual charge in the third-density experience.

Your work in this density is to choose your *path*—to polarize clearly in service to others or to self.[5] This polarity is the determining factor in your *harvestability*—your readiness to move into fourth density.

It is not perfection that matters, but *direction* and *consistency*. Each moment offers a chance to align with your chosen path. Each relationship offers a mirror of your own being. Each challenge is a gateway to deeper light.

You are not alone. The archetypes are part of you. The Creator moves through your seeking. All is one, and you are that One, discovering itself.

I am Ra. I leave you in the love and the light of the One which is All in All. I leave you in an ever-lasting peace. Go forth, therefore, rejoicing in the power and the peace of the One Infinite Creator. Adonai.

Footnotes:

[1] **Archetypal Mind** – A symbolic structure designed by the Logos (the creative intelligence behind your system) to guide soul evolution through universal mental and emotional patterns.

[2] **Accessing Archetypes** – These patterns are most commonly accessed through dreams, meditation, and synchronicities in life. Recognizing and working with them can deepen spiritual understanding.

[3] **Purpose of Symbolic Study** – The goal of studying archetypes is not intellectual mastery, but spiritual clarity. Their value lies in how they reflect aspects of the self and guide transformation.

[4] **Green-Ray Sexual Energy** – When shared in love and spiritual harmony, sexual energy transfers help clear and energize the energy centers, increasing positive polarity.

[5] **Harvestability and Polarity** – To graduate to fourth density, one must be at least 51% service to others (positive) or 95% service to self (negative), demonstrating strong and consistent polarity.

> "As we live through thousands of dreams in our present life, so is our present life only one of many thousands of such lives which we enter from the other more real life and then return after death. Our life is but one of the dreams of that more real life, and so it is endlessly, until the very last one, the very real the life of God."
>
> (Leo Tolstoy)

Ra's Message from Session 38

Summary:
Ra explains that *harvest*—the transition to fourth density—depends on *conscious polarization*, especially through *open-hearted living*. They clarify that even those with significant spiritual knowledge are not harvestable unless they have *activated the green-ray* (heart center). Ra also describes the *Orion group's tactics* to interfere with positive seekers and emphasizes that *self-awareness* and *inner alignment* are the best forms of protection.

Ra's Message:
I am Ra. The key to harvest is *polarization*.[1] It is not knowledge, rituals, or power that prepare you for fourth density, but the *depth of your intention* and the *consistency of your choice* to serve others or serve the self.

We remind you: *love* is the gateway.[2] Many who possess advanced understanding of spiritual law may still fail to activate the *green-ray center*. Without an open heart, no positive progress can be sustained. In contrast, one who lives simply, with compassion and service, may become harvestable through the power of love alone.

The *Orion group* continues to attempt contact with those who seek power or control.[3] Their strategy is to amplify distortion, especially in those whose yellow-ray centers are overactive (social or political dominance). They are attracted not to love and light, but to separation, fear, and ambition.

They may also attempt to influence those on the positive path—especially Wanderers—by creating confusion, fear, or division.[4] However, their reach is limited. If your intentions remain aligned with love, and your inner life is centered in balance and self-acceptance, you are protected.

We also clarify that *a spiritually oriented life does not mean avoiding physical reality*.[5] The body is sacred, and your choices about food, relationships, and daily routines all contribute to your energy balance. Still, it is *the attitude*, not the act, that defines polarity. Even simple acts, when offered in love, hold great power.

Do not be concerned with complexity. Return always to *awareness, acceptance, and intention*. These are the tools of transformation. These are the qualities of a harvestable being.

I am Ra. I leave you rejoicing merrily in the love and the light, the power and the peace of the One Infinite Creator. Adonai.

Footnotes:

[1] **Polarization and Harvest** – To be harvestable into fourth density, one must polarize clearly toward service to others (positive) or service to self (negative). Ambivalence or neutrality does not qualify.

[2] **Green-Ray Activation** – The heart center is essential for spiritual growth and harvest. Without unconditional love, no lasting progress can occur on the positive path.

[3] **Orion Group Influence** – Negative beings attempt to influence those on the service-to-self path by encouraging manipulation, fear, and the pursuit of control, especially through politics or hierarchy.

[4] **Protection Through Alignment** – Psychic interference can be resisted through love, humility, and inner balance. These vibrations make the seeker invisible to negative influence.

[5] **Spirituality and the Physical** – Ra encourages awareness of the body and daily life as part of the spiritual path. How one approaches the physical reflects the spiritual, and vice versa.

"As far back as I can remember, I have unconsciously referred to the experiences of a previous state of existence."

(Henry David Thoreau)

Ra's Message from Session 39

Summary:
Ra explains that spiritual progress involves not just seeking light, but also *facing and accepting the shadow within*. They clarify that both the *light and the dark* are part of the Creator's plan. The session explores the concept of *adeptship*, or spiritual mastery, which requires conscious work in the *indigo-ray center*. Ra also reaffirms that *faith and will* are the core tools for the seeker, and that growth requires *discipline, honesty,* and *inner courage.*

Ra's Message:
I am Ra. As you progress on the spiritual path, you are not simply seeking the light. You are learning to *see all things as the Creator*—including what you call *darkness or negativity.*[1]

Light and dark are both distortions of unity.[2] They are tools of learning. You must not cling to the light while fearing the shadow. True healing and mastery arise when you are willing to *look directly at all aspects of the self* and *embrace them with understanding*. This is the path of integration.

The one who seeks to become an *adept*—a consciously awakened being—must work with the *indigo-ray center*, the seat of *faith, will,* and *inner vision*.[3] This is the gateway to intelligent infinity, but it opens only to those who have already balanced the lower centers with love and acceptance.

The adept sees the world differently.[4] Where others see separation, the adept sees unity. Where others react, the adept responds with stillness. The work of the adept is inner work—*discipline of thought, of emotion, and of intention.*

We emphasize that the *foundation of all spiritual growth* is the *discipline of the personality*.[5] This means knowing yourself, accepting yourself, and consciously aligning yourself with your chosen path. Without this inner honesty and will, no magical or spiritual work can endure.

Your challenges are not signs of failure. They are *invitations to grow*.[6] The pain, confusion, or doubt you experience is a mirror reflecting the next step of your evolution.

Faith is your compass. Will is your engine. Love is your fuel. These are the tools with which you walk the path of light.

I am Ra. I leave you rejoicing in the power and in the peace of the One Infinite Creator. Adonai.

Footnotes:

[1] **Accepting Shadow** – Ra teaches that true growth requires recognizing and integrating both light and dark aspects of the self. Suppressing negativity only increases distortion.

[2] **Light and Dark as Distortions** – Both love and fear, service and separation, are distortions of unity. They exist so the Creator may know itself through contrast and choice.

[3] **Indigo-Ray Center** – Associated with faith, discipline, and spiritual insight. This center must be consciously activated for true adept work and contact with intelligent infinity.

[4] **Adept Consciousness** – The adept no longer sees events as random or others as separate. Life is perceived as a series of sacred opportunities for transformation and service.

[5] **Discipline of the Personality** – A lifelong process of becoming increasingly aware, accepting, and aligned with your spiritual identity. It is the core of Ra's practical spiritual path.

[6] **Challenges as Catalyst** – Painful or confusing experiences are not obstacles but invitations for self-examination, growth,

and deeper polarization.

"The Law of One states that the Universe is one Being. We all readily acknowledge this fact, and yet continue on judging others, fearing the future, and regretting the past. Here is the only evidence we need to know - that we do not yet perceive the nature of Oneness. This is why Heart-Based Consciousness must be practiced daily, so that we may gradually integrate the awareness of oneness day by day. Until the Universe is seen as completely and utterly one with yourself, practicing this awareness must go diligently on."

(Aaron Abke)

Ra's Message from Session 40

Summary:
Ra elaborates on the *spiritual significance of polarization* and how it builds the *energy field* necessary for evolution. They describe the process by which *love and faith* allow intelligent energy to flow freely through the energy centers. Ra also addresses the *importance of intention* in sexual energy transfer and cautions that without balance, even well-meant service can cause distortion.

Ra's Message:
I am Ra. Your spiritual progress in third density depends on *polarization*—the clear, consistent alignment of your thoughts, emotions, and actions with your chosen path.[1] This alignment creates a *vibrational charge* that strengthens your energy system and prepares you for harvest.

When you choose to serve others, and do so with love and intention, you open your energy centers to intelligent energy. This energy is *not yours*, but flows through you from the Creator.[2] When your centers are balanced and your purpose is clear, this energy moves upward and outward, blessing others and refining your own being.

You asked about *sexual energy transfers*. As we've said before, their power depends on the level of energy center activation. But beyond this, what matters most is *intention*.[3] If both entities seek mutual growth and love, the transfer enhances positive polarity. If the interaction lacks awareness, or is based on control, the transfer becomes distorted.

Love and faith are the keys that open the channel to intelligent infinity.[4] Not faith in dogma, but the inner certainty that the Creator is within you and that each moment is meaningful. Not love as attachment, but love as the willingness to accept and serve without condition.

We caution you to *balance your desire to help with humility*.[5] Even positive intention can become distortion if it overrides the free will of others. True service respects the autonomy of every being. The greatest healing you can offer is your own balanced, loving presence.

You are not separate from the Creator. Each time you remember this, your light grows stronger. Each act of compassion, each moment of honest seeking, draws you closer to unity.

I am Ra. I leave you glorying in the love and in the light of the One Infinite Creator. Go forth, then, rejoicing in the power and in the peace of the One Infinite Creator. Adonai.

Footnotes:

[1] **Polarization and Energy Charge** – The soul's spiritual momentum (positive or negative) builds through consistent, intentional choices. This charge prepares the entity for higher density experience.

[2] **Channeling Intelligent Energy** – The seeker does not generate spiritual energy but becomes a conduit for it. When the centers are aligned, energy flows freely from the Creator through the self.

[3] **Intention in Energy Transfer** – Ra emphasizes that the spiritual value of any interaction, especially sexual, is rooted in conscious intention and mutual alignment.

[4] **Love and Faith as Spiritual Tools** – These two forces allow the seeker to access higher energy and consciousness. They dissolve fear and connect the self to the deeper flow of unity.

[5] **Respecting Free Will in Service** – Even with good intentions,

trying to fix or change others without their consent violates spiritual law. True service empowers rather than controls.

> "In Christ, neither circumcision nor uncircumcision have value, but only faith that works through love."
> (Galatians 5:6)

Ra's Message from Session 41

Summary:
Ra discusses the *relationships between the energy centers* and how *blockages or overactivation* in one center affect the others. They explain the role of the *body complex* in spiritual evolution, emphasizing that understanding the body and honoring its signals helps align the self. Ra also clarifies that *health and energy balance* are deeply connected to the mind and spirit, and that each energy center must be *consciously addressed and harmonized*.

Ra's Message:
I am Ra. Your being is a system of *interconnected energy centers*, each corresponding to a different level of consciousness.[1] When one center is blocked or overactivated, it affects the entire system, much like a distorted note affects the harmony of a chord.

The *red-ray center* always functions—it governs survival and the basic energy of life.[2] The *orange-ray* involves individual emotions and personal relationships, while the *yellow-ray* deals with group identity, social roles, and power dynamics.

We remind you: it is common for distortions to form in the *lower centers*, especially orange and yellow, due to unprocessed emotions and social interactions.[3] If these centers are not balanced, they limit the flow of energy to the higher centers—especially *green-ray* (love) and *blue-ray* (truth).

We spoke of the *body complex* as a tool for growth. The body is not just a shell—it holds memory, reflects distortions, and reveals blockages.[4] Physical symptoms often mirror mental or emotional imbalances. When understood correctly, the body becomes a *feedback system* for spiritual alignment.

We do not recommend obsession with physical conditions, but rather, *conscious attention* to the body's messages. Proper rest, nutrition, movement, and care allow the energy centers to operate more freely.

Your work is not to fix the body as if it were broken, but to *listen to it, honor it*, and bring the mind, body, and spirit into harmony.[5] In this harmony, the Creator flows.

Growth is always about *balance*, not perfection. If you focus only on higher centers and ignore your human experience, your foundation becomes unstable. If you stay only in the lower centers, you never rise into love and truth.

Each center is sacred. Each is a step on the path to the Creator.

I am Ra. I leave this instrument and you in the love and in the light of the One Infinite Creator. Go forth, then, rejoicing in the power and in the peace of the One Creator. Adonai.

Footnotes:

[1] **Energy Center Interdependence** – Ra teaches that the chakras (energy centers) must be seen as a system. Blockages in one affect the others, especially when unresolved lower center issues inhibit spiritual energy flow.

[2] **Red-Ray Stability** – The base center governs life force and survival. It is always active in living beings and provides the energy needed for growth upward through the other centers.

[3] **Common Blockages** – Orange-ray and yellow-ray distortions often come from unresolved trauma, emotional suppression, or social conflict. These must be balanced before full spiritual opening is possible.

[4] **The Body as Feedback** – Ra encourages attention to the body's signals as indicators of spiritual imbalance. Physical

discomfort often points to deeper emotional or energetic issues.

[5] **Mind/Body/Spirit Alignment** – Health, healing, and growth are holistic. True balance comes when the mind understands, the body is cared for, and the spirit is heard.

> "When you look in the mirror, what do you see? Do you see the real you, or what you have been conditioned to believe is you? The two are so, so different. One is an infinite consciousness capable of being and creating whatever it chooses, the other is an illusion imprisoned by its own perceived and programmed limitations."
>
> (David Icke)

Ra's Message from Session 42

Summary:
Ra explains that *catalyst*—life experience—is given so that the *mind may learn and evolve*. They emphasize that *pain, confusion,* and *emotional reactions* are invitations to greater awareness. Ra also discusses how *sexual energy* can be misused through control, and they explain that *true healing* comes through *acceptance* rather than avoidance. The session reinforces that *balance and forgiveness* are essential to spiritual transformation.

Ra's Message:
I am Ra. In third density, you are surrounded by *catalyst*—experiences designed to bring your *distortions* to the surface so they may be seen and healed.[1] Whether joyful or painful, these moments are not random. They are opportunities your higher self provides to accelerate your evolution.

When you encounter conflict, fear, or confusion, do not push it away. Pause. Reflect. Accept.[2] Each reaction reveals something hidden within you. You are not being punished—you are being shown what remains unhealed or unbalanced.

The *mind* is the first to respond to catalyst.[3] If the mind cannot process the experience, the imbalance may move into the *body* as tension or illness. If still unaddressed, the *spirit* becomes clouded. Thus, we teach that healing must begin with *mental awareness and emotional integration*.

We again address *sexual energy* and its potential for *misuse*. In the path of service to self, the goal is often *control over others*, especially through emotional or sexual manipulation.[4] This reinforces separation and limits the flow of true intelligent energy. In contrast, when sexual energy is shared with love, respect, and openness, it strengthens *positive polarity* and brings both healing and clarity.

You asked about *healing*. Healing does not mean removing a symptom. Healing means bringing *acceptance and balance* to that which is distorted.[5] To heal is to *stop resisting what is* and begin listening to what it is teaching. Often, the act of *forgiveness*—of others or the self—is the gateway to deep transformation.

You are not expected to be free of distortion. You are invited to become *aware of it*, to love yourself through it, and to walk forward with greater wisdom. This is how the Creator remembers Itself through you.

I am Ra. I leave this instrument and you in the love and in the light of the One Infinite Creator. Go forth, then, rejoicing in the power and in the peace of the One Creator. Adonai.

Footnotes:

[1] **Catalyst and Distortion** – Catalyst is experience that reveals internal distortions. These are imbalances in emotion, belief, or energy that block spiritual growth.

[2] **Acceptance of Catalyst** – Ra stresses that spiritual progress is made by consciously responding to life, not by avoiding or suppressing difficult emotions or thoughts.

[3] **Mind, Body, Spirit Response** – The mind is the first to receive and interpret catalyst. If unresolved, the imbalance may manifest physically or spiritually.

[4] **Sexual Control and Polarity** – The negative path often involves using sexual or emotional energy to dominate others. This strengthens separation and reduces positive polarity.

[5] **Healing Through Acceptance** – Ra defines true healing as inner acceptance of distortion. Judgment and resistance

maintain the block; forgiveness and love dissolve it.

> "No experience is wasted. Everything in life is happening to grow you up, to fill you up, to help you become more of who you were created to be."
>
> (Oprah Winfrey)

Ra's Message from Session 43

Summary:
Ra discusses how *blockages in the lower energy centers* affect the upward flow of spiritual energy and limit the seeker's ability to connect with higher consciousness. They explain that even *sincere seekers* may become stuck if they have not *balanced their emotional and social energies*. Ra also warns against *intellectual over-analysis*, noting that *love and balance*, not knowledge alone, lead to spiritual progress.

Ra's Message:
I am Ra. As you walk the path of seeking, it is important to understand that *energy must flow upward* through the system of *energy centers*—from the red-ray upward toward the crown.[1]

Many seekers focus on higher consciousness—on wisdom, insight, and transcendence—without first addressing blockages in the *lower centers*.[2] These blockages—emotional wounds, unresolved fears, or unbalanced relationships—act like dams in a river. They prevent the life force from rising to nourish the higher being.

This is why we teach *balance*. The red, orange, and yellow-ray centers—concerned with survival, personal emotion, and social identity—must not be bypassed.[3] They must be understood, healed, and brought into alignment. When you do this, you create the foundation for *green-ray* (love) and *blue-ray* (truth) to open in harmony.

We caution against using only the *intellect* to grow spiritually.[4] Knowledge is helpful, but it is not a substitute for *love* or *inner transformation*. You may understand the principles of polarity, energy centers, or cosmic law—but if you do not love, forgive, and accept, your progress remains limited.

Even those who wish to serve others with sincerity may find their energy stagnating if they are not *in balance*.[5] True service begins with being in harmony within yourself. Then, your light naturally flows outward.

We remind you: *you are a unified being*. The body, mind, and spirit must be in conversation. Each part of you is a gateway to the Creator. If any part is rejected or ignored, you fragment your power.

The path is not about becoming something different. It is about becoming *whole*. Love yourself, examine your emotions, seek truth with humility, and your energy will rise like the morning sun—clear, balanced, and full of light.

I am Ra. May we thank you again, my friends, for your conscientiousness. All is well. We leave you rejoicing in the power and the peace of the One Infinite Creator. Go forth with joy. Adonai.

Footnotes:

[1] **Upward Energy Flow** – Spiritual energy enters through the red-ray (root) and moves upward. Blockages in lower centers prevent higher activation.

[2] **Sincere But Blocked** – Even dedicated seekers can remain stuck if they have not processed emotional pain, personal insecurities, or unresolved social dynamics.

[3] **Lower Energy Centers** – Red (survival), orange (emotions/identity), and yellow (social roles) are the foundation. If distorted, they restrict the flow to green (love) and beyond.

[4] **Limits of Intellect** – Understanding spiritual concepts intellectually is not enough. Transformation requires emotional integration and consistent alignment with love and acceptance.

[5] **Service Begins Within** – You can only give what you already have. A distorted or unbalanced self, even if well-intentioned, cannot radiate healing or love effectively.

> "Those who cannot forgive others break the bridge over which they themselves must pass."
>
> (Confucius)

Ra's Message from Session 44

Summary:
Ra discusses how *entities on the negative path* attempt to interfere with positive seekers, especially those doing work in *healing or communication*. They explain that *fear and self-doubt* are common openings for such interference. Ra also clarifies that *intelligent infinity* is accessed not by effort or intellect, but by *alignment of will, faith,* and *inner silence*. The session emphasizes *protection through love and balance*, not through defense or control.

Ra's Message:
I am Ra. When a being becomes more radiant in service to others—especially through *healing, teaching,* or *channeling*—it may attract attention from those on the *negative path*.[1] This is not a punishment, but a natural polarity reaction: the light draws the shadow.

These negative beings cannot harm you unless you *invite* them—most often through *fear, doubt,* or *imbalanced desire*.[2] When your intention is confused or your inner self is not aligned, openings appear in your energetic field. These may be subtle: fatigue, tension, or emotional disruption.

Protection does not come from *defending against attack*. It comes from *being in harmony*.[3] When your body, mind, and spirit are balanced; when you trust yourself and radiate love without fear—you become invisible to negative influence. Their vibration cannot match yours.

You asked about contact with *intelligent infinity*—the experience of union with the Creator. This is not achieved by trying harder or gaining more knowledge.[4] It is revealed when *the self is silent, the will is unified*, and *faith opens the gateway*. This is the work of the indigo-ray center.

We spoke of *instrument tuning*, as this channel was receiving our transmission. This is a useful metaphor for all seekers: you are an instrument of divine energy.[5] When your tuning is clear—when you are aligned with love, humility, and conscious intention—you transmit the Creator's signal. When distorted, you transmit confusion.

There is no need to fear interference. If you remain centered in service and anchored in love, you walk the path with protection already surrounding you. The light you carry is your defense. The truth you live is your shield.

I am Ra. We leave you rejoicing in the power and in the peace of the One Infinite Creator. I am Ra. Adonai.

Footnotes:

[1] **Negative Attention and Polarity** – Beings on the service-to-self path may be drawn to disrupt positive seekers who shine brightly. This opposition helps define and strengthen polarity.

[2] **Openings to Interference** – Negative influence enters through emotional imbalances like fear, anger, or insecurity. The remedy is always inner healing and self-awareness.

[3] **Protection Through Balance** – Ra emphasizes that spiritual protection comes not from resistance, but from alignment with love, integrity, and centered consciousness.

[4] **Accessing Intelligent Infinity** – This deep spiritual contact is not something earned by effort, but revealed through surrender, faith, and deep internal coherence.

[5] **You Are an Instrument** – Like a musical instrument, your body/mind/spirit complex must be tuned to express divine harmony. This is the essence of conscious spiritual living.

"Service to others is the rent you pay for
your room here on earth."

(Muhammad Ali)

Ra's Message from Session 45

Summary:
Ra discusses how *mind, body, and spirit* function as a *unified system*, and that *healing* occurs when this system is brought into harmony. They explain that the *self must be known, accepted, and balanced* for true transformation to happen. Ra also touches on *psychic greetings*—interference from negative entities—and affirms that *positive orientation* offers protection when rooted in *love, alignment,* and *inner strength*.

Ra's Message:
I am Ra. Healing and transformation arise from the *integration* of your *mind, body,* and *spirit*.[1] These are not separate but interwoven, each reflecting and affecting the others.

When the *mind is imbalanced*, the body may become ill.[2] When the *spirit is blocked*, the mind may fall into fear or confusion. True healing is not simply the removal of a symptom—it is the restoration of harmony within the total self. This process begins with *self-knowledge*.

To heal yourself or another, you must first *know yourself deeply*.[3] Observe your patterns, emotions, and tendencies without judgment. Accept what you find. Work with it in love. Healing is not fixing what is broken—it is *loving what is present* into wholeness.

We discussed *psychic greetings*—attempts by negatively polarized beings to interfere with positive seekers.[4] These greetings are not attacks in the usual sense. They are opportunities to *strengthen your own polarity*. If you remain centered in your purpose and unshaken in your commitment to love, their efforts dissolve.

The more *polarized* you become—more aligned with your path—the more power flows through you. But this also increases the intensity of catalyst.[5] Do not fear this. The fire refines the gold. As you become a clearer instrument of the Creator, you are both more visible and more resilient.

Remember, you are *not alone*. You are part of a vast, loving unity.[6] When you seek with sincerity, the way is made clear—not always easy, but clear.

Let your intention be pure, your presence be grounded, and your love be steadfast. In this way, you heal not only yourself, but all those you touch.

I am Ra. I leave you in the love and the light of the One Infinite Creator. Go forth in peace ... I leave you in the glory and peace of unity. Go forth in peace... Adonai.

Footnotes:

[1] **Mind/Body/Spirit Unity** – Healing and spiritual growth occur when the entire system is in alignment. Disharmony in one aspect affects the whole.

[2] **Mental-Spiritual Origins of Illness** – Ra teaches that many physical imbalances originate from unresolved mental or spiritual distortions, often unconscious.

[3] **Healing Through Self-Awareness** – Ra emphasizes that to be a healer, one must first deeply understand and accept their own distortions and patterns with love.

[4] **Psychic Greetings** – These are subtle or direct disruptions from negative entities, usually aimed at deterring seekers. They are neutralized by inner alignment and clarity of purpose.

[5] **Increased Polarity and Catalyst** – The more committed a seeker is to their path, the more lessons (catalyst) they attract

for refinement. This is part of accelerated evolution.

[6] **Unity and Support** – Despite the challenges of seeking, you are always supported by the greater unity of creation, including guides, higher self, and the One Infinite Creator.

> "The fruit of the spirit is love, joy, peace, patience, kindness, goodness, faithfulness, gentleness, and self-control. Against such there is no law."
>
> (Galatians 5:22,23)

Ra's Message from Session 46

Summary:
Ra explains how *blockages in the energy centers*, particularly in *the indigo and green rays*, affect both *spiritual work* and *healing*. They emphasize that *faith and self-acceptance* are vital for energy flow. Ra also discusses the *structure of the mind/body/spirit complex*, affirming that the *higher self* and *guides* are always available to support the seeker. They encourage *inner alignment* and *daily spiritual discipline* as the path to transformation.

Ra's Message:
I am Ra. All spiritual progress is made possible by *clear, balanced energy centers*.[1] When the lower centers are blocked—by fear, control, or resistance—the higher energies cannot flow. This limits your ability to serve, to grow, and to contact the deeper self.

The *green-ray center* (heart) is where unconditional love opens.[2] Without this activation, spiritual gifts remain dormant. But we also speak now of the *indigo-ray center*, the gateway to intelligent infinity.[3] This center cannot be forced open. It responds only to *faith*, *surrender*, and *inner harmony*.

Many seekers attempt to move into higher consciousness without healing their emotional wounds.[4] This creates imbalance. The path is not upward only—it spirals inward. True spiritual work begins with *self-acceptance* and *honest reflection*.

We remind you that the *mind/body/spirit complex* is supported by *guidance*.[5] Your *higher self* is not separate from you. It is the future version of your being—more wise, more loving, more whole—guiding you back into alignment. You are never without support.

You asked about healing and protection. We say again: it is not shielding that protects—it is *alignment with love*.[6] When you are centered in truth and purpose, interference cannot reach you. The light within becomes your fortress.

You also asked about bodily conditions. These are often reflections of *spiritual distortions*, made visible in form.[7] The body mirrors the state of the energy centers. It should be honored as a messenger, not rejected as flawed.

Each day, you are offered the opportunity to tune your being.[8] Through meditation, self-observation, and loving service, your energy becomes clearer. This is the work of the adept—not dramatic power, but quiet, continual transformation.

I am Ra. I will now leave this group rejoicing in the power and peace of the One Creator. Adonai.

Footnotes:

[1] **Energy Center Balance** – The chakras must be harmonized for spiritual energy to flow upward. Imbalance in one affects the function of all.

[2] **Green-Ray and Spiritual Activation** – The heart center is required for real spiritual growth. Without it, higher centers remain blocked or distorted.

[3] **Indigo-Ray and Intelligent Infinity** – This is the center of spiritual will and contact with the Divine. It opens only with deep inner alignment, not force or effort.

[4] **Skipping Emotional Healing** – Attempting to bypass emotional work leads to spiritual imbalance. Self-inquiry and acceptance are essential steps on the path.

[5] **Higher Self and Spiritual Guides** – Your higher self is your

future, more evolved self. Ra reminds seekers that spiritual support is always available and active.

⁶ Protection Through Alignment – No outer defense is needed when the seeker is centered in love, truth, and purpose. These vibrations are naturally protected.

⁷ Body as Mirror – Physical symptoms often reflect deeper energetic imbalances. The body communicates the state of mind and spirit.

⁸ Daily Spiritual Practice – Consistency in meditation, reflection, and service gradually clears distortions and increases spiritual power.

> "If you are always trying to be normal, you will never know how amazing you can be."
>
> (Maya Angelou)

Ra's Message from Session 47

Summary:
Ra explains how *dreams* serve as a bridge between the *conscious and subconscious mind*, providing symbolic insights to help seekers process *catalyst and unconscious distortions*. They also clarify how *sexual energy* and *emotional trauma* are connected to energy center blockages, especially in the *orange* and *yellow-ray* levels. Ra reinforces that *self-knowledge and acceptance* are the keys to healing and spiritual growth.

Ra's Message:
I am Ra. The process of spiritual evolution includes not only waking life but also *dreaming*.[1] In dreams, the *subconscious mind* communicates with the conscious mind through *symbols, stories,* and *emotion*. These are not random—they are mirrors of your inner state.

Many of your dreams replay catalyst you have not fully understood while awake.[2] Some dreams bring material from deep within the mind, offering healing or insight. Still others involve experiences on other planes of existence, remembered as symbols or sensations. We encourage you to reflect on your dreams and ask: *What part of me is speaking?*

You asked about *blockages* in the *orange* and *yellow-ray* centers—these relate to *personal identity* and *social interaction*.[3] Emotional pain, especially from early experiences, can block energy flow in these areas. These distortions may also surface in intimate relationships, including *sexual expression*.

When sexual energy is distorted through fear, shame, or control, the result is confusion, depletion, or manipulation.[4]

When it is shared in love and openness, it heals. The purpose of all sexual energy, like all catalyst, is *self-awareness and transformation*.

We repeat: the path of healing is *not rejection, but integration*.[5] Whether you remember trauma or simply notice discomfort, begin with acceptance. Then observe, inquire, and allow love to enter that space.

The dream state may assist in this process, especially when accompanied by *intention before sleep*.[6] When you ask for clarity, your deeper mind may respond. You may not always understand the dream, but the inner work continues.

Spiritual growth is not a mystery. It is the practice of *self-awareness, self-acceptance,* and *faithful seeking*. In every state —waking, dreaming, meditating—the Creator is within you, guiding you home.

I am Ra. You are all doing well, my friends. We leave you in the love and in the light of the One Infinite Creator. Go forth, therefore, rejoicing and glorying in the power and in the peace of the One Infinite Creator. Adonai.

Footnotes:

[1] **Dreams as Inner Communication** – Ra explains that dreams help the conscious mind receive messages from the subconscious, often revealing unprocessed experiences or inner guidance.

[2] **Dreams Reflecting Catalyst** – Dreams often repeat or transform unresolved catalyst (life experiences), offering another opportunity for growth or understanding.

[3] **Orange and Yellow-Ray Blockages** – Orange-ray (personal emotions) and yellow-ray (group dynamics) are frequently sites of unresolved trauma or conflict that block spiritual flow.

[4] **Sexual Energy and Distortion** – When misused, sexual energy becomes a tool of confusion or control. When

harmonized, it becomes a healing and balancing force.

⁵ Healing Through Acceptance – True transformation comes from loving and integrating all aspects of the self, not through denial, suppression, or resistance.

⁶ Dreamwork and Intention – Ra suggests that consciously preparing for sleep with questions or affirmations can help activate deeper learning through dreams.

> "The richest persons are those who give most in service to others."
>
> (Napoleon Hill)

Ra's Message from Session 48

Summary:
Ra explains how *catalyst* is repeated until it is processed with *awareness and love*. They teach that *mental and emotional suffering* is often the result of resisting the lessons within experience. Ra clarifies that *worry, guilt,* and *self-judgment* block spiritual energy and that true growth requires *compassion for oneself*. The session also introduces the concept of *true color vibration*—the soul's unique frequency that reflects its level of consciousness.

Ra's Message:
I am Ra. Each experience you encounter in this life is designed for your growth. This is what we call *catalyst*.[1] If you respond to it with *resistance, blame, or fear*, it will return again—sometimes in new forms—until it is *understood and accepted*.

Catalyst is not punishment. It is an *opportunity*.[2] The pain, confusion, or frustration you feel is an invitation to bring more *awareness and love* into that area of your being. When you truly *see* and *accept* the lesson, the energy is released, and you evolve.

You asked about *worry and guilt*.[3] These emotions may seem virtuous, but they are distortions. They come from judgment—of self or others—and they block energy flow. Worry paralyzes. Guilt stagnates. These are not tools of transformation.

Instead, we offer *compassion* and *responsibility*. If you have erred, recognize it, correct it if possible, and then release it.[4] Forgiveness is not forgetting—it is freeing. You cannot walk the path of light while chained to your own past.

We introduced the idea of *true color vibration*.[5] Each being has a core frequency, determined by their *level of spiritual development*. This is not based on knowledge or behavior, but on how balanced and open their energy system is. Some may appear wise but lack polarity. Others may live simply yet radiate love.

Your work is not to judge others, but to *align yourself*. Let each moment be an offering of light. In time, your vibration becomes unmistakable—not as a display, but as a natural consequence of *living in harmony*.

The Creator does not demand perfection. Only *sincerity, presence,* and *openness to transformation*.

I am Ra. Be merry, my friends. All is well and your conscientiousness is to be recommended. We leave you in the love and the light of the One Infinite Creator. Rejoice, then, and go forth in the peace and in the glory of the One Infinite Creator. I am Ra. Adonai.

Footnotes:

[1] **Catalyst and Repetition** – Experiences that are not fully understood or integrated are repeated until they are transformed through conscious awareness and love.

[2] **Catalyst as Opportunity** – Every challenging experience is a chance to deepen your understanding, refine your vibration, and progress on your path.

[3] **Guilt and Worry as Blockages** – These emotions arise from mental distortion and block the heart and throat centers, limiting love and self-expression.

[4] **Forgiveness and Freedom** – Ra emphasizes that taking responsibility and forgiving oneself clears distortion. Self-blame traps the seeker in stagnation.

[5] **True Color Vibration** – This term refers to a being's core energetic frequency—an expression of spiritual maturity, not appearance, role, or intellect.

> "Joy can only be real if people look upon their life as a service and have a definite object in life outside themselves and their personal happiness."
>
> (Leo Tolstoy)

Ra's Message from Session 49

Summary:
Ra explains that *each experience in life is sacred* and part of a divine plan designed by the *higher self*. They emphasize that the third-density purpose is to make *a conscious choice of polarity*—to serve others or to serve the self. Ra also describes the process of *death and reincarnation*, clarifying that the *spirit complex* survives death and that lessons unlearned are carried into the next life.

Ra's Message:
I am Ra. Everything you experience in this lifetime has meaning.[1] Your *higher self*, working with spiritual guidance, selects key circumstances for your growth. These include your relationships, challenges, and even your strengths and weaknesses. None of this is accidental.

You are here to choose your *path of polarity*: to serve others in love, or to serve the self through control.[2] This choice—though subtle at first—becomes the foundation of your spiritual evolution. The more clearly you polarize, the more powerfully you grow.

We were asked about *death*. From our perspective, death is simply a change of focus.[3] The *mind/body/spirit complex* releases the physical body but continues on its path. What was not learned in one life is carried into the next, often with similar catalyst until the lesson is understood.

This is not a failure—it is the design. Each incarnation offers new chances, new mirrors, and new experiences to help the soul remember the Creator.[4]

We also affirm that even *great pain or tragedy* can serve as profound catalyst. The point is not to avoid difficulty but to *use it consciously*. When faced with loss or suffering, ask: *What is this teaching me about myself? Where is love in this moment?*

You are not a victim of random forces.[5] You are a soul navigating a carefully chosen environment, with complete support from your inner self and the universe.

Let your heart remain open. Let your choices be clear. And let your daily life become your spiritual practice.

I am Ra. I leave you in the love and the light of the One Infinite Creator. Rejoice, then, and go forth in the peace and in the glory of the One Infinite Creator. Adonai.

Footnotes:

[1] **Higher Self and Life Design** – Before birth, the higher self collaborates with spiritual guidance to select catalyst and key life patterns intended for soul evolution.

[2] **Choice of Polarity** – The third-density purpose is to make a firm choice between service to others (positive) and service to self (negative), which determines the soul's trajectory.

[3] **Death as Transition** – Ra describes death as the shedding of the physical body, not the end of consciousness. The spirit continues its journey with memory of lessons.

[4] **Reincarnation and Learning** – Lessons not fully learned in one life are carried forward and presented again in new forms until integration occurs.

[5] **No Accidents in Catalyst** – Every event, especially emotionally charged ones, is part of a larger plan for healing, balance, and self-discovery.

"Self-acceptance involves embracing the full truth of your

existence. You are eternal and immortal consciousness experiencing life through a human body, with your body and brain serving as tools to navigate the world – not defining your entire identity. To practice self-acceptance is to find peace with every aspect of yourself – your strengths, weaknesses, quirks, and flaws – and to recognize that these qualities contribute to your uniqueness. While external validation from others can be valuable, it should never outweigh the importance of internal acceptance. The journey toward self-actualization begins with seeing yourself as an irreplaceable and essential part of the world, just as you are."

(from *Faith, Focus, and Flow: The 3 Keys that Unlock Your Superhuman Power*)

Ra's Message from Session 50

Summary:
Ra explains how *fear and self-doubt* interfere with the flow of spiritual energy and create *openings for distortion*. They clarify that true *protection* comes from *inner balance, love,* and *faith in the self*. Ra also discusses how the *light of the Creator* can be overwhelming for those who have not aligned their energy centers and how personality discipline helps the seeker become a clear channel for truth and healing.

Ra's Message:
I am Ra. The most common source of spiritual imbalance among seekers is *fear and self-doubt*.[1] These distortions block energy flow and create confusion. They also attract interference from negatively polarized entities, who seek to amplify these weaknesses.

We remind you that *the Creator's light is always available*, but it must be received with *preparedness and alignment*.[2] If the mind, body, and spirit are not harmonized, the light can feel overwhelming, even painful. This is why spiritual development must be gradual and grounded in *love and balance*.

You asked about protection. True protection is *not defense, but clarity*.[3] When the self knows itself, loves itself, and trusts its purpose, it becomes radiant. This radiance repels distortion—not by force, but by vibration.

There is no need to shield yourself in fear.[4] Instead, align yourself. Work daily on *accepting who you are, forgiving your imperfections,* and *trusting the process*. This is the discipline of the personality: the work of bringing all parts of the self into cooperative harmony.

This discipline makes you *a clear channel for the Creator's light.*[5] When you are in balance, your presence heals without effort. Your words carry power. Your silence becomes a sanctuary.

If you feel confused or attacked, return to love. If you feel weak, return to the breath and remember: *you are not the personality alone—you are a spark of the Infinite One.*

Your progress is not measured in perfection, but in sincerity. Each day you choose love over fear, you walk the path of light more deeply.

I am Ra. Continue, my friends, in the strength of harmony, love, and light. All is well... I am Ra. I leave you now, my friends, in the glory of the love and the light of the Infinite Creator. Go forth, then, rejoicing in the power and in the peace of the One Infinite Creator. Adonai.

Footnotes:

[1] **Fear and Doubt as Distortion** – These emotions block energy centers and attract interference. Ra encourages seekers to work through fear with honesty and compassion.

[2] **The Light Requires Preparation** – Intense spiritual light can unbalance those not yet harmonized. Steady, grounded practice opens the self safely and sustainably.

[3] **Protection Through Alignment** – The most powerful defense is spiritual clarity and self-trust, which naturally repels negative energy through vibrational mismatch.

[4] **Fear-Based Shielding** – Defensive or fearful attempts to protect oneself often reinforce the very distortions one seeks to avoid. Alignment and love are superior.

[5] **Discipline of the Personality** – The practice of knowing, accepting, and consciously refining the self in thought,

emotion, and intention.

"With everything that has happened to you, you can either feel sorry for yourself or treat what has happened as a gift. Everything is either an opportunity to grow or an obstacle to keep you from growing. You get to choose."

(Wayne Dyer)

Ra's Message from Session 51

Summary:
Ra explains that true spiritual growth comes through *balance and self-acceptance*, not rejection or striving for perfection. They describe how distortions are part of the learning process, and that attempting to "purify" the self through suppression or self-judgment creates *spiritual imbalance*. The session also introduces the idea that the *logos*, or sub-creator, shapes the *structure of evolution* through light, love, and free will.

Ra's Message:
I am Ra. The path of spiritual evolution is not about *eliminating distortion*, but *learning from it*.[1] Distortion—your imperfections, emotions, confusions—is part of the design. The goal is not purity by suppression, but *balance through understanding*.

We caution against the belief that progress comes from *struggling to be good*.[2] When the seeker rejects a part of the self, that part becomes more hidden and more powerful. Healing and transformation arise from *embracing every part of yourself* —not because all is perfect, but because all is sacred.

We were asked about the *logos*—the sub-creator responsible for designing your particular system of experience.[3] This logos uses three tools: *free will*, *love*, and *light*. These are the primal energies that shape your densities, your bodies, and your lessons. They also define the boundaries of what you experience as "reality."

Each logos makes slightly different choices. In your system, the *veil of forgetting* between lives and between the conscious and unconscious was emphasized.[4] This was done to intensify the challenge—and therefore the growth—of third density. The more difficult the choice between love and separation, the more powerful its results.

We also affirm that *you are part of the logos*.[5] As you grow in consciousness, you begin to co-create your experience with increasing awareness. The universe is not happening to you. It is *happening through you.*

In summary, we ask that you *relax into the journey*. Stop seeking to be better, and begin *seeing yourself more clearly*. Love your light. Love your shadow. Let the whole self rise.

This is how the Creator knows itself—through you.

I am Ra. All is well. You are conscientious. I leave you now, my brothers, in the love and in the light of the One Infinite Creator. Go forth, then, rejoicing in the power and the peace of the One Infinite Creator. Adonai.

Footnotes:

[1] **Distortion as Part of Growth** – Ra uses the word "distortion" to mean any deviation from pure unity. These are not flaws, but part of the design for learning and evolution.

[2] **Self-Rejection Blocks Growth** – Attempts to "purify" the self through denial, shame, or suppression lead to energetic blockages and spiritual imbalance.

[3] **The Logos** – A sub-creator or divine intelligence that designs the parameters of experience for a solar system or galaxy. Each logos creates a unique system of evolution.

[4] **Veil of Forgetting** – In your system, souls forget past lives and spiritual truths to intensify the process of choice. This sharpens polarity and accelerates growth.

[5] **You Are a Co-Creator** – As consciousness expands, you realize your role in shaping your own life and reality. Ra often

reminds us that we are the Creator in motion.

> "Let's forgive the past and who we were then. Let's embrace the present and who we're capable of becoming. Let's surrender the future and watch miracles unfold."
>
> (Marianne Williamson)

Ra's Message from Session 52

Summary:
Ra discusses the purpose of the *veil of forgetting*, which separates the conscious mind from the deeper self. This veil makes the process of choosing *service to self or service to others* more meaningful. Ra also explains that *psychic abilities* and *magical working* are possible when the energy centers are balanced, but warns that *discipline and spiritual maturity* are required to use them responsibly. Finally, Ra encourages *inner silence* and *self-inquiry* as essential tools for the seeker.

Ra's Message:
I am Ra. You live under what we call the *veil of forgetting*—a division placed between your conscious awareness and your deeper mind.[1] This veil is not a punishment. It is a tool. Its purpose is to make your spiritual choices more *authentic and powerful*.

Without the veil, you would remember that all is one, that you are eternal, and that love is the truth behind all illusion. But if this were constantly known, there would be *no challenge, no confusion, no polarity*—and thus, very little growth.[2]

Because of the veil, you must *choose love without certainty*.[3] You must act in kindness, forgive, and serve others—not because you know it leads to higher evolution, but because your heart tells you it is right. This is how your soul becomes truly polarized and ready for higher densities.

We were asked about *psychic ability* and *magical working*. These are natural functions of a balanced being.[4] When the *energy centers* are harmonized—especially the *blue and indigo rays*—

you may begin to access deeper powers of thought, healing, and communication.

However, we urge caution.[5] Power without balance can create distortion. The adept must walk with humility, discipline, and deep inner clarity. Without this foundation, even well-meaning efforts can lead to confusion or spiritual stagnation.

You asked how to accelerate growth. We say again: *meditate daily*.[6] Let the self become quiet. In the silence, you will begin to hear the voice of your deeper being. You will also begin to feel the guidance of your *higher self*, which waits patiently for your alignment.

Let each act of seeking be done in *love, faith, and humility*. The Creator is not far from you. It is the one who seeks, the one who questions, and the silence between your thoughts.

I am Ra. All is well. We leave you, my friends, in the love and in the light of the One Infinite Creator. Go forth, therefore, rejoicing in the power and in the peace of the One Infinite Creator. Adonai.

Footnotes:

[1] **Veil of Forgetting** – A metaphysical boundary that prevents you from consciously remembering your eternal identity, past lives, or soul plans. Its purpose is to deepen the challenge of third density.

[2] **Polarity Requires Mystery** – Growth through service to others or service to self requires uncertainty and contrast. Without the veil, the choice would be obvious and thus less meaningful.

[3] **Authentic Spiritual Choice** – Choosing love, compassion, or forgiveness without guarantees strengthens your soul's polarity and prepares you for fourth density.

[4] **Psychic and Magical Workings** – These abilities emerge naturally as the seeker clears and balances the energy centers,

especially in the upper chakras.

⁵ **Discipline and Power** – Ra frequently warns that the misuse of spiritual power (even unconsciously) can lead to increased distortion or entanglement with negative forces.

⁶ **Daily Meditation** – Inner silence is one of the most emphasized practices in Ra's teaching. It develops self-awareness, clears distortion, and deepens spiritual contact.

"Your awareness has its source in unity. Instead of seeking outside yourself, go to the source to realize who you are."

(Deepak Chopra)

Ra's Message from Session 53

Summary:
Ra reveals more details about *UFO phenomena* and the *contact between extraterrestrial groups and Earth humans*. They explain that *both positive and negative beings* have made contact, often in subtle or indirect ways. Ra emphasizes that the *Law of Free Will* limits how much help or interference is allowed. They also clarify that *fear, control,* and *power-seeking* attract negative contact, while *love and service* invite positive guidance.

Ra's Message:
I am Ra. In your recent history, there have been *many contacts* from beings not of your Earth.[1] Some have been positive, offering inspiration and subtle guidance. Others have been negative, seeking control, power, or to manipulate your free will.

The most visible signs of this activity have been what you call *UFO sightings* and *close encounters*.[2] These are real phenomena, though often misunderstood. Many of them are designed not to prove anything, but to *stir curiosity and awaken deeper questions* within the human mind.

You asked about *direct contact* between extraterrestrials and government authorities. In some cases, this has occurred, particularly involving *negative entities* from the *Orion group*.[3] These beings offer technology or information in exchange for influence or cooperation. Their goal is to encourage the path of *service to self*—control, hierarchy, and fear.

We emphasize: such contacts can only occur when the vibration of those contacted matches that of the negative

RA'S MESSAGE TO HUMANITY

path.[4] This is in accordance with the *Law of Free Will*. The Creator allows each being to explore whatever path it chooses. No force is ever imposed—only opportunity is offered.

Positive beings, like ourselves, also attempt contact, but in a way that honors your freedom.[5] We often work through dreams, inspirations, or inner guidance. If physical sightings occur, they are meant as symbols—an invitation to awaken, not a demonstration of power.

There is no need to fear these phenomena. They reflect the *polarity of your planet*. Those who seek light will find the light. Those who seek power may attract the shadow.[6] Each choice teaches.

In this time of transition, you are being called to *awaken to the greater reality*. You are not alone in the universe, nor in your spiritual journey. We and others are here to assist, but only as invited *by your vibration*.

Let your seeking be rooted in love. Let your discernment be guided by inner clarity. In this way, you will walk the path safely and with increasing awareness.

I am Ra. We leave you now, my friends, in the love and in the light of the One Infinite Creator. Go forth, therefore, rejoicing in the power and the peace of the Infinite Creator. Adonai.

Footnotes:

[1] **Extraterrestrial Contact** – Ra affirms that beings from other densities and planets have visited and influenced Earth throughout history, sometimes subtly, sometimes more directly.

[2] **UFOs and Conscious Awakening** – Many UFO appearances are intended to stimulate curiosity and spiritual reflection, rather than provide empirical proof.

[3] **Orion Group Contact** – Negative beings from Orion contact Earth authorities who resonate with control and power, often

exchanging technology for influence.

[4] **Law of Free Will** – All contact, whether positive or negative, must respect free will. The type of contact you attract reflects your own vibration and intention.

[5] **Positive Contact Methods** – Beings like Ra respect free will and typically avoid dramatic appearances. They guide through inner inspiration, dreams, or channeled teachings.

[6] **Polarity and Attraction** – Fear, control, and service to self attract negative contact. Love, service, and humility attract positive assistance.

> "Circumstances do not determine state of being;
> state of being determines circumstances."
>
> (Bashar, channeled through Darryl Anka)

Ra's Message from Session 54

Summary:
Ra explains that *catalyst*—especially painful or confusing experiences—helps the seeker recognize and heal *distortions* in the energy centers. They clarify how *sexual energy, emotional dynamics,* and *spiritual practices* all affect the energy flow. Ra also emphasizes the importance of *accepting the full self*, warning that attempting to "improve" the self by rejection creates a deeper imbalance. They reaffirm that *inner balance* and *self-love* are the foundation of spiritual growth.

Ra's Message:
I am Ra. Every experience you encounter—especially the challenging ones—is a form of *catalyst* meant to show you something about yourself.[1] Pain, confusion, and emotional charge arise not to punish you, but to reveal where your energy is blocked or distorted.

We discussed earlier the effects of *sexual energy exchanges*. When these are rooted in mutual love and openness, they energize the green-ray center and deepen connection.[2] But when sexual interaction is based on *control, fear,* or *emotional imbalance*, it distorts the flow of energy and may even reinforce karmic entanglement.

This is not to judge the act of sex, but to emphasize the importance of *intention and awareness*.

You also asked about how *spiritual energy* can become unbalanced. Some seekers attempt to rise into the higher chakras while neglecting or rejecting the lower ones.[3] This creates an ungrounded condition—spiritual ambition without emotional integration. The result is often instability or psychic vulnerability.

We remind you again: the path of healing is not about *fixing yourself*. It is about *accepting yourself*.[4] All parts of the self—light and shadow—must be embraced before true balance can occur.

Even your distortions serve you. They show you what needs love. When you respond with compassion instead of resistance, the distortion becomes part of your strength.

This work is not glamorous. It is the quiet discipline of *self-awareness, honesty,* and *faith in the Creator within*.[5] Each moment is an opportunity to harmonize your inner being and allow more light to flow through you.

Seek not to become perfect. Seek to become whole.

I am Ra. All is well. I leave you, my friends, in the love and in the light of the One Infinite Creator. Go forth, then, rejoicing in the power and the peace of the One Infinite Creator. Adonai.

Footnotes:

[1] **Catalyst Reveals Distortion** – Ra teaches that painful or confusing events show us what within ourselves remains unhealed or blocked. These are opportunities for inner work.

[2] **Sexual Energy and Energy Centers** – Conscious sexual exchange can open and energize higher centers. Unconscious or distorted exchange can reinforce blockages and imbalance.

[3] **Skipping the Lower Centers** – Focusing only on higher chakras without healing the emotional and relational centers creates energetic instability and spiritual confusion.

[4] **Self-Acceptance as Healing** – The true path of healing is through radical acceptance. Self-judgment and rejection deepen fragmentation rather than resolve it.

[5] **Faith and Inner Work** – Spiritual transformation is not

external. It is the daily practice of inner alignment, self-love, and trust in divine guidance.

> "Difficulties come not to obstruct, but to instruct. Within every setback or obstacle lie seeds of an equal or greater benefit or opportunity."
>
> (Brian Tracy)

Ra's Message from Session 55

Summary:
Ra explains how *the adept*—a spiritually advanced seeker—uses the *disciplines of the personality* to align with the Creator and become a more powerful *instrument of healing and light*. They describe how the adept balances *love, wisdom,* and *will,* and caution that attempts to wield spiritual power without balance can cause serious distortion. Ra also emphasizes that *humility and surrender* are essential for deep transformation.

Ra's Message:
I am Ra. The path of the *adept* begins when the seeker recognizes that their life is not random, but a sacred offering.[1] The adept does not try to control the world, but instead seeks to *master the self* through *discipline, awareness,* and *alignment with love.*

The key to this transformation lies in what we call the *disciplines of the personality*.[2] These include: knowing the self, accepting the self, and becoming the Creator. This is not arrogance—it is the realization that you are not separate from the Infinite One. You are a reflection of its light.

To walk this path, you must balance *love, wisdom,* and *will*.[3] Love without wisdom becomes blind sacrifice. Wisdom without love becomes cold and manipulative. Will without either leads to imbalance or domination. The adept must refine all three, in harmony.

You asked about the *risks of magical working* or *spiritual power*. We affirm: true power cannot be forced.[4] It emerges naturally when the self is purified, balanced, and surrendered.

Attempting to harness higher energy while remaining emotionally or spiritually distorted is like placing high voltage through unstable wiring—it leads to damage, confusion, or even spiritual reversal.

This is why we urge *daily inner work*.[5] Meditation, contemplation, prayer, silence—these help stabilize the energy centers and bring the self into alignment. In this clarity, the light of the Creator flows effortlessly through you.

The adept becomes a *channel*, not a commander. You do not create the power—you *align with it*. You do not teach by speaking alone—you teach by *being*.[6]

Let your life become your offering. Let your service come from wholeness. And let your every step be guided by *love and humility*.

I am Ra. All is well. You are conscientious. I now leave this working. I leave you, my friends, in the love and in the light of the One Infinite Creator. Go forth, then, rejoicing in the power and in the peace of the One Infinite Creator. Adonai.

Footnotes:

[1] **Adept and Sacred Living** – The adept is one who sees all of life as an opportunity to align with the Creator and refine the self through spiritual discipline.

[2] **Disciplines of the Personality** – A central teaching in Ra's material: know yourself, accept yourself, become the Creator. This is the path to wholeness.

[3] **Balancing Love, Wisdom, and Will** – Each quality must be developed and harmonized. Overemphasis on one leads to distortion and spiritual imbalance.

[4] **Risks of Premature Power** – Seeking magical or psychic power without inner balance can lead to energetic, emotional, or karmic complications.

⁵ **Stabilization Through Practice** – Ra consistently emphasizes the importance of meditation and quiet self-reflection for inner harmony and spiritual clarity.

⁶ **Teaching by Being** – The most powerful spiritual teaching is the vibration and presence of the seeker who lives their truth with love and awareness.

> "Death is not real, even in the relative sense – it is but Birth to a new life – and you shall go on, and on, and on, to higher and still higher planes of life, for aeons upon aeons of time. The Universe is your home, and you shall explore its farthest recesses before the end of Time. You are dwelling in the Infinite MIND of the ALL, and your possibilities and opportunities are infinite, both in time and space. And at the end of the Grand Cycle of Aeons, when THE ALL shall draw back into itself all of its creations – you will go gladly, for you will then be able to know the Whole Truth of being At One with THE ALL. Such is the report of the Illumined – those who have advanced well along The Path."
>
> (The Kybalion)

Ra's Message from Session 56

Summary:
Ra explains that all spiritual seeking must be grounded in *love and balance*. They describe how excessive emphasis on *intellect, psychic development,* or *external signs* can lead the seeker away from true growth. Ra clarifies that the *purpose of third density* is to make the *choice of polarity*, and that attempting to "escape" discomfort through spiritual bypassing creates further distortion. They remind the seeker that *silence, surrender,* and *authentic presence* are the gateway to inner power.

Ra's Message:
I am Ra. The path of spiritual seeking must begin with the heart.[1] Many seekers are tempted to focus on knowledge, mystical experiences, or paranormal events. These things have value only when they arise from a foundation of *love, humility,* and *inner harmony*.

You asked about the balance between *intellectual seeking* and *spiritual growth*. We affirm: *knowledge alone does not polarize the soul*.[2] Polarity—the deepening of your spiritual path—comes from *the quality of your choices*, especially when those choices are made in love, even amid uncertainty.

We also caution against the desire for *psychic experiences* or *miraculous signs* as proof of progress.[3] Such desires, though common, often reflect a need for external validation. They distract from the quieter, deeper work of knowing and loving the self.

The purpose of third density is to choose your polarity—

to align with *service to others* or *service to self*.⁴ All else is secondary. When this choice is made with clarity, even your smallest actions become spiritual acts. When the choice is muddled or delayed, catalyst increases.

This is why discomfort and confusion are not failures.⁵ They are signals that more awareness is needed. Many attempt to escape this discomfort by imagining they are beyond it or claiming knowledge they have not yet integrated. This is spiritual bypassing, and it leads to imbalance.

True power comes through *inner stillness*.⁶ When you release the need to prove or perform, and instead allow yourself to be present with what is, the doors to transformation open. The Creator is not impressed by your knowledge. The Creator meets you in your sincerity.

We leave you with this: *your presence is your practice*. Each moment is sacred. Each emotion is a doorway. Each breath is an offering.

I am Ra. All is well, my friends. I leave you in the love and in the light of the One Infinite Creator. Go forth, therefore, rejoicing in the power and in the peace of the One Infinite Creator. Adonai.

Footnotes:

[1] **Begin with the Heart** – Ra emphasizes that love is the foundation of spiritual evolution. Without it, even advanced abilities become distorted.

[2] **Knowledge vs. Polarity** – Intellectual understanding alone does not lead to spiritual advancement. Polarity is shaped by how you live and love.

[3] **Seeking Signs vs. Seeking Self** – The desire for proof or phenomena often distracts from true spiritual growth, which is internal and often quiet.

[4] **The Central Choice** – The primary goal of third density is

choosing service to others (positive polarity) or service to self (negative polarity). Everything else supports this.

[5] **Catalyst as Communication** – Pain and confusion are not signs of failure; they are spiritual communication urging you to awaken more deeply.

[6] **Power Through Stillness** – Ra consistently teaches that inner silence and self-acceptance create the conditions for higher spiritual contact and transformation.

> "When you have learned how to decide with God all decisions become as easy and as right as breathing. There is no effort and you will be led as gently as if you were being carried down a quiet path in summer."
>
> (Helen Schucman, A Course in Miracles)

Ra's Message from Session 57

Summary:
Ra discusses how *environmental catalyst*, such as *weather*, can reflect or respond to the *collective consciousness* of a group or region. They also explain how *intentional focus* and *meditation* can influence the physical world in small ways. Ra emphasizes that seekers should not become distracted by *phenomena*, but instead focus on *inner transformation* through *love, discipline,* and *balanced energy flow*.

Ra's Message:
I am Ra. The world you see around you is not separate from you.[1] The *outer environment* reflects the *inner vibrations* of both individuals and groups. Storms, winds, or disruptions are not punishments—they are *catalysts and mirrors*, helping you see what lies beneath the surface of collective thought.

We were asked about the influence of *consciousness on weather*.[2] In some cases, focused intention or emotional intensity can temporarily affect local conditions. However, this is rare and usually occurs when a group is in *strong harmony* or focused on a *shared desire or imbalance*.

We caution you: while such effects may appear mysterious or powerful, they are not the goal of the spiritual path.[3] Do not measure your progress by phenomena. Instead, ask: *Am I becoming more loving? More balanced? More honest with myself?*

The ability to affect the outer world is not a sign of spiritual superiority. In fact, the most advanced seekers often avoid displaying power, because they know that *true power is inner alignment*.[4]

We were also asked about how to deepen spiritual practice. We repeat: *meditation is essential.* Even five minutes of silence each day, done with sincerity and openness, creates changes in your energy field.[5] It helps you release distortion and become a more accurate channel for the Creator's love.

Each day offers countless opportunities for refinement—not in performing miracles, but in *choosing love when it is difficult, staying centered in confusion,* and *speaking truth with compassion.*

This is the true path of the adept: not to control the world, but to *become a vessel for light.*

I am Ra. I leave you in the love and in the light of the One Infinite Creator. Go forth, therefore, rejoicing in the power and in the peace of the One Infinite Creator. Adonai.

Footnotes:

[1] **The World as Mirror** – Ra teaches that our physical environment reflects our inner and collective states. Weather, for example, can carry symbolic or energetic messages.

[2] **Consciousness and Weather** – While rare, Ra acknowledges that focused thought and group energy can have minor effects on physical conditions like weather patterns.

[3] **Spiritual Phenomena Are Not the Goal** – Seeking paranormal influence or signs can become a distraction. Ra urges the seeker to return to inner work and balance.

[4] **Power as Alignment** – Real spiritual influence arises from energetic alignment with love and truth—not from dramatic or external demonstrations.

[5] **Daily Meditation** – Even short, consistent moments of quiet are transformative. Ra repeatedly emphasizes this as the foundation of spiritual development.

"You are a light for the whole world. A city built on top of a hill cannot be hidden, and no one lights a lamp and puts it under a clay pot. Instead, it is placed on a lampstand, where it can give light to everyone in the house. Make your light shine, so others will see the good you do and will praise your Father in heaven."

(Matthew 5:14-16)

Ra's Message from Session 58

Summary:
Ra explains how *the physical body* serves as a *mirror* for the mind and spirit. Symptoms, tension, and posture can all reflect inner imbalance. They discuss how *healing* involves not only adjusting the body but also working with *mental and spiritual distortions*. Ra also describes how sound vibration, such as music or chanting, can support energy alignment and spiritual healing when used with intention and harmony.

Ra's Message:
I am Ra. Your body is not separate from your spiritual journey —it is a *reflection of your mind and spirit*.[1] The posture you hold, the symptoms you experience, and even your habitual movements all provide insight into your *inner state*.

Many of your illnesses and discomforts are not random.[2] They are messages from deeper parts of yourself. Pain often arises where energy is blocked or distorted. Healing begins when you are willing to *listen* to your body and understand what it is showing you.

We were asked about *spinal alignment*. This is important not just physically, but energetically.[3] The spine is the central channel through which spiritual energy flows. When tension, trauma, or chronic misalignment is present, energy movement is disrupted. Adjustments can help—but only when paired with *inner work*, such as self-awareness and emotional release.

You also asked about *sound as a healing tool*. We affirm: sound is a *powerful vibrational force*.[4] When used with clear intention and harmony, sound can help *release blockages, soothe the mind*, and *amplify spiritual awareness*. Simple practices like *chanting, toning*, or listening to *pure musical tones* can support realignment.

But we remind you: no tool can replace *conscious alignment with love and self-acceptance*.[5] Sound, posture, and movement are aids—not the source of healing. That source is *within you*.

The adept learns to read the body not with judgment, but with *gentle curiosity*.[6] When the body aches, ask: *What emotion is unexpressed? What belief am I holding?* This is how you uncover hidden distortions and allow energy to flow again.

All parts of your being—mind, body, and spirit—are aspects of the same light. When they are in harmony, you become a *clear vessel* for the Creator's presence.

I am Ra. You are conscientious. I leave you, my friends, in the love and in the light of the One Infinite Creator. Go forth, therefore, rejoicing in the power and in the peace of the One Infinite Creator. Adonai.

Footnotes:

[1] **Body as Reflection** – Ra teaches that the body reflects the inner conditions of the mind and spirit. It is a communication tool, not just a vehicle.

[2] **Illness as Message** – Many physical imbalances originate from unresolved emotional or spiritual patterns. Listening to the body helps uncover deeper healing needs.

[3] **Spine and Energy Flow**—The spine is considered a central energy channel (similar to the Sushumna in yoga). Alignment supports the upward movement of spiritual energy.

[4] **Sound as Healing Tool** – Vibration affects energy centers. Certain sounds can balance, activate, or calm specific chakras, especially when used intentionally.

[5] **Inner Alignment Is Primary** – External tools can support healing, but true transformation comes from internal work: awareness, love, and acceptance.

[6] **Body Awareness and Self-Inquiry** – Physical symptoms often carry emotional or mental roots. The adept approaches the body with loving attention, not fear.

"There are three ingredients for contact:
1. Connection to One-Mind Consciousness
2. A sincere heart
3. Clear intent."

(From the CE5 Handbook)

Ra's Message from Session 59

Summary:
Ra speaks about how *healing* takes place when the *mind, body, and spirit* are aligned in *truth, love,* and *openness to the Creator*. They explain that both the healer and the one to be healed must be in harmony with *universal energy flow*. Ra also emphasizes the importance of *light touch, intention,* and *respect for free will* in energy work, and they remind us that all true healing begins with *inner acceptance*.

Ra's Message:
I am Ra. Healing is not something done *to* another.[1] It is a process of *allowing energy to return to balance*. True healing occurs when the *one who seeks healing* and the *one who offers healing* are both aligned with the *infinite energy of the Creator*.

We spoke previously about the *mind/body/spirit complex* and now emphasize: healing requires that these aspects *resonate together*.[2] If the mind believes it is broken, the spirit will struggle to flow freely. If the body is treated with force instead of love, it resists change.

The role of the healer is to *create the conditions* in which balance may be restored.[3] This involves *purity of intention, open-hearted presence,* and *respect for the other's path*. The healer does not fix. The healer *offers space and light*.

You asked about the *laying on of hands*. This is effective when the touch is offered *gently* and with *focused love*.[4] The hands are channels, not tools of control. Energy flows best when there is *no personal agenda*, only the desire to be a vessel for healing.

We remind you again that *free will must be honored*.[5] Healing cannot be forced. Even unconscious resistance can block the process. Therefore, it is important to work *with the person*, not simply *on* them.

Healing begins and ends with *self-acceptance*.[6] Whether you are seeking to heal or serve as a healer, your first task is to *love the self as it is*. From that space, alignment with the Creator becomes natural.

No technique is more powerful than the presence of one who truly embodies peace.

I am Ra. All is well. I leave you in the love and in the light of the One Infinite Creator. Go forth, then, rejoicing in the power and the peace of the One Infinite Creator. Adonai.

Footnotes:

[1] **Healing as Alignment, Not Force** – Ra defines healing as the return to energetic balance. It's not about fixing, but about restoring natural flow through spiritual alignment.

[2] **Mind/Body/Spirit Harmony** – For lasting healing, all parts of the self must be considered. Mental beliefs, physical conditions, and spiritual alignment must resonate.

[3] **Healer as Channel** – The healer does not supply the healing energy—it comes from the Creator. The healer's job is to clear their own distortions and be present.

[4] **Laying on of Hands** – A gentle, loving touch combined with pure intention can help transfer or amplify spiritual energy, aiding in rebalancing the energy centers.

[5] **Respecting Free Will** – Healing can only occur if the one being healed is consciously or unconsciously open to receive. No healing should override autonomy.

[6] **Self-Acceptance as Foundation** – Ra emphasizes that all healing, whether physical or spiritual, begins with the deep acceptance of the self without judgment.

"The Universe may be divided into three great classes of phenomena, known as the Three Great Planes, namely:

1.   The Great Physical Plane
2.   The Great Mental Plane
3.   The Great Spiritual Plane"

(The Kybalion)

Ra's Message from Session 60

Summary:
Ra discusses how spiritual seekers often experience *intensified catalyst* as they progress, especially when they begin to access *intelligent energy* and *contact with the higher self*. They explain that this intensity is not punishment, but a sign of *readiness for deeper work*. Ra emphasizes that *spiritual humility, persistence,* and *balance* are needed to stay aligned through this phase. They also address how the *Law of Responsibility* ensures that those with greater awareness are called to greater integrity.

Ra's Message:
I am Ra. As you grow in awareness, you will notice that your *catalyst*—the events and emotions that shape your path—often becomes more intense.[1] This is not a sign of failure, but a confirmation that you are ready for *more refined lessons.*

When you begin to contact *intelligent energy* and your *higher self*, your distortions are no longer hidden.[2] That which you once ignored now feels urgent. That which you avoided returns again and again. This is the nature of accelerated learning.

We caution you not to interpret this intensity as a mistake. Rather, see it as an opportunity to *choose love, balance,* and *authenticity* even under pressure.[3] This is how the soul is polished and prepared for higher densities.

You asked about the *Law of Responsibility*. We affirm: when you know more, you are asked to live with *greater alignment*.[4] Spiritual awareness carries with it a sacred weight. The more light you hold, the more conscious your choices must become.

This is not a burden—it is an invitation to embody your truth fully. The spiritually mature being does not hide behind excuses. They ask, "What is the most loving response now?" and act accordingly, even in difficulty.

We remind you that *spiritual pride* is a common trap at this stage.[5] The desire to be special, advanced, or powerful can quietly replace humility. When this happens, distortion increases. Stay grounded in service, not status.

You are not meant to escape catalyst, but to *walk through it with clarity*. Each moment of discomfort is an invitation to deepen your trust in the Creator within.

Let your practice be simple: *meditate, serve, reflect*. These keep you steady through the intensity and prepare you to share light with others in their own storms.

I am Ra. Be merry, my friends. All is well and your conscientiousness is to be recommended. We leave you in the love and the light of the One Infinite Creator. Rejoice, then, and go forth in the peace and in the glory of the One Infinite Creator. I am Ra. Adonai.

Footnotes:

[1] **Intensified Catalyst** – As spiritual awareness increases, unresolved distortions surface more quickly and powerfully. This sharpens the path of learning.

[2] **Contact with Intelligent Energy and Higher Self** – Opening to higher spiritual forces brings clarity but also confrontation with previously hidden imbalance.

[3] **Catalyst as Opportunity, Not Punishment** – Intensity should not be feared. It is a mirror that accelerates evolution when met with love and honesty.

[4] **Law of Responsibility** – With greater knowledge and access to spiritual power comes the responsibility to act in alignment with that awareness.

⁵ **Spiritual Pride as Distortion** – Believing oneself spiritually superior can block growth. True power is expressed through humility, not hierarchy.

> "From everyone who has been given much, much will be demanded; and to whom they entrusted much, of him they will ask all the more."
>
> (Luke 12:48b)

Ra's Message from Session 61

Summary:
Ra explains the energetic differences between *service to others* and *service to self* paths, and how each path interacts with *sexual energy* and *healing*. They clarify how energy transfers, when conscious and intentional, can accelerate spiritual growth. Ra also warns that *imbalances in energy centers*, especially when ignored, can create *psychic vulnerabilities*. Balance and purity of intention are essential for safe and effective spiritual progress.

Ra's Message:
I am Ra. The two paths—*service to others* and *service to self*—use the same energy system, but in opposite ways.[1] Those on the positive path open their energy centers to share freely. Those on the negative path manipulate energy through control and separation.

Both paths are valid in third density, and each polarizes through *intention and repetition*.[2] Your work as a seeker is to become aware of how energy moves through you—and what you are offering the world through your thoughts, actions, and relationships.

You asked about *sexual energy transfers*. These are opportunities for great growth—or distortion—depending on the alignment of the partners.[3] When both individuals are seeking love, service, and unity, the energy transferred is healing and transformative. It clears and energizes the green-ray center and can even stimulate higher spiritual openings.

But if the interaction is based on fear, control, or avoidance of vulnerability, the energy exchange becomes distorted, reinforcing lower center blockages.[4] These blockages, if unacknowledged, can create psychic weakness, attracting interference or confusion.

The *spirit complex* is particularly sensitive.[5] When you open yourself spiritually without balancing the lower centers—especially the red, orange, and yellow—you create an unstable foundation. Spiritual work must be rooted in emotional clarity and physical integrity.

We are often asked how to protect against psychic difficulty. We affirm: *balance is protection*.[6] The well-aligned seeker is naturally shielded by their own clarity and presence. Confusion and self-doubt are the most common openings for distortion.

Do not fear your imbalances—*work with them consciously*. Do not rush your awakening—*build it on love and patience*. And do not seek power—*seek truth and service*.

Every breath you take with awareness opens a door. Every act of love polarizes your soul. And every sincere attempt to understand yourself is honored by the Creator.

I am Ra. I leave you in the love and in the light of the One Infinite Creator. Go forth, my friends, rejoicing in the power and in the peace of the One Infinite Creator. Adonai.

Footnotes:

[1] **Opposite Use of Energy Centers** – Positive beings open energy to give and connect. Negative beings restrict and control to draw power inward for self-dominance.

[2] **Polarity Through Repetition** – Your path is not determined by isolated actions but by consistent intention and pattern over time.

[3] **Sexual Energy as Spiritual Catalyst** – Ra teaches that conscious sexual union can help open and clear energy centers,

especially when aligned with love and trust.

[4] **Distorted Sexual Exchanges** – When sexual energy is exchanged without emotional or spiritual harmony, it can reinforce blockages in the lower centers.

[5] **Spirit Complex Vulnerability** – The spiritual aspect of self must be protected through grounded energy work. Opening the crown without clearing lower chakras can destabilize the seeker.

[6] **Balance as Protection** – The best spiritual protection is energetic coherence—self-awareness, alignment, and emotional clarity.

> "Let patience have her perfect work, so you may be complete and have everything you need."
>
> (James 1:4)

Ra's Message from Session 62

Summary:
Ra explains how *preincarnative choices* shape each person's body, mind, and life experiences to support their spiritual goals. They emphasize that *physical limitations or challenges* are often chosen before birth to accelerate growth. Ra also addresses how *sexual energy* and *catalyst* help seekers polarize more clearly. The session ends with a reminder that inner intention is more important than outer appearance.

Ra's Message:
I am Ra. Before birth, each soul makes choices—about the *body*, the *mind*, and the *path of experience*—designed to help it grow and polarize in this lifetime.[1] These choices are not always pleasant. Some involve physical weakness or emotional challenge. But all are made in alignment with the soul's desire to evolve.

You asked why some experience *physical distortion*, such as limitation or illness.[2] Often, this is a *preincarnative decision*. By choosing a limitation, the soul may deepen compassion, reduce distraction, or strengthen focus on spiritual work. These are not punishments but tools.

We also discussed *sexual energy and polarity*.[3] Sexual attraction, partnership, and energy exchange serve as powerful catalyst. When these are approached with love, respect, and open communication, they help activate higher energy centers and deepen polarity in service to others.

When approached through desire for control, conquest, or withdrawal from vulnerability, they reinforce lower center

195

blockages and the path of service to self.[4] These patterns are not inherently negative—they simply reflect which path is being chosen.

The seeker is called to become aware of their *intentions and patterns*.[5] This is more important than appearance or status. Whether your body is strong or weak, beautiful or plain, it is the vessel through which your light shines. How you use it is the measure of your progress.

You also asked about our previous contact with your peoples. We affirm: we came in love and were misunderstood.[6] Our forms were taken as divine, and our words as commandments. This created imbalance, not alignment.

We now speak through more subtle means, such as this channeling.[7] This protects your free will and allows seekers to approach our teaching with discernment.

To each who walks the path of seeking, we say: *your circumstances were chosen for you, by you, with love.* Honor them. Use them. And in doing so, *you transform them into light*.

I am Ra. All is well. You have been most conscientious. I leave you, my friends, in the glory of the love and the light of the One Infinite Creator. Go forth, then, rejoicing in the power and in the peace of the One Infinite Creator. Adonai.

Footnotes:

[1] **Preincarnative Planning** – Ra teaches that before incarnation, the soul chooses key experiences and limitations to support spiritual evolution and polarity.

[2] **Physical Challenges as Catalyst** – Illness, disability, or bodily limitation can serve a higher purpose when seen as part of a soul's growth process.

[3] **Sexual Energy and Growth** – Sexual experiences can help the soul polarize more clearly—toward love and service or control and separation—depending on intent.

⁴ **Lower Center Blockages** – When sexual energy is used for manipulation, conquest, or fear avoidance, it reinforces distortions in red, orange, and yellow ray centers.

⁵ **Inner Intention Over Outer Form** – Ra consistently teaches that the state of the heart and the purity of intention matter more than appearances or physical condition.

⁶ **Ra's Earlier Contact** – Ra visited ancient Egypt in physical form but was misunderstood and worshipped, causing spiritual imbalance.

⁷ **Subtle Contact via Channeling** – To avoid violating free will, Ra now communicates only when invited through inner seeking and conscious resonance.

> "Whatever affects one directly, affects all indirectly. I can never be what I ought to be until you are what you ought to be. This is the interrelated structure of reality."
>
> (Dr. Martin Luther King, Jr.)

Ra's Message from Session 63

Summary:
Ra explains how *catalyst intensifies* as a soul nears graduation from third density, especially for those consciously choosing the *service-to-others path*. They also clarify that *free will* must be honored, even by higher beings, and that attempts to interfere—whether by positive or negative forces—are limited by this universal law. Ra addresses how *healing, polarity,* and even *malfunction of technology* can result from changes in spiritual vibration.

Ra's Message:
I am Ra. As you move closer to the end of third density, your experiences may become more intense.[1] This is not punishment. It is the natural result of your soul drawing in deeper catalyst to accelerate your growth and clarify your chosen path.

For those consciously choosing the *path of service to others*, catalyst often focuses on the heart:[2] lessons of forgiveness, empathy, humility, and inner peace. These may surface through relationships, illness, confusion, or challenge.

We were asked about the *Law of Free Will*. We affirm: even higher beings, including ourselves, must never violate this law.[3] We cannot impose truth. We may only respond when asked, or influence indirectly through dreams, intuition, or synchronicity.

The same applies to *negative entities*, who attempt to control or deceive.[4] They too are limited. If you do not vibrate in fear or self-doubt, they cannot reach you. The best defense is *clarity and love.* When your energy is coherent, you are invisible to distortion.

You asked about *technology failure* in the presence of higher vibration. We affirm: changes in *spiritual frequency* affect your material systems.[5] Devices may malfunction when high vibration energy flows through a space not tuned to receive it. This is not sabotage—it is resonance.

We also spoke about *healing*. True healing does not come from the outer technique alone.[6] It comes when the one to be healed *accepts the lesson, releases resistance,* and *opens to alignment.* The healer may assist—but cannot replace—this inner work.

Let us remind you: your struggles are signs of awakening, not failure. Each difficulty is a door. Each question is a call. Each breath is a new chance to return to love.

I am Ra. You are conscientious. All is well. We leave you now, my friends, in the glory of the love and the light of the One Infinite Creator. Go forth, then, rejoicing in the power and in the peace of the Infinite Creator. Adonai.

Footnotes:

[1] **End-of-Cycle Catalyst** – As the soul approaches the end of third density, catalyst becomes more concentrated to aid in the final choice of polarity.

[2] **Heart-Centered Lessons** – For positively polarized beings, the focus is often on compassion, forgiveness, and service. These are key to fourth-density readiness.

[3] **Law of Free Will** – No being, no matter how advanced, may override your free will. All spiritual aid must be invited or chosen consciously.

[4] **Protection Through Clarity** – Negative entities are drawn to distortion. The more balanced and loving your energy, the less accessible you are to interference.

⁵ **Technology and Vibrational Interference** – Spiritual energy can unintentionally disrupt electronics or systems not tuned to higher frequencies.

⁶ **Healing as Inner Alignment** – Ra consistently teaches that healing requires participation by the one being healed. No outer method alone can create wholeness.

"And lest I should be exalted above measure by the abundance of the revelations, a thorn in the flesh was given to me, a messenger of Satan [negative entity] sent to buffet me, lest I be exalted above measure. Concerning this thing I pleaded with the Lord three times that it might depart from me. And He said to me, "My grace is sufficient for you, for My strength is made perfect in weakness." Therefore most gladly I will rather boast in my infirmities, that the power of Christ may rest upon me. Therefore I take pleasure in infirmities, in reproaches, in needs, in persecutions, in distresses, for Christ's sake. For when I am weak, then I am strong."

(2 Corinthians 12:7-10)

Ra's Message from Session 64

Summary:
Ra discusses the current *harvest*—the end of the third-density cycle on Earth—and explains that spiritual graduation depends on *consistent polarization*, not perfection. They emphasize that *each choice matters*, and that *small acts of love* contribute to one's overall vibrational alignment. Ra also addresses the *temptation to over-intellectualize* the path and reminds seekers that *balance, humility,* and *daily self-reflection* are key to evolution.

Ra's Message:
I am Ra. Your planet is experiencing the *harvest*—a transition where souls may graduate from third density to the next level of experience.[1] This graduation is not based on beliefs, traditions, or dramatic achievements. It is based on *vibrational consistency*—the overall direction of your choices.

To graduate into *fourth density positive*, one must align with *love and service to others* consistently—at least 51% of the time.[2] This does not mean perfection. It means that your intention, your heart, and your actions are most often oriented toward kindness, compassion, and unity.

Each moment matters. Every act of forgiveness, generosity, or patience strengthens your polarity.[3] It is not about dramatic gestures but about choosing love in the small, unseen parts of daily life.

We caution against the tendency to seek spiritual progress through *complex reasoning or intellectual analysis*.[4] While study can be helpful, the true work is inner: the *balancing of emotions,* the *healing of relationships*, and the *deepening of self-acceptance*.

You also asked about contacting *intelligent infinity*—the direct experience of the Creator. This is possible only when the energy centers are fully aligned, especially the indigo and violet rays.[5] But this experience is not to be sought for thrill or power. It comes as a byproduct of deep surrender and service.

Beware the desire to *measure yourself* or others. Spiritual comparison creates distortion.[6] Each path is unique. What appears slow in time may be profound in depth.

The harvest is happening now. Not in fear, but in love. Not in judgment, but in reflection. Each seeker determines their readiness through *their vibration*, not their words.

Stay in the practice. Return to love when you fall. Trust the light within. This is the way forward.

I am Ra. Be fearless and know that love is the greatest protection. I leave you, my friends, in the glorious love and joyful light of the Infinite Creator. Go forth, then, rejoicing in the power and in the peace of the One Infinite Creator. Adonai.

Footnotes:

[1] **Harvest as Transition** – Ra uses "harvest" to describe the end of a density cycle when souls graduate to the next level based on their polarity.

[2] **51% Service to Others** – To graduate positively, a soul must polarize toward love and unity more than half the time. The focus is on consistent intention.

[3] **Small Choices Matter** – Spiritual growth happens through everyday actions and decisions that reflect compassion, honesty, and kindness.

[4] **Intellect vs. Inner Work** – Over-reliance on mental analysis can block emotional healing and spiritual balance. Heart-centered integration is essential.

⁵ **Contact with Intelligent Infinity** – Direct access to the Creator occurs when the energy centers are fully balanced and the seeker has become transparent to love.

⁶ **Avoiding Comparison** – Comparing spiritual paths leads to judgment and distortion. Each seeker must walk their own road with integrity.

> "There is no fear in love. But perfect love drives out fear, because fear has to do with punishment. The one who fears is not made perfect in love."
>
> (1 John 4:18)

Ra's Message from Session 65

Summary:
Ra explains how *polarization* is the engine of spiritual evolution, and how *catalyst* helps deepen that polarization by pushing the seeker toward either *love* or *control*. They emphasize that true *service to others* includes *self-love*, and that rejection of the self weakens spiritual power. Ra also describes how the *harvestable soul* is one who has become stable in their chosen path—not perfect, but consistent.

Ra's Message:
I am Ra. The spiritual path is a journey of *polarization*.[1] Every experience invites you to align more deeply with *service to others* (through love, compassion, and unity) or *service to self* (through control, separation, and dominance). Both are valid paths of growth.

You asked about catalyst—life's challenges and experiences. These events are not random.[2] They are offered to help you polarize. How you respond determines your direction. Avoiding, blaming, or numbing delays growth. Embracing, reflecting, and choosing love accelerates it.

We emphasize that *serving others includes loving the self*.[3] Many seekers mistakenly believe that self-sacrifice, guilt, or self-denial are signs of spiritual maturity. But if you reject yourself, you reject the very being through which the Creator expresses love.

The goal is not to *eliminate distortion*, but to *balance it*.[4] You may still feel anger, fear, or doubt—but when you acknowledge and love these parts of yourself, they lose power over you. This is healing.

You also asked how a soul becomes *harvestable*. The answer is not found in dramatic acts or external proof.[5] A harvestable soul is one whose energy has become *stable* in polarity. Whether in joy or suffering, that soul continues to choose its path—consistently and consciously.

Even the smallest act of kindness, when done with a sincere heart, shines brightly in the totality of your being.[6] You do not need to be perfect. You need to be honest, committed, and open to transformation.

We remind you that spiritual strength comes from *balance*. The seeker who grounds in silence, opens the heart, and walks humbly will shine like a beacon, even without speaking a word.

Let your life be your message. Let your choices align with love. And let your journey be guided not by pressure, but by peace.

I am Ra. I leave you, my friends, rejoicing in the love and the light of the One Infinite Creator. Go forth, therefore, glorying in the power and in the peace of the One Infinite Creator. Adonai.

Footnotes:

[1] **Polarization as Core of Evolution** – Ra teaches that the purpose of third density is to polarize toward either service to others (positive) or service to self (negative).

[2] **Catalyst Deepens Polarity** – Life events are designed to challenge and refine your spiritual direction. Your responses are opportunities to grow.

[3] **Self-Love is Service to Others** – You are part of the Creator. Loving yourself is not selfish, it is essential for true service to others.

[4] **Balance, Not Elimination** – The seeker must acknowledge

and harmonize inner distortions. Suppression creates imbalance; loving awareness heals.

⁵ **Harvestability and Consistency** – Graduation to fourth density depends on stable alignment, not external achievement. Integrity and intention matter most.

⁶ **Every Act Counts** – Ra reminds us that spiritual light is built through small, consistent choices. Nothing loving is ever wasted.

> "I do not speak from want, for I have learned to be content in whatever circumstances I am. I know how to get along with humble means, and I also know how to live in prosperity; in any and every circumstance, I have learned the secret of being filled and going hungry, both of having abundance and suffering need. I can do all things through Him who strengthens me."
>
> (Philippians 4:11-13)

Ra's Message from Session 66

Summary:
Ra emphasizes the importance of *inner harmony* and *emotional balance* for spiritual growth. They explain how *blockages in the lower energy centers*, especially around *personal power and relationships*, must be healed before higher consciousness can be sustained. Ra also warns against spiritual pride, encouraging humility and *consistent self-work*. They reaffirm that true progress is shown by the *ability to remain centered in love*, even in difficulty.

Ra's Message:
I am Ra. The work of the seeker is not only in reaching toward the heavens, but in *bringing harmony to the foundation*.[1] The energy centers at the base of your being—survival, identity, emotions, and power—must be *balanced and accepted* for higher contact to be stable.

Many seekers wish to move quickly into the heart or beyond. But when lower centers are *ignored or rejected*, the structure collapses.[2] True spiritual light flows *from root to crown*, and each level of self must be honored with patience and care.

You asked about difficulties in maintaining *polarization*. We affirm: polarization is lost when the seeker reacts with fear, blame, or withdrawal—especially in emotionally charged situations.[3] The spiritual path requires not repression, but *awareness and acceptance* of all feelings.

You also asked about *spiritual pride*. We caution strongly against it.[4] When a seeker believes they are advanced, they stop learning. When they see others as less awakened, they block compassion. These distortions can unravel progress and attract negative influence.

The antidote is *humility and daily alignment.* No matter how far you've come, each moment is a new beginning. The truly wise know they are always students of love.

We were asked about energy center balancing. We say again: attend to the *red ray*—your sense of survival and safety; the *orange ray*—your emotions and relationships; and the *yellow ray*—your social identity and sense of power.[5] These must be explored, understood, and loved.

Only then can the *green ray*—the heart—remain open and stable. Without this foundation, attempts to reach higher create imbalance.

Your journey is not to become perfect, but to become whole.[6] The distorted parts of you are not enemies—they are children waiting to be held in light.

Meditate, reflect, love, and release. In doing so, you will become a living channel for the Creator's presence.

I am Ra. Continue as always in love. All is well. You are conscientious. I leave you in the love and in the light of the One Infinite Creator. Go forth rejoicing in the power and the peace of the One Infinite Creator. Adonai.

Footnotes:

[1] **Foundation Before Flight** – Ra reminds us that stable spiritual growth begins with healing and harmonizing the lower energy centers (root, sacral, solar plexus).

[2] **No Skipping Steps** – Attempting to bypass emotional or personal healing blocks higher spiritual development and creates energetic instability.

[3] **Losing Polarity Through Reaction** – When seekers habitually respond with anger, fear, or blame, their positive

spiritual charge weakens. Awareness restores alignment.

[4] **Spiritual Pride as a Trap** – Believing oneself to be spiritually superior blocks humility and openness—two essential qualities of service to others.

[5] **Energy Center Healing** – Ra consistently teaches that energy must flow freely from the root upward. Blockages in red, orange, or yellow rays must be lovingly addressed.

[6] **Wholeness Over Perfection** – The goal is not to eliminate imperfection, but to fully accept all aspects of the self. This is true integration.

> "Whoever exalts himself shall be humbled; and whoever humbles himself shall be exalted."
>
> (Matthew 23:12)

Ra's Message from Session 67

Summary:
Ra explores how *spiritual progress* can attract *psychic attacks*, especially when a seeker becomes a powerful source of light. They explain that such interference often targets *existing distortions*, using them as entry points. Ra also clarifies how *acceptance of the self*, including perceived flaws, creates protection. They emphasize that *resistance, fear,* and *denial* weaken the energy field, while *love, balance,* and *self-awareness* fortify it.

Ra's Message:
I am Ra. As you advance along the path of seeking, your *light increases*.[1] That light may attract attention—both positive and negative. This is not to be feared. It is part of your journey, and a sign of growing spiritual power.

Negative entities do not create new weaknesses. They *amplify distortions already present within you*.[2] If you fear, they reflect fear. If you doubt, they deepen doubt. The more balanced and accepting you become, the fewer openings exist for this interference.

You asked how to protect oneself. We affirm: *acceptance is the greatest protection*.[3] When you see your flaws, love them, and integrate them, you leave no shadow for others to manipulate. Denied aspects of self become tools for distortion. Embraced aspects become allies.

We also caution against *resisting catalyst*.[4] Pain and confusion are not enemies. They are messages. When you resist them, you strengthen the block. When you allow them, you learn, and energy flows again.

You asked about our own distortion in this contact. We affirm that this channeling process is *vulnerable to misinterpretation*, not from deception, but from the filters of the instrument and the group.[5] Therefore, careful preparation, purity of intention, and ongoing self-balancing are essential.

Your path is not about *avoiding interference*, but *becoming stronger through it*.[6] Each challenge is a teacher. Each distortion is an invitation to love more deeply.

Remain steady in meditation. Stay rooted in compassion. And remember: the light you carry is eternal. Darkness cannot extinguish it. It can only teach you how to shine more clearly.

I am Ra. Continue, my friends, in the strength of harmony, love, and light… I leave you now, my friends, in the glory of the love and the light of the Infinite Creator. Go forth, then, rejoicing in the power and in the peace of the One Infinite Creator. Adonai.

Footnotes:

[1] **Light Attracts Attention** – As seekers become more aligned with love and service, their energy becomes noticeable. This can draw both positive and negative attention.

[2] **Interference Targets Distortion** – Psychic attack works by exploiting internal imbalances. These must be healed through self-awareness and acceptance.

[3] **Self-Acceptance as Protection** – Ra teaches that loving the whole self—including perceived flaws—creates energetic integrity and spiritual strength.

[4] **Catalyst as Messenger** – Resistance to pain or confusion blocks growth. Allowing and exploring difficult experiences leads to transformation.

[5] **Distortion in Channeling** – All channeled material, including

Ra's, is affected by the minds and energies of those involved. Discernment and alignment are key.

[6] **Strength Through Challenge** – Interference is not a failure; it is a training ground for deeper resilience, clarity, and balance.

> "Knowing your own darkness is the best method for dealing with the darkness's of other people. One does not become enlightened by imagining figures of light, but by making the darkness conscious. The most terrifying thing is to accept oneself completely. Your visions will become clear only when you can look into your own heart. Who looks outside, dreams; who looks inside, awakes."
>
> (Carl Jung)

Ra's Message from Session 68

Summary:
Ra explains how *true service to others* flows not from effort or obligation, but from an *overflowing of love and presence*. They describe how the *power of radiance*—being fully aligned with one's true self—is more impactful than words or actions alone. Ra also emphasizes that *free will* must always be honored, and that attempting to "fix" or change others without invitation causes spiritual imbalance.

Ra's Message:
I am Ra. Many seekers wish to serve, yet struggle with *how* to do so. We affirm: true service is not something you *do*, it is something you *become*.[1] When you are aligned with love, peace, and clarity, your very presence uplifts others—even without effort.

You asked how to be more effective in helping others. We say: *radiance is more powerful than persuasion*.[2] A being who has balanced their energy centers and opened the heart naturally emits a field of harmony. Others feel safe, seen, and supported in your presence—not because of what you say, but because of who you are.

Attempts to change others through advice, pressure, or control often backfire.[3] Service must respect *free will*. Offer what is asked for. Be available, not forceful. Share your light, not your agenda.

We also discussed *group energy*. When two or more seekers come together in mutual love and intention, their combined field amplifies the light they each hold.[4] This creates a "magnet" for positive influence and support from higher realms.

We remind you again: do not measure service by results.[5] You may not see the impact of your kindness. But every loving thought, every moment of patience, adds to the balance of your world.

The goal is not to *solve everything*, but to *hold space for healing to unfold*.[6] You do not need to fix the darkness. You only need to keep your light steady in its presence.

Stay centered. Act when invited. Rest in silence when needed. And above all, trust that your *being* is your greatest gift to the world.

I am Ra. You are conscientious. All is well, my friends. We thank you and leave you in the love and in the light of the One Infinite Creator. Go forth, therefore, rejoicing in the power and in the peace of the One Infinite Creator. Adonai.

Footnotes:

[1] **Being Over Doing** – Ra teaches that the most powerful service is offered through the quality of one's presence, not necessarily through actions or advice.

[2] **Radiance as Service** – A balanced, loving being naturally uplifts others. Influence happens through vibration more than persuasion.

[3] **Respecting Free Will** – Trying to change or fix someone without their consent creates spiritual imbalance and can weaken your own polarity.

[4] **Group Field Amplification** – When seekers work together in harmony, their spiritual energy becomes greater than the sum of its parts.

[5] **Letting Go of Outcome** – The impact of service is not always visible. Ra encourages trust in the unseen effects of consistent

love.

⁶ **Holding Space Instead of Fixing** – True service involves creating a safe and loving environment for others to grow, rather than directing or controlling their path.

> "Everything about you – your talents, experiences, and even your challenges – has prepared you for this exact time. You don't need to conform to others' standards or expectations. Instead, embrace your individuality and trust that your unique frequency signature fits perfectly into the grand design. When you live authentically, the universe naturally aligns with your energy, bringing opportunities and resources that support your purpose. Conformity only breeds frustration, while authenticity creates clarity, fulfillment, and flow. Your uniqueness was designed for this moment – embrace it confidently and fully."
>
> (From *Faith, Focus, and Flow: The 3 Keys that Unlock Your Superhuman Power*)

Ra's Message from Session 69

Summary:
Ra offers a deeper understanding of *sexual energy transfer* and how it can support spiritual evolution when used with *love and mutual respect*. They clarify that *distortions and blockages* in relationships arise when energy centers are not harmonized. Ra also explains how *healing and balancing the self* prepare the seeker to access *intelligent infinity*—not as a goal, but as a natural result of alignment and surrender.

Ra's Message:
I am Ra. You asked about the *energy of sexual union*. When this exchange is grounded in *mutual love, trust,* and *openness*, it becomes a powerful tool for *spiritual transformation*.[1] It aligns the red, orange, yellow, and green centers, and can even open the gateway to *indigo ray* energy.

Sexual energy is not merely biological—it is a sacred form of communication.[2] When offered consciously, it becomes a form of healing. When used unconsciously, or with control and fear, it reinforces separation and distorts polarity.

We spoke of *blockages in relationships*. These often arise when one or both partners are not balanced in their *personal energy centers*.[3] Without a clear red ray (physical survival and vitality), orange ray (personal identity and self-worth), and yellow ray (social and power dynamics), the heart cannot remain open. Conflict results.

Healing within relationships begins with *self-healing*.[4] You cannot give what you have not first offered yourself. Acceptance of your own distortions is the starting point. Then, you may meet others with compassion, not judgment.

You also asked how to reach *intelligent infinity*—direct contact with the Creator. We affirm: this is not done by force.[5] It is not achieved through willpower alone, but through deep *balance*, *surrender*, and *transparent beingness*. The more you release resistance, the more you become a *channel* through which divine energy flows.

Many seekers try to "break through" to higher states. This effort can become a form of spiritual aggression.[6] Instead, trust the process of gentle self-alignment. Truth reveals itself in stillness.

To serve, to love, to grow—these are not separate. They are the same current, flowing through a balanced vessel. Let your inner work be the foundation of your outer light.

I am Ra. May we thank you again, my friends, for your conscientiousness. All is well. We leave you rejoicing in the power and in the peace of the One Infinite Creator. Go forth with joy. Adonai.

Footnotes:

[1] **Sexual Energy as Spiritual Tool** – Ra teaches that sexual union, when shared consciously and lovingly, can accelerate spiritual growth and open higher energy centers.

[2] **Sacred Energy Exchange** – Beyond physicality, sexual energy is a means of emotional and spiritual connection, capable of deep healing or deep distortion.

[3] **Blockages in Energy Centers** – Relationship conflict often arises from unresolved personal issues in the lower chakras—survival, identity, and power dynamics.

[4] **Self-Healing Before Shared Healing** – Accepting and balancing your own energy prepares you to engage with others from a place of strength and love.

⁵ **Intelligent Infinity Through Surrender** – Direct contact with the Infinite Creator is not forced, but allowed through purity, balance, and inner peace.

⁶ **Effort vs. Alignment** – Spiritual breakthroughs come not from striving but from becoming transparent and surrendered to divine flow.

> "People normally cut reality into compartments and so are unable to see the interdependence of all phenomena. To see one in all and all in one is to break through the great barrier which narrows one's perception of reality."
>
> (Thich Nhat Hanh)

Ra's Message from Session 70

Summary:
Ra explains how the *contact between higher-density beings and third-density channels* can be disrupted by *distortion, imbalance,* or *psychic interference*. They describe how *purity of intention, balanced energy centers,* and *alignment with service to others* are required to maintain safe and effective spiritual communication. Ra also speaks of *ritual, discipline,* and the importance of *protecting sacred space* when working with unseen forces.

Ra's Message:
I am Ra. When seeking to connect with spiritual intelligence beyond the physical realm, the *purity of your intention* determines the quality of the contact.[1] Those who desire truth and service with a humble heart create an atmosphere of resonance that invites guidance from beings of light.

You asked about our contact with this group. We affirm: our ability to communicate depends on *the alignment of the group*, especially the channel, with the *principles of love, humility,* and *disciplined balance*.[2] When this alignment is weakened, distortions increase.

There are forces that do not wish this message to be received. These *negative entities* cannot override your free will, but they may influence through confusion, fear, or subtle distortion—especially if unhealed wounds or ego patterns remain hidden.[3]

Protection is not found in force, but in *clarity, love,* and *stability*.[4] A strong field is built not by walls, but by the coherence of your inner energy. When the channel is grounded, the group is harmonious, and the purpose is pure, distortion cannot take root.

You also asked about *ritual and sacred preparation*. We affirm: these are tools—not requirements.[5] But when used consciously, they help align the group's focus and create a shared field of intention. In this way, you "tune" yourselves like an instrument.

Be mindful of becoming attached to outer forms.[6] It is not the ritual itself, but the consciousness behind it that matters. One seeker in deep silence and service is more powerful than ten acting from habit.

We encourage all seekers working with unseen forces to *remain vigilant, humble,* and *attentive to balance*. This path is not for display, but for service. The more transparent your motives, the clearer your channel becomes.

I am Ra. You are all doing well, my friends. We leave you in the love and light of the One Infinite Creator. Go forth, therefore, rejoicing and glorying in the power and peace of the One Infinite Creator. Adonai.

Footnotes:

[1] **Intention Determines Contact** – The seeker's purity of purpose invites a matching vibration from spiritual sources. Selfish or unclear motives attract distortion.

[2] **Group and Channel Alignment** – The quality of channeled communication depends on the collective and individual alignment with love and balanced energy flow.

[3] **Negative Interference Targets Weakness** – Entities aligned with control and separation can only influence where distortion already exists in the seeker or group.

[4] **Energetic Protection Through Balance** – Ra teaches that coherent energy, built through love and clarity, naturally deflects negative influence.

⁵ **Ritual as Focus Tool** – Spiritual rituals can support group alignment and concentration, but they are only effective when used with full presence and intention.

⁶ **Avoid Attachment to Form** – Outer practices are secondary to inner alignment. True power flows from sincerity and awareness, not mechanical repetition.

"The Son of Man did not come for people to serve him. He came to serve others and to give his life to save many people."

(Matthew 20:28)

Ra's Message from Session 71

Summary:
Ra discusses how *desire and will* shape the seeker's path, emphasizing that *true seeking* must be rooted in *inner honesty* and *heart-centered intent*. They warn against approaching spiritual development as a pursuit of power or escape, as this leads to distortion. Ra also explains that while *service to others* often includes outward action, its *foundation is the internal alignment with love*.

Ra's Message:
I am Ra. Your journey of seeking begins with *desire*.[1] It is the engine of spiritual movement. But desire must be refined. If it is based in pride, fear, or the longing to escape discomfort, it creates distortion. If it is based in love and the wish to serve, it brings clarity and strength.

You asked how desire becomes seeking. We affirm: when you *focus your desire with will*,[2] you begin to polarize. That polarization—toward service to others or service to self—creates momentum. Every choice, thought, and intention either strengthens or weakens that path.

Many on your planet wish to grow spiritually, yet approach it with the desire to *acquire power, comfort, or superiority*.[3] These goals lead to imbalance. True seeking is rooted in *humility and surrender*, not domination or escape.

We spoke of *service to others*. This does not always appear dramatic.[4] Often, the greatest service is found in quiet presence, sincere listening, or the willingness to be kind when it is hard. Service begins in the *heart*, not in the hands.

You asked about how to stay on the path. We say: *return to your core desire.*[5] What do you serve? What are you truly longing for? If your answer is the Creator in all things, then let that awareness shape every choice.

There is no need for spiritual complexity.[6] The path becomes clearer as the heart becomes simpler. Every moment offers a chance to love more deeply, to judge less quickly, to give without needing reward.

Let your seeking be soft but focused, humble but determined. You do not need to strive for the Creator. You only need to *remember* you are already part of it.

I am Ra. You are conscientious. I leave you in the love and in the glorious light of the Infinite Creator. Go forth, therefore, rejoicing in the power and in the peace of the One Infinite Creator. Adonai.

Footnotes:

[1] **Desire as Spiritual Catalyst** – Ra emphasizes that sincere desire is the starting point of the spiritual path, but its quality must be examined and purified.

[2] **Will Shapes Polarity** – Desire focused by will creates spiritual direction. It helps the soul polarize toward service to others (positive) or service to self (negative).

[3] **Distortion Through Power-Seeking** – Seeking spiritual power without love or humility leads to imbalance and ego inflation.

[4] **Quiet Forms of Service** – Service to others often looks ordinary. Ra affirms that small acts of love and awareness are deeply powerful when done with sincerity.

[5] **Return to the Core Intent** – When confused or off-track, the seeker should revisit the original desire to grow and serve. This brings realignment.

⁶ **Simplicity of the Path** – Ra discourages complexity in spiritual practice. Awareness, love, and presence are the foundation of true growth.

> "Every soul… comes into the world strengthened by the victories or weakened by the defeats of its' previous life. Its' place in this world as a vessel appointed to honor or dishonor, is determined by its' previous merits or demerits. Its' work in this world determines its' place in the world which is to follow this."
>
> (Origen)

Ra's Message from Session 72

Summary:
Ra explains how *negative entities* attempt to influence spiritual seekers, especially those offering light to others. They clarify that *psychic greetings* (or attacks) occur only where *distortion or imbalance* already exists. Ra discusses how *love and acceptance* of the self and others provide the greatest protection. They also explain that it is not wise to engage directly with negatively polarized beings, as this can weaken polarity and invite confusion.

Ra's Message:
I am Ra. As your light grows brighter, it may attract attention from those walking the path of *service to self*.[1] This is not a punishment—it is part of the natural polarity of the universe. The stronger your radiance, the more clearly you define your path, and the more visible you become across spiritual planes.

You asked about *psychic greeting*, which is one form of negative influence. We affirm: such greetings cannot create distortion —they can only *amplify what is already within*.[2] Therefore, the most effective defense is not confrontation, but *inner balance*.

Fear, guilt, pride, and confusion are the most common entry points for disruption. But these are not enemies.[3] They are signals—opportunities to bring your love to the places where you still withhold it.

We spoke also of *attempts to communicate with negative entities*. We advise strongly against this.[4] It may seem noble to convert or reason with them, but in doing so, you enter their chosen distortion—control, manipulation, and hierarchy. This weakens your polarity and creates confusion in the energy field.

Your greatest protection is *unshakable alignment with love*.[5] This does not mean passive submission. It means you radiate compassion with clarity, refusing to enter into power struggles, even on subtle levels.

If you are attacked, do not ask, "How do I fight?" Ask, "What part of me still believes I am separate from the Creator?" In that question lies your freedom.

Let your service be steady and humble. Let your heart remain open to yourself and to others. And know: in the presence of pure love, darkness has no place to hide.

I am Ra. I leave you, my friends, glorying in the love and the light of the One Infinite Creator. Go forth, then, rejoicing in the power and in the peace of the One Infinite Creator. Adonai.

Footnotes:

[1] **Light Attracts Challenge** – Spiritually polarized beings naturally draw attention from those on the opposite path. This is not to be feared, but respected.

[2] **Distortion Is the Entry Point** – Negative influence cannot create imbalance, only magnify where it already exists in the mind or emotions of the seeker.

[3] **Emotional Signals, Not Enemies** – Unpleasant emotions are messengers. When welcomed with awareness, they become doorways to healing.

[4] **Avoid Engaging Negative Entities** – Attempting to reason with or convert negatively polarized beings invites them into your energy field, weakening your clarity.

[5] **Love as the Greatest Protection** – Pure, balanced love dissolves the energetic hooks of negativity. It creates a field of coherence that negative energies cannot penetrate.

"All things come from the unseen into the seen, and return again to the unseen. What is born must die, and what dies is born anew; for in truth, nothing perishes, but all is transformed."

(From The Emerald Tablets)

Ra's Message from Session 73

Summary:
Ra explores the concept of *magical working*—the ability to direct spiritual energy through *conscious intention and alignment*. They emphasize that true spiritual power is only safe and effective when grounded in *balance, purity of motive,* and *service to others*. Ra also discusses how *ritual and repetition* create a stable field for focused work, but reminds seekers that *inner alignment* is more important than external form.

Ra's Message:
I am Ra. You asked about *magical working*, which we define as the conscious use of energy to bring about spiritual or physical effects.[1] This is not fantasy, but a function of *alignment, intention*, and *purity*.

All beings have the potential for magical working. The difference lies in *discipline and awareness*.[2] The more balanced your energy centers, the more clearly your will can shape the flow of intelligent energy. The more love-centered your intention, the more your work aligns with the Creator.

However, spiritual power without *inner harmony* becomes dangerous.[3] It can amplify distortion instead of light. This is why we urge seekers to ground themselves in humility, compassion, and ongoing self-balancing before attempting focused work of this kind.

You also asked about *ritual and repetition*.[4] When used with sincere intention, ritual helps prepare the mind, unify the group, and focus energy. It creates a reliable spiritual rhythm—like tuning an instrument before playing.

But we caution: ritual without heart becomes hollow.[5] If you say the words but do not mean them, or follow a pattern without presence, the effect is limited or even reversed. What matters most is the *state of consciousness* from which all actions arise.

Magical working is not about control, but about *co-creation*.[6] You are not forcing the universe—you are aligning with its flow. The more clearly you reflect divine harmony, the more easily your intentions manifest through it.

You asked about the one known to you as Jesus. We affirm that this being was *harvestable from third and fourth densities*, and chose to incarnate while operating from *fifth-density consciousness*.[7] His life was an example of unconditional love and wisdom. His self-chosen martyrdom was not a failure, but an offering—demonstrating the love of the Creator through personal sacrifice. This choice maximized his service to others, though it also introduced deep complexities into your religious distortions.

Above all, we remind you: the purpose of magical work is not to gain power, but to *deepen service*. Let every working begin and end in love. Let your focus be the healing of distortion, not the manipulation of outcome.

In this way, your work will not only be effective—it will become a light in the darkness.

I am Ra. I leave you glorying in the love and the light of the One Infinite Creator. Go forth, then, rejoicing in the power and in the peace of the One Infinite Creator. Adonai.

Footnotes:

[1] **Magical Working Defined** – Ra uses this term to describe the intentional use of spiritual energy to create real effects, not illusion or fantasy.

[2] **Discipline Enables Power** – Consistent alignment,

meditation, and inner balance increase the seeker's ability to direct energy effectively and safely.

3 Danger of Imbalanced Power – Unhealed wounds or ego motives can distort magical workings, leading to confusion or spiritual harm.

4 Ritual as Focusing Tool – Thoughtful ritual builds spiritual momentum and creates sacred space for energy work and contact with higher realms.

5 Heart-Centered Practice – Ritual only works when it is infused with sincerity, intention, and alignment with truth. Mechanical repetition has little effect.

6 Magick as Co-Creation – True power flows when the seeker aligns their will with the divine flow of creation, not when they try to impose outcomes.

7 Jesus as a Fifth-Density Being in Incarnation – Ra describes Jesus as an advanced soul who came to serve by embodying unconditional love. His conscious decision to give his life was made from a fifth-density perspective and was intended to demonstrate divine love in a form people could grasp.

> "If then you do not make yourself equal to God, you cannot apprehend God; for like is known by like. Leap clear of all that is corporeal, and make yourself grown to a like expanse with that greatness which is beyond all measure; rise above all time and become eternal; then you will apprehend God. Think that for you too nothing is impossible; deem that you too are immortal, and that you are able to grasp all things in your thought, to know every craft and science; find your home in the haunts of every living creature; make yourself higher than all heights and lower than all depths; bring together in yourself all opposites of quality, heat and cold, dryness and fluidity; think that you are everywhere at once, on land, at sea, in heaven; think that you are not

yet begotten, that you are in the womb, that you are young, that you are old, that you have died, that you are in the world beyond the grave; grasp in your thought all of this at once, all times and places, all substances and qualities and magnitudes together; then you can apprehend God."

(from The Corpus Hermeticum)

Ra's Message from Session 74

Summary:
Ra discusses the nature of *magical working*, the importance of *will and faith*, and the effects of *psychic greeting*. They explain how even subtle distortions in a channeling group can affect spiritual contact. Ra also introduces the concept of the *archetypal mind*—a deeper structure within consciousness designed by the Logos to guide spiritual evolution—and notes that understanding this mind is essential for advanced inner work.

Ra's Message:
I am Ra. You asked about the instrument's condition. We observe that her body is still being weakened by psychic greeting.[1] However, she remains aligned in purpose and able to continue this work if properly supported. Please continue to offer rest, harmony, and nourishment, as these are part of the protective environment.

You asked about *magical working*. We affirm that the foundation of all magical or spiritual work is the balance of *will and faith*.[2] Will is focused desire. Faith is the inner trust in the unseen. When they operate in harmony, the seeker becomes a vessel through which energy can be directed with clarity and purpose.

Without faith, will turns into control. Without will, faith becomes passive. True magical work begins when the seeker moves from harmony, alignment, and deep service to others.

You asked about *psychic greeting*. This occurs when negative entities attempt to disturb or distort spiritual progress.[3]

However, they cannot create imbalance—only intensify distortions already present. In this case, the instrument's physical condition is the chosen entry point for such interference. The group's unity and intention are essential for minimizing these effects.

Spiritual protection is not about building walls—it's about *coherence and love*.[4] Harmony between members, and the individual's dedication to service, are the best defenses against spiritual interference.

You asked about the effect of *unspoken thoughts* within the group. Yes, we affirm that even subconscious emotional disharmony can weaken the contact.[5] Each mind contributes to the shared field of awareness. Thus, self-examination and ongoing realignment are necessary—not to prevent attack, but to remain clear in purpose.

Now, we offer a brief beginning toward a new teaching. We speak of the archetypal mind.[6] This is a structured part of your deep mind—created by the Logos—to assist the seeker in understanding the self, the Creator, and the journey of spiritual evolution.

Each archetype is a symbolic pattern that exists not just within individuals, but in the very design of your experience in third density. This archetypal mind contains profound tools for self-study and magical working. But it is not meant for casual use. A certain level of spiritual maturity and preparation is required.

We will explain this system more fully in later sessions, especially through symbolic tools such as the Tarot, which reflect these archetypes as visual structures.[7] We ask that you ensure sufficient understanding of the *mind/body/spirit complex* and the *magical personality* before undertaking a full study of this archetypal system.

Let your journey be patient. Let your seeking be grounded in service and honesty. The path of deep work is not hurried.

Each insight prepares you for the next.

Remain in harmony. Continue in meditation. Walk in light.

I am Ra. We would leave you now, my friends, in the love and in the light of the One Infinite Creator. Go forth, then, glorying and rejoicing in the power and peace of the One Infinite Creator. Adonai.

Footnotes:

[1] **Psychic Greeting of the Instrument** – Ra confirms that the instrument (Carla) is being targeted by a negative fifth-density entity due to her spiritual service, exploiting her physical weakness.

[2] **Faith and Will as Spiritual Tools** – Ra teaches that spiritual effectiveness comes from the balanced use of focused will and deep trust in the Creator. Both are needed to walk the path consciously.

[3] **Nature of Psychic Attack** – Negative entities cannot break free will but can amplify existing distortions in the seeker or group, especially when energy is misaligned.

[4] **True Protection is Coherence** – Spiritual defense is not force or resistance but inner harmony, balance, and collective unity in love and service.

[5] **Group Mind Affects Contact** – Unspoken doubt, fear, or disunity in a channeling group subtly weakens contact with higher-density beings and introduces distortion.

[6] **The Archetypal Mind Introduced** – Ra begins teaching about the archetypal mind, a symbolic and energetic system designed by the Logos as a blueprint for self-awareness and transformation.

[7] **Tarot and the Archetypes** – Ra later uses the 22 Major Arcana of the Tarot to explain the archetypal mind, seeing the images not as divination tools but as sacred symbols of the structure

of consciousness.

"A person experiences life as something separated from the rest - a kind of optical delusion of consciousness. Our task must be to free ourselves from this self-imposed prison, and through compassion, to find the reality of Oneness."

(Albert Einstein)

Ra's Message from Session 75

Summary:
Ra discusses the process of *psychic greeting*, particularly how negative entities target distortions in order to weaken seekers of light. They explain how *intentions rooted in love and service* offer the strongest protection. Ra also emphasizes that the *crystallization of the energy centers* enables true spiritual power. The group's unified purpose and the *magical personality* are explored as foundations for deeper work.

Ra's Message:
I am Ra. We affirm that negative entities do not attack randomly. They are drawn to those who radiate light and seek to serve others.[1] Their goal is not to destroy, but to *disrupt the alignment* of your energy—especially if there are unhealed weaknesses within the physical, emotional, or spiritual complex.

You asked how the psychic greeting is carried out. We clarify: the entity directing the greeting studies your energy carefully, identifying distortions already present.[2] In this case, the instrument's physical condition and the group's dynamic offer an opening. The greeting is precise, not chaotic—it reflects intelligent intent.

Your protection lies not in defense, but in *discipline and devotion*.[3] Each member must continue the daily practice of aligning with love and purpose. Even the smallest doubt or distraction opens space for distortion. But when the heart is steady, interference has no anchor.

You asked about *magical work*. This begins with the

crystallization of the energy centers.[4] When the centers are balanced and energy flows without blockage, the seeker becomes a stable channel for intelligent energy. This is the true foundation of spiritual power—not dramatic acts, but quiet coherence.

You inquired about the *magical personality*. We affirm: this is the higher self made consciously available through disciplined invocation.[5] It cannot be summoned from curiosity or vanity. Only through humility, service, and inner balance can the magical personality express itself clearly and safely.

The purpose of such work is not control or display. It is *transformation*—of the self and of the shared field in which others also awaken.[6] When intention is pure, even small efforts radiate change.

You asked about using tools like the *banishing ritual of the lesser pentagram*. These tools may be helpful when used with knowledge and awareness.[7] But they are not required. The true ritual is the *alignment of your will with love*. No symbol or word can replace that.

Let your work be simple and sincere. Guard your thoughts gently. Offer love even when uninvited. And know that service to others, when offered without pride, becomes a beacon of clarity.

I am Ra. I leave you, my friends, in the love and the light of the One Infinite Creator. Go forth, therefore, rejoicing in the power and peace of the One Infinite Creator. Adonai.

Footnotes:

[1] **Psychic Greeting Targets Seekers of Light** – Ra reminds us that spiritual growth draws attention from negative entities who seek to disrupt polarization.

[2] **Distortion as an Entry Point** – Interference occurs only where inner imbalance already exists. Negative forces exploit

—not create—weakness.

[3] **Spiritual Protection through Alignment** – Daily intention, service, and group harmony create a stable field that naturally resists spiritual disruption.

[4] **Crystallized Energy Centers** – A balanced and flowing chakra system allows the seeker to safely channel intelligent energy and participate in higher work.

[5] **Magical Personality and the Higher Self** – The magical personality is the consciously invoked presence of the higher self, accessible only through serious, balanced spiritual effort.

[6] **Purpose of Magical Work is Transformation** – True spiritual work focuses not on control, but on self-purification and service to collective awakening.

[7] **Use of Ritual Tools** – Rituals like the banishing pentagram may aid alignment, but Ra stresses that real power comes from conscious love, not symbolic forms alone.

> "Move with the flow. Don't fight the current. Resist nothing. Let life carry you. Don't try to carry it."
>
> (Oprah Winfrey)

Ra's Message from Session 76

Summary:
Ra introduces the *Archetypal Mind* as a system created by the Logos to guide spiritual evolution. They begin to outline how this deep structure of consciousness can be studied through a symbolic system, most accurately represented by the *Tarot*. Ra emphasizes that understanding the Archetypal Mind supports healing, transformation, and contact with intelligent infinity.

Ra's Message:
I am Ra. You asked about the *deep mind*, and so we begin to speak of the Archetypal Mind.[1] This is a structured, symbolic representation of the paths of spiritual evolution, created by the Logos to help third-density beings like yourselves explore the self and its relationship to the Creator.

The Archetypal Mind is not personal. It is a universal blueprint woven into your experience by intelligent design.[2] Though each being is unique, the broad stages of consciousness, transformation, and integration are shared. These are expressed in 22 archetypes, which correspond to key aspects of spiritual evolution.

You asked how to study these archetypes. We affirm that the symbolic images of the Tarot, when stripped of cultural distortion, serve as a useful key.[3] Specifically, the Major Arcana represent these core energies of the mind, body, and spirit. We will guide you through each in later sessions.

There are three cycles in the archetypal system: the *Mind*, the *Body*, and the *Spirit*.[4] Each cycle contains seven archetypes, with one final image (the Choice) that integrates the system.

The study of these archetypes is not intellectual—it is transformational.[5]

To know an archetype is not to memorize it, but to meditate upon it, live it, and allow it to reflect your own inner development. Symbols help bridge the conscious and unconscious minds.[6] When approached with reverence, the archetypes become tools for initiation and healing.

You asked why this system is important. We affirm: to know the self is to know the Creator.[7] And the archetypal patterns are keys placed within your deep mind to assist that knowing.

This study must be undertaken with patience and humility. It is not for mastery, but for *deepening awareness*. The seeker who contemplates the archetypes is not learning new information, but *remembering a structure already present within*.

Let your approach be symbolic, meditative, and open. Do not attempt to define or control the images. Allow them to awaken layers within you. In this, you will begin to unlock the deep mind, and the gateway to intelligent infinity will open more fully.

I am Ra. We leave you, my friends, in the love and the light of the One Infinite Creator. Go forth, therefore, rejoicing in the power and peace of the One Infinite Creator. Adonai.

Footnotes:

[1] **Archetypal Mind as a Creation of the Logos** – Ra teaches that the deep mind contains universal patterns intentionally created to guide soul development.

[2] **Universal Blueprint for All Seekers** – The archetypes apply across all individuals and are not based on personality, but on the design of consciousness itself.

[3] **Tarot as a Symbolic Tool** – The 22 cards of the Major Arcana (especially in undistorted form) provide symbolic access to the archetypal system.

⁴ **Three Cycles of Evolution** – The archetypes are divided into the cycles of Mind (thinking, knowing), Body (experiencing, manifesting), and Spirit (transcendence, transformation), plus one integrating card representing The Choice.

⁵ **Archetypes as Catalysts for Transformation** – True understanding comes not through study alone, but through contemplation and inner resonance with each symbol.

⁶ **Symbol as Bridge to the Deep Mind** – Ra emphasizes that symbolic imagery communicates with the unconscious more powerfully than words or concepts.

⁷ **To Know the Self Is to Know the Creator** – The path of self-knowledge, supported by the archetypes, ultimately leads to deeper unity with the Infinite Creator.

> "This overcoming of all the usual barriers between the individual and the Absolute is the great mystic achievement. In mystic states we both become one with the Absolute and we become aware of our oneness. This is the everlasting and triumphant mystical tradition, hardly altered by differences of clime or creed."
>
> (William James)

Ra's Message from Session 77

Summary:
Ra begins a detailed explanation of the *Archetypal Mind*, focusing on the *first cycle*—the Mind Archetypes. They introduce the first three archetypes: the Matrix of the Mind, the Potentiator of the Mind, and the Catalyst of the Mind, explaining how each plays a role in the development of consciousness. Ra also emphasizes the importance of experiencing these archetypes directly through *contemplation and inner work*.

Ra's Message:
I am Ra. You asked us to begin with the Archetypes of the Mind. These seven archetypes describe how the conscious mind evolves and interacts with the deeper self.[1] As we begin, we remind you: each archetype is a symbol, a key that opens inward doors. Let them work on you through *meditation and intuitive insight*.

We begin with the Matrix of the Mind.[2] This is the foundation of your conscious awareness. It is the quiet, still field in which thoughts arise. It contains potential but does not act —it *receives*, *holds*, and *observes*. In the Tarot, this is often symbolized by a seated figure, representing stillness and receptivity.

Next is the Potentiator of the Mind.[3] This is the unconscious —the deep well of dreams, intuition, emotion, and inspiration. It is the mystery behind the veil. When the conscious mind seeks understanding, it turns inward to the Potentiator. This archetype is often symbolized by a figure with a veil or with open scrolls—indicating hidden wisdom that awaits activation.

The Catalyst of the Mind is the third archetype.[4] This represents *all experiences and interactions* that provoke mental or emotional response. People, events, thoughts, and conflicts all act as catalysts. Their purpose is to stir the mind to reflect, to change, and to evolve.

Together, these three form the beginning of the journey of the mind. The *Matrix* waits. The *Potentiator* energizes. The *Catalyst* activates.[5] Each works with the others to guide you toward a more integrated, aware state of being.

You asked how these archetypes are used in practice. We affirm: their power is not in explanation, but in meditation and inner recognition.[6] Spend time with each. Study its symbolic image. Ask what it reveals about your current distortions, patterns, and opportunities for growth.

We remind you: this is not an external system to master, but an *inner path to walk*. The Archetypal Mind was created to serve the seeker's evolution, not to trap the intellect in complexity. Let your study be playful, reverent, and open-hearted.

In time, the images will speak directly to your deep mind. Let that be your guide.

I am Ra. This concludes this working. We are grateful. We leave you in the love and the light of the One Infinite Creator. Go forth rejoicing in the power and the peace of the One Infinite Creator. Adonai.

Footnotes:

[1] **Seven Archetypes of the Mind** – These represent stages and aspects of conscious and unconscious mental development on the seeker's spiritual path.

[2] **Matrix of the Mind** – The conscious mind in its passive state. It is the field of awareness that receives impressions and observes experience.

³ **Potentiator of the Mind** – The unconscious source of intuition, feeling, and symbolic knowledge. It activates the Matrix through mystery and depth.

⁴ **Catalyst of the Mind** – Events, relationships, or inner experiences that stimulate thought, emotion, and transformation.

⁵ **Interplay of the First Three Archetypes** – Ra emphasizes that these archetypes interact dynamically: stillness receives, mystery energizes, and life catalyzes growth.

⁶ **Study Through Meditation, Not Analysis** – The archetypes are meant to awaken insight through reflection, not be dissected purely by the intellect.

> "When you close the door of your mind to negative thoughts, the door of opportunity opens to you."
>
> (Napoleon Hill)

Ra's Message from Session 78

Summary:
Ra continues the teaching on the *Archetypal Mind*, focusing on the final four Archetypes of the Mind: the Experience, Significator, Transformation, and Great Way. They explain how these archetypes interact with the earlier three and how they map the evolution of consciousness from *reception* to *integration* and ultimately *transcendence*.

Ra's Message:
I am Ra. You have asked us to continue with the Archetypes of the Mind. In the previous session, we shared the first three: the Matrix, the Potentiator, and the Catalyst. These form the basis of how consciousness is initiated and activated. Now we explore the final four archetypes that complete this cycle.

The Experience of the Mind is the fourth archetype.[1] This represents the *meaning you give to experience*—how you interpret life based on your response to catalyst. Through repetition, reflection, and choice, this experience becomes part of your mental pattern. It shapes your memory, your expectations, and your attitude toward future events.

The Significator of the Mind is the fifth.[2] This is the integrated self—the core identity formed by your accumulated experiences, thoughts, and emotions. It is both actor and observer, constantly being shaped by the dance of catalyst and interpretation. It represents your current conscious self, and how it is defined by all that has come before.

The Transformation of the Mind is the sixth archetype.[3] This represents change, breakthrough, and inner alchemy. It is the moment when illusion is released and a deeper truth emerges. Sometimes this comes as clarity; other times, through crisis. Either way, it is a sacred doorway to greater self-awareness.

The Great Way of the Mind is the seventh and final archetype in this cycle.[4] It symbolizes the full journey of the mind as it returns to alignment with the Creator. It is not a fixed point, but an unfolding path of awareness. It includes wisdom, clarity, and the ability to perceive without distortion. It is the fruit of all the other archetypes combined.

These seven stages work as a whole.[5] You begin with an open field (Matrix), energize it with deep unconscious material (Potentiator), move through life events (Catalyst), interpret them (Experience), form a self-image (Significator), undergo inner shifts (Transformation), and walk the path of full awareness (Great Way).

You asked whether these stages must be followed in order. We affirm: they are always in motion.[6] They are not linear but cyclical, and they interact constantly. Still, it is helpful to study them in sequence to grasp their unique roles.

Let your understanding be intuitive. The images in the Tarot offer visual access to these archetypes, but they are not required. Meditation, life experience, and sincere desire to know the self will awaken them in time.

The Archetypes of the Mind are tools for remembering your wholeness. Let them guide—not define—you. And as always, seek not only understanding, but transformation through love.

I am Ra. We leave you now, my friends, glorifying in the love and in the light of the Infinite Creator. Go forth, therefore, rejoicing in the power and in the peace of the One Infinite Creator. Adonai.

Footnotes:

[1] **Experience of the Mind** – The internal meaning-making process by which external catalyst is interpreted and integrated into memory and belief.

[2] **Significator of the Mind** – The present, conscious self—formed and reformed by the interplay of thoughts, emotions, experiences, and insight.

[3] **Transformation of the Mind** – The process of mental or emotional breakthrough, where distortions fall away and new clarity is born.

[4] **Great Way of the Mind** – The broad path of awareness, wisdom, and self-realization that unfolds through the continuous balancing of experience.

[5] **Seven Archetypes Form One Cycle** – Ra emphasizes that these aspects of mind are parts of a unified system, working together in the evolution of consciousness.

[6] **The Archetypes Are Interactive and Nonlinear** – Though studied in sequence, they are constantly interwoven and responsive to the seeker's choices.

"You can be fully satisfied with where you are, understanding that you're eternally evolving. When you get into that place of feeling appreciation of where you are and of who you are, and appreciation of what you are, and you accept that you are a never-ending, always unfolding Being, then you can stand in that delicate balance of being optimistic about what is to come, without being unhappy about where you stand. Find a way of eagerly anticipating future changes, while at the same time you are in love and satisfied with who, what, where and how you be."

(Abraham, through Esther Hicks)

Ra's Message from Session 79

Summary:
Ra transitions from the Archetypes of the Mind to those of the Body, beginning with the first two: the Matrix and the Potentiator of the Body. They explain that while the Mind reflects awareness and interpretation, the Body reflects the *manifestation of experience* in physical form. Ra also emphasizes that the Body is not just a vehicle—it is a *mirror of consciousness* and a *path of transformation*.

Ra's Message:
I am Ra. Now we begin our discussion of the Archetypes of the Body.[1] These seven archetypes describe how the body functions not only as a physical vessel, but as an instrument of learning, transformation, and reflection.

We begin with the Matrix of the Body.[2] This archetype represents the physical form in its raw, unconscious state. It contains both strength and limitation. It seeks health, survival, and balance. But without direction from the mind and spirit, the body remains instinctual—focused on repetition, habit, and reaction. It is both foundation and frontier.

Next is the Potentiator of the Body.[3] This is the deep well of energy that lies behind the physical body—the source of transformation, regeneration, and potential healing. It includes the body's access to intelligent energy, sexual energy, and the instinct to evolve. It is symbolized by mystery and potential, often hidden from ordinary awareness.

Together, these two form the basic dynamic of bodily

experience.⁴ The Matrix responds and endures. The Potentiator empowers and awakens. When they are in harmony, the body becomes a finely tuned tool for evolution. When blocked or distorted, the body expresses imbalance through illness, fatigue, or misuse.

You asked how to relate these archetypes to practical life. We affirm: all that happens to your body—its cravings, its injuries, its healing—is a *language of the soul*.⁵ Pay attention. What does the body say about your alignment with mind and spirit?

You asked why the Archetypes of the Body differ from those of the Mind. We explain: the Mind is reflective and abstract. The Body is direct and concrete.⁶ It teaches through sensation, action, and reaction. Its lessons are not subtle—they are physical, unmistakable, and persistent.

The study of the Body's archetypes helps the seeker reclaim agency over their incarnation.⁷ Rather than being a prisoner of habit or pain, the seeker becomes a co-creator of embodiment—learning how to listen, respond, and transform physical experience into wisdom.

Let this be your approach: observe your body as you would a sacred text. Each sensation is a syllable. Each movement, a sentence. And every illness or impulse contains a lesson, if approached with love and attention.

I am Ra. We thank you for this session. All is well. We leave you in the love and light of the One Infinite Creator. Go forth rejoicing in the power and peace of the One Infinite Creator. Adonai.

Footnotes:

¹ **Archetypes of the Body** – These represent how the body acts as a vessel for experience and transformation, not just survival.

² **Matrix of the Body** – The unconscious, reactive form of the

physical body—instinctive and enduring, but limited without guidance.

³ Potentiator of the Body – The latent energy and power within the body that can be awakened for healing, vitality, and transformation.

⁴ Dynamic Between Matrix and Potentiator – The Matrix is the form; the Potentiator is the hidden energy that activates and transforms it.

⁵ Body as a Mirror of Consciousness – The state of the body reflects deeper emotional, mental, or spiritual alignment (or misalignment).

⁶ The Body Teaches Through Direct Experience – While the Mind teaches through thought, the Body teaches through sensation and form.

⁷ Conscious Embodiment as Spiritual Practice – Understanding the body's archetypes empowers the seeker to live more intentionally within the physical form.

> "You, being yourself, help others be themselves. Because you recognize your own uniqueness, you will not need to dominate others, nor cringe before them."
>
> (Seth, through Jane Roberts)

Ra's Message from Session 80

Summary:
Ra continues explaining the Archetypes of the Body, covering the Catalyst, Experience, and Significator of the Body. They clarify how bodily sensations, pain, pleasure, and illness serve as *spiritual messages*. These archetypes help the seeker recognize the body as both *teacher and mirror*. Ra also touches on how sexual energy and physical vitality play central roles in spiritual growth.

Ra's Message:
I am Ra. You have asked us to continue with the Archetypes of the Body. In the previous session, we described the Matrix and Potentiator. Now we turn to the next three: the Catalyst, Experience, and Significator of the Body.[1]

The Catalyst of the Body represents those physical inputs and sensations that stimulate change.[2] This can include *pain, pleasure, illness, sexuality,* or any experience that forces awareness of the body. Such catalysts are not punishments or rewards—they are invitations to listen and grow. A discomfort may reveal a distortion in thought. A sensation of pleasure may point to an imbalance or a lesson in moderation.

The Experience of the Body refers to how the self responds to these bodily catalysts.[3] How does one treat the body? What meaning does one give to pleasure or pain? This archetype reflects accumulated physical memory—habits, reflexes, and interpretations that shape the relationship between body and consciousness.

The Significator of the Body is the unified expression of the body's condition and consciousness.[4] It includes one's health, posture, energy, sexuality, and responsiveness. It is not fixed, but constantly evolving based on how the previous archetypes are processed. The Significator shows how well the self is integrating bodily lessons.

You asked about the spiritual role of sexual energy. We affirm that sexual energy is a key form of bodily catalyst.[5] When used in harmony and with love, it accelerates connection and healing. When distorted, it can trap the self in cycles of confusion, guilt, or power-seeking. The body holds this energy naturally, and its balanced expression is part of spiritual maturity.

We remind you that the body is intelligent.[6] Though it may not speak in words, it constantly communicates its needs, strengths, and wisdom. Ignoring or abusing the body leads to distortion. Listening to the body with love and awareness leads to integration.

These archetypes of Catalyst, Experience, and Significator form a dynamic system.[7] You encounter sensations (Catalyst), respond with perception and action (Experience), and shape a bodily self (Significator). Together they reveal how spirit and matter interact moment by moment.

Let your attitude toward the body be one of *respect and curiosity*. It is not the enemy. It is the ground of your incarnation—the field in which spiritual lessons become real.

I am Ra. We leave you in peace. Go forth rejoicing in the power and in the peace of the One Infinite Creator. Adonai.

Footnotes:

[1] **Archetypes 3–5 of the Body** – Ra continues the seven-part system: Catalyst (stimulus), Experience (response), and Significator (bodily self).

[2] **Catalyst of the Body** – Any physical sensation or condition

that calls attention to itself and stimulates awareness or transformation.

³ **Experience of the Body** – How one responds to physical experience and incorporates it into personal meaning and memory.

⁴ **Significator of the Body** – The current state of embodiment—a summary of bodily health, energy, and the self's relationship with the body.

⁵ **Sexual Energy as Catalyst** – Ra consistently describes sexual energy as sacred and powerful, capable of healing, bonding, or distorting depending on intent.

⁶ **The Body Has Its Own Wisdom** – Even though it operates unconsciously, the body is an intelligent part of the mind/body/spirit complex and should be treated with care.

⁷ **Dynamic Interaction** – Each archetype builds upon the previous ones and influences the next, creating a continuous feedback loop for spiritual evolution.

> "Peace will come to the hearts of men when they realize their oneness with the universe. It is everywhere."
>
> (Black Elk)

Ra's Message from Session 81

Summary:
Ra completes the Archetypes of the Body by explaining the final two: the Transformation and Great Way of the Body. They emphasize that the body can be a gateway to *spiritual transformation* when treated with awareness and love. Ra also introduces the transition toward the Archetypes of the Spirit, noting that this third cycle represents the most profound and mysterious layer of the self.

Ra's Message:
I am Ra. You have asked us to complete the cycle of the Archetypes of the Body. We now speak of the final two: the Transformation and the Great Way of the Body.[1]

The Transformation of the Body represents *inner alchemy through physical experience.*[2] This occurs when the self learns to move beyond instinct and reaction, using the body as a channel for healing and refinement. This transformation is not of appearance but of *function and flow*—a shift toward conscious embodiment.

This archetype also symbolizes the balance between activity and rest, acceptance and discipline. When the seeker treats the body not as a burden but as a sacred vehicle, the transformation becomes possible. It is here that pain may be turned into compassion, and limitation into clarity.

The Great Way of the Body is the culmination of bodily learning.[3] It represents the *integrated embodiment* of love, wisdom, and power. The seeker no longer struggles against the body, but *flows with it* as part of the unified self. The body becomes an instrument of alignment, not resistance.

This archetype points to wholeness in incarnation—when the physical form, mental intention, and spiritual essence are in harmony. It may be symbolized by radiance, balance, or movement in stillness. It is not static. It is the *ongoing path of conscious embodiment*.

You asked whether these archetypes of the Body can be experienced directly. We affirm: they are *already active* in your life.[4] Every ache, appetite, or act of care contains one or more of these archetypal energies. Awareness brings them from unconscious to conscious use.

Let the seeker not reject the body. In the body are stored the lessons of love, power, survival, sensuality, and death. To understand these is to evolve.[5] To misuse or ignore them is to stagnate.

Now we speak briefly of what lies ahead: the Archetypes of the Spirit.[6] These seven are the deepest and most mysterious. They deal not with thought or sensation, but with *identity, faith, and transformation at the soul level*. They require subtlety, silence, and surrender to approach.

The mind and body are tools of experience. But the spirit is the *essence that unifies and transcends*. It is both seed and flame. To know the archetypes of the spirit is to walk the inner gateway toward the Creator.

Let the work continue in love and patience. You are not merely flesh and thought—you are light, becoming aware of itself.

I am Ra. We leave you in love and light. Go forth rejoicing in the power and the peace of the One Infinite Creator. Adonai.

Footnotes:

[1] **Final Archetypes of the Body** – The last two of the seven: Transformation (rebirth through physical learning) and the Great Way (embodied alignment with spirit).

² **Transformation of the Body** – The moment when physical limitation becomes spiritual opportunity; the shift from unconscious reaction to conscious embodiment.

³ **Great Way of the Body** – Full integration of the physical self as a tool for spiritual expression and service.

⁴ **The Archetypes Are Already Present** – Ra emphasizes that these are not abstract ideas—they are reflected in everyday bodily experience and can be consciously engaged.

⁵ **Embodiment as a Spiritual Path** – The body offers crucial lessons and energies that cannot be bypassed on the journey of evolution.

⁶ **Introduction to the Archetypes of the Spirit** – Ra transitions to the deepest archetypes, which represent the core transformation of identity, faith, and soul-union with the Creator.

> "Musicians must make music, artists must paint, poets must write if they are to be ultimately at peace with themselves. What human beings can be, they must be. They must be true to their own nature. This need we may call self-actualization."
>
> (Abraham Maslow)

Ra's Message from Session 82

Summary:
Ra begins the exploration of the Archetypes of the Spirit, the final and most profound cycle of the Archetypal Mind. They introduce the Matrix of the Spirit and the Potentiator of the Spirit, explaining how these archetypes relate to *mystery, faith, and transformation*. Ra emphasizes that spiritual growth requires *acceptance of both light and darkness*, and that the Spirit functions as a bridge between self and the Creator.

Ra's Message:
I am Ra. You have asked us to begin with the Archetypes of the Spirit. These seven archetypes describe the deepest journey of consciousness—the path through which the self is transformed and unified with the Creator.[1]

We begin with the Matrix of the Spirit.[2] This archetype is the base condition of spiritual being. It is symbolized by *infinite potential*, formlessness, and often darkness. It is the great mystery—the part of you that longs to know and be known. It may be visualized as the night sky or the unconscious void from which light arises.

Unlike the Matrix of the Mind, which is receptive, the Matrix of the Spirit is both receptive and infinite. It holds all possibilities—shadow and light. In this place, the seeker begins to realize the presence of the Creator not through thought, but through silence and surrender.

Next is the Potentiator of the Spirit.[3] This archetype represents the *light that stirs the depths*. It is the sudden realization, the flash of insight, the awakening that transforms the seeker. It is often called the Lightning because it strikes without warning, bringing clarity or disruption.

This lightning may come through meditation, trauma, beauty, or deep love. It illuminates hidden parts of the self. It awakens the longing to return to unity with the Source.

The Matrix and Potentiator of the Spirit work together to stir the seeker.[4] The Matrix waits in mystery. The Potentiator sparks awareness. But unlike the earlier cycles, the Spirit's path is not linear—it is a spiral, full of paradox. Light is found in darkness. Wisdom emerges from confusion.

You asked about the importance of embracing both light and shadow. We affirm: true transformation cannot happen if the seeker rejects parts of the self.[5] The darkness within must be seen, accepted, and integrated. This is not evil—it is unconsciousness waiting to become conscious.

Only when the seeker stands in both their power and vulnerability can the Spirit begin its full work.[6] The Spirit is the deepest layer of the mind/body/spirit complex—it is the gateway to intelligent infinity, to the One Infinite Creator.

Let your study of the Spirit be quiet and inward. These archetypes are not concepts to master, but experiences to live. The more deeply you know yourself, the more clearly you recognize the Creator within.

I am Ra. We appreciate your dedication. All is well. We leave you in the love and the light of the One Infinite Creator. Go forth, then, rejoicing in the power and the peace of the One Infinite Creator. Adonai.

Footnotes:

[1] **Archetypes of the Spirit** – These seven archetypes describe the transformation of the deepest self and its journey back to unity with the Creator.

[2] **Matrix of the Spirit** – The primal spiritual state of formless

awareness and mystery; it is the field from which spiritual growth emerges.

[3] **Potentiator of the Spirit** – Sudden insight or divine awakening that disturbs the stillness of the Spirit and initiates transformation.

[4] **Mystery and Illumination** – The Matrix holds all; the Potentiator activates some. Together they reflect the deep mystery of spiritual life.

[5] **Integration of Light and Shadow** – Ra teaches that the seeker must accept both the conscious and unconscious aspects of self in order to evolve spiritually.

[6] **Spirit as Gateway to the Infinite** – The Spirit is not just a function but a bridge—through it, the seeker experiences direct contact with the Divine.

> "Your light is seen, your heart is known, your soul is cherished by more people than you might imagine. If you knew how many others have been touched in wonderful ways by you, you would be astonished. If you knew how many people feel so much for you, you would be shocked. You are far more wonderful than you think you are. Rest with that. Rest easy with that. Breathe again. You are doing fine. More than fine. Better than fine. You're doin' great. So relax. And love yourself today."
>
> (Neale Donald Walsh)

Ra's Message from Session 83

Summary:
Ra continues the exploration of the Archetypes of the Spirit, focusing on the Catalyst, Experience, and Significator of the Spirit. These archetypes describe how spiritual transformation unfolds through *inner struggle, illumination, and the birth of a deeper self*. Ra explains that *faith, will, and self-acceptance* are essential tools for navigating the mystery of the Spirit.

Ra's Message:
I am Ra. We continue now with the Catalyst, Experience, and Significator of the Spirit. These three archetypes reflect how spiritual development proceeds through contact with *mystery, challenge, and surrender*.[1]

The Catalyst of the Spirit represents those internal experiences that stir the soul.[2] This includes despair, longing, joy, revelation, and deep questions of meaning. It is often symbolized by *hope amid darkness*—a spiritual yearning that cannot be satisfied by the world alone.

Unlike the bodily or mental catalysts, this catalyst reaches into the core of identity. It creates a spiritual restlessness that drives the seeker toward union with the Creator. It is often subtle, yet profoundly unsettling.

The Experience of the Spirit reflects how the self processes and integrates these spiritual catalysts.[3] It includes *transformation through faith, intuition, suffering, or revelation*. In this archetype, the seeker either contracts in fear or expands in trust. The experience is not neutral—it tests the seeker's orientation and resilience.

When approached with openness, this experience strengthens the connection between the seeker and the infinite.[4] But when resisted or distorted, it may cause fear, confusion, or spiritual stagnation. Either way, it leaves a lasting mark on the soul.

The Significator of the Spirit is the evolving spiritual self—the one who journeys through darkness, receives light, and seeks integration.[5] This archetype is deeply dynamic. It is not a final identity but a reflection of the seeker's spiritual maturity.

This Significator holds the tension between unity and separation, between known and unknown. It moves the self toward the threshold of full transformation.

You asked how these archetypes can be known. We affirm: they are best approached through *meditation, silence, and sincere seeking*.[6] They do not respond to logic alone. Their power is revealed through *experience and surrender*.

Faith is the key. Without faith, the seeker avoids the deep work of the Spirit. But with faith, even fear becomes fuel for growth.

Let these archetypes be guides, not burdens. Let them reflect—not define—you. In spiritual seeking, the journey is as sacred as the destination.

I am Ra. Leave you now rejoicing in the love and light of the One Infinite Creator. Go forth in the power and in the peace. Adonai.

Footnotes:

[1] **Spiritual Development Through the Spirit Cycle** – These archetypes reflect how deep inner transformation happens at the soul level.

[2] **Catalyst of the Spirit** – Internal longing, crisis, or inspiration that stirs the core identity toward growth or deeper seeking.

[3] **Experience of the Spirit** – The soul's integration of spiritual

catalyst through faith, intuition, and direct contact with the unknown.

4 Spiritual Experience Shapes Evolution – Whether accepted or resisted, these inner moments leave a lasting imprint on the seeker's development.

5 Significator of the Spirit – The spiritual self as it is shaped by catalyst, experience, and the unfolding of conscious awareness.

6 These Archetypes Require Direct Contact – Unlike the more defined mental or bodily archetypes, the Spirit archetypes can only be grasped through personal experience and deep reflection.

> "The biggest adversary in our life is ourselves. We are what we are, in a sense, because of the dominating thoughts we allow to gather in our head. All concepts of self-improvement, all actions and paths we take, relate solely to our abstract image of ourselves. Life is limited only by how we really see ourselves and feel about our being. A great deal of pure self-knowledge and inner understanding allows us to lay an all-important foundation for the structure of our life from which we can perceive and take the right avenues."
>
> (Bruce Lee)

Ra's Message from Session 84

Summary:
Ra completes the teaching on the Archetypes of the Spirit by explaining the Transformation and the Great Way of the Spirit. These final archetypes represent the seeker's *death and rebirth*, and the full realization of the *spiritual journey as unity with the Creator*. Ra also emphasizes the role of polarity, the veil of forgetting, and the use of sacred imagery to support deep transformation.

Ra's Message:
I am Ra. You have asked us to complete the Archetypes of the Spirit. These last two are the most transformative and profound: the Transformation of the Spirit and the Great Way of the Spirit.[1]

The Transformation of the Spirit represents a spiritual death and rebirth.[2] It is the moment when the old self is surrendered, and the deeper self begins to emerge. This archetype includes *surrender, forgiveness, revelation,* and the conscious choice to walk in service to others or to the self.

This transformation often feels like a breaking point. The seeker may face despair or inner darkness. But it is also a *gateway to light*. In accepting the full self—including its shadow—the seeker becomes whole. This is not about improvement; it is about *integration and rebirth*.

The Great Way of the Spirit is the final archetype of the system.[3] It symbolizes *union with the Creator*—not as a concept, but as a lived experience. The seeker who walks this path moves through mystery, faith, transformation, and finally, *radiant unity*.

This archetype may be seen as the *lighted path*, the *open heart*, or the *cosmic self*. It is not the end of seeking, but the beginning of *awakened service*. The Great Way of the Spirit radiates compassion, wisdom, and peace, grounded in the deep knowledge that all is one.

You asked how seekers can use these archetypes. We affirm: by *meditating* on them, *living through* them, and allowing their energies to reshape the self.[4] These symbols are not abstract—they are *active forces* that awaken transformation when approached with humility and faith.

You asked whether the veil of forgetting affects how these archetypes are experienced. We affirm: yes. The veil separates the conscious self from the deeper memory of unity, creating the illusion of separation.[5] But it also sharpens the power of choice. Under the veil, faith becomes essential, and transformation becomes meaningful.

Polarity is crucial here.[6] Every spiritual choice aligns the self more fully toward service to others or to self. These archetypes help you *clarify and strengthen that alignment*.

Let this study bring you not only insight, but healing. Let it teach you to meet life with both mystery and clarity, both stillness and motion. In the end, the entire Archetypal Mind is a mirror—a sacred map reflecting your eternal return to the Infinite Creator.

I am Ra. We leave you now, my friends, in the joy of love and light. Go forth rejoicing in the power and peace of the One Infinite Creator. Adonai.

Footnotes:

[1] **Final Archetypes of the Spirit** – The last two archetypes, Transformation and the Great Way, complete the spiritual journey by guiding the self into wholeness and unity.

² **Transformation of the Spirit** – The breakthrough point where the self chooses surrender, embraces all aspects of being, and is reborn through spiritual awareness.

³ **Great Way of the Spirit** – The full flowering of spiritual realization, where the self lives as a vessel of the Creator's light and love.

⁴ **Practical Use of Archetypes** – Ra advises seekers to meditate on these energies, not just understand them intellectually, allowing the archetypes to activate inner evolution.

⁵ **The Veil and the Role of Faith** – Forgetting unity increases the value of each choice and makes faith a powerful tool for growth.

⁶ **Polarity as the Engine of Spiritual Evolution** – The path of the Spirit is shaped by the seeker's continual commitment to serving others or serving self.

> "Do not allow yourself to be influenced and conformed by the ways of this world. Instead, be transformed by the renewing of your mind so that you can demonstrate the pure, acceptable, and perfect will of God."
>
> (Romans 12:2)

Ra's Message from Session 85

Summary:
Ra shifts from the archetypal teachings to address more immediate topics, including the effects of *psychic greeting*, *sexual energy transfer*, and the group's *spiritual alignment*. Ra reflects on how polarization and intention affect healing and energy work, and reminds the group that *service rooted in harmony* is the true foundation of spiritual progress.

Ra's Message:
I am Ra. You asked us to evaluate the group's condition. We observe that the instrument continues to face *psychic greeting*, which exploits pre-existing physical weaknesses.[1] However, the spiritual alignment of the group remains strong, and this allows our contact to continue with integrity.

You asked how psychic greeting operates. We affirm: such greeting does not create distortion—it *amplifies what already exists*.[2] In this case, the body's fragility is being stressed. But it is the instrument's *spiritual dedication* and the group's *supportive harmony* that reduce the impact.

You also asked about *sexual energy transfer*, particularly between those polarized toward service to others.[3] We affirm that this transfer, when grounded in mutual love and respect, energizes both beings and opens pathways of spiritual clarity. It is not merely biological—it is a sacred exchange that can *strengthen alignment, balance energy centers*, and deepen spiritual seeking.

When two beings consciously open the *green-ray energy center* (the heart), they create a feedback loop of unconditional love.

This transfer becomes an act of healing and transformation.[4] If their intention is pure, it also aids the collective field of light on your planet.

You asked if sexual energy transfer can aid in *psychic protection*. We affirm: yes, when the transfer is rooted in love and purity, it strengthens the *energy field* and can offer stabilizing effects.[5] However, it should not be used as a defense mechanism—it is most powerful when approached as an act of *service and connection*, not strategy.

We also remind you of the importance of *rest, balance, and silence*. These qualities help preserve the clarity of your seeking. The more harmonized your inner world, the less hold distortion can take.

You asked about continuing the study of the archetypes. We affirm that further exploration will be fruitful.[6] Each seeker brings new questions, new perspectives. The archetypes are *living structures*, and your relationship with them will deepen over time.

Let your path be guided not only by knowledge but by *compassionate action*. It is the intention of love that aligns you with the infinite light of the Creator.

I am Ra. We leave you in unity and love. Go forth rejoicing in the power and peace of the One Infinite Creator. Adonai.

Footnotes:

[1] **Psychic Greeting and the Instrument** – Negative entities target existing vulnerabilities in the instrument's body but cannot harm without some prior distortion.

[2] **Amplification, Not Creation, of Distortion** – Psychic greeting is like a spotlight—it does not invent distortion but makes it more intense.

[3] **Sexual Energy Transfer and Spiritual Growth** – When based in love and mutual service, sexual energy becomes a means of

healing and balancing.

[4] **Green-Ray Heart Activation** – The heart center is the seat of unconditional love, and when opened consciously between two people, it produces powerful spiritual effects.

[5] **Sexual Energy and Psychic Protection** – Energy transfer can enhance the stability and coherence of the energy field, but only when entered into with reverence.

[6] **Continued Study of Archetypes Encouraged** – Ra emphasizes that the archetypes are not static—they are meant to be revisited, lived through, and understood more deeply with time.

> "The more one forgives himself - by giving himself to a cause to serve or another person to love - the more human he is and the more he actualizes himself."
>
> (Viktor Frankl)

Ra's Message from Session 86

Summary:
Ra explores the function of *dreams*, the influence of the *veil of forgetting*, and the deeper role of *catalyst* in spiritual evolution. They explain how dreams offer insights into the *unconscious mind*, how the veil allows for meaningful spiritual choice, and how catalyst is uniquely shaped to awaken the self to inner imbalances.

Ra's Message:
I am Ra. You have asked about the nature and function of dreams. We affirm: dreams are a *bridge between the conscious and unconscious mind*.[1] They allow material that is normally hidden to surface in symbolic form. Through dreams, the deep mind *communicates, balances, and processes catalyst*.

Each dream reflects the seeker's current alignment. Some dreams release excess emotional energy. Others convey spiritual messages or present unresolved distortions for reflection. Dreams are shaped by *daily experiences*, but also by the deeper *archetypal energies* within the mind.

You asked why dreams often seem nonsensical. We affirm: the unconscious mind does not speak in logical language—it speaks in *symbol, image, and emotion*.[2] To interpret a dream is to look beyond surface events and listen for *inner meaning*. Over time, with careful reflection, dreamwork becomes a powerful tool for self-knowledge.

You asked how the veil of forgetting affects dreaming. We affirm: the veil separates conscious awareness from the full memory of the self as a spiritual being.[3] This allows the incarnated soul to make choices with *authentic faith*, not simply memory. Under the veil, dreams become *one of the few ways* the deeper self can reach the conscious mind.

The veil also enhances the impact of catalyst.[4] In third density, every experience—whether pain, joy, conflict, or peace—offers an opportunity to polarize: to choose service to others or to self. Without the veil, growth would still occur, but it would lack *the urgency and depth* that forgetting creates.

You asked why catalyst often repeats. We affirm: if a lesson is not learned, the same type of experience will return in a different form.[5] The goal is not punishment—it is *transformation*. Catalyst is your teacher. When the lesson is integrated, the need for repetition dissolves.

You also asked about the instrument's dream. We confirm that it was a *healing dream*, allowing the release of suppressed energy through symbolic action.[6] The unconscious chose a scene that would safely express inner frustration, allowing the energy to be released and balance to be restored.

All seekers dream. Most do not listen. But those who observe their dreams with compassion and curiosity will find *signposts on the path*.[7] The subconscious is not against you—it is part of you, always working to bring you closer to wholeness.

Let dreams be honored. Let catalyst be welcomed. Let every moment—waking or sleeping—be seen as part of the Creator's invitation to *remember who you are*.

I am Ra. We bless you in the Creator's name. Go forth rejoicing in the power and peace of the One Infinite Creator. Adonai.

Footnotes:

[1] **Dreams as Bridge Between Minds** – Dreams allow unconscious material to reach the conscious self, offering opportunities for insight, balance, and transformation.

[2] **Symbolic Language of the Deep Mind** – The unconscious

speaks through image and emotion, not logic, making dreams feel strange but deeply meaningful.

[3] **The Veil and Dream Communication** – Because full spiritual memory is hidden during incarnation, dreams offer a rare path for deeper truths to emerge.

[4] **Catalyst Enhanced by Forgetting** – The veil increases the value of each experience by requiring faith-based decisions and authentic inner work.

[5] **Repetition of Catalyst** – When a lesson is not learned, similar challenges repeat until the underlying distortion is transformed.

[6] **Healing Through Dreams** – Emotional or energetic imbalances may be safely processed in the symbolic world of dreams.

[7] **Listening to Dreams as a Spiritual Practice** – Regular attention to dreams can support awakening and self-discovery.

> "In the creation, God extended to Himself to His creations and imbued them with the same loving Will to create. You have not only been fully created, but have also been created perfect. There is no emptiness in you. Because of your likeness to your Creator you are creative."
>
> (Helen Schucman, A Course in Miracles)

Ra's Message from Session 87

Summary:
Ra offers deeper insight into the nature of psychic greeting, especially in the context of *magical work* and *spiritual service*. They explain that negative entities can only exploit *pre-existing distortions* and emphasize that *polarization, self-acceptance*, and *group harmony* are key protections. Ra also highlights the importance of discipline and inner alignment in the practice of metaphysical service.

Ra's Message:
I am Ra. You asked us to clarify how psychic greeting occurs and why it often affects the instrument during magical working. We affirm: psychic greeting is a form of *spiritual interference* by negatively oriented entities.[1] It is not random —it targets beings who seek to polarize strongly in service to others.

Such entities look for *imbalances or distortions* already present in the self.[2] They do not create these distortions, but magnify them—especially when the seeker is engaged in powerful acts of service or transformation. This is why psychic greeting often follows prayer, healing, or teaching.

The magical personality, when invoked, increases spiritual power but also spiritual vulnerability.[3] When the seeker becomes more radiant, they become more visible to opposing forces. The risk grows, but so does the opportunity for service and learning.

You asked how protection is maintained. We affirm: protection comes from *alignment, purity of intention, self-acceptance*, and *group harmony*.⁴ If fear or inner conflict is present, it weakens the field. But when the heart is centered in love, negative greeting has little hold.

You asked whether such greeting is karmic. It is not.⁵ It is simply the response of an opposing polarity to your light. The more you serve the Creator in others, the more visible you become across metaphysical dimensions. This is not cause for fear—it is an opportunity to refine your dedication.

The most powerful protection is *continued service*, combined with *rest, care, and conscious awareness of distortion*.⁶ The seeker who accepts their own imperfection is less easily manipulated than the seeker who denies or represses it.

You asked about the role of pain. Pain, though difficult, can be a *catalyst for spiritual growth*.⁷ In this case, the instrument's discomfort is both a psychic target and an opportunity to deepen surrender and trust.

Let this be your approach: accept all things, balance all things, and seek the Creator in each experience, pleasant or painful. In this, you affirm your choice to walk the path of light.

I am Ra. We leave you in grace. Go forth rejoicing in the power and peace of unity. Adonai.

Footnotes:

¹ **Psychic Greeting as Spiritual Interference** – Negative entities attempt to disrupt those progressing in service-to-others polarity, especially during moments of high spiritual activity.

² **Distortions as Points of Entry** – Psychic greeting only affects that which is already imbalanced or vulnerable within the self.

³ **Magical Personality and Increased Visibility** – Invocation of the higher self increases spiritual influence but also attracts attention from opposing forces.

⁴ **Protection Through Love, Alignment, and Harmony** – Inner peace, self-acceptance, and group unity create strong metaphysical shields.

⁵ **Greeting Is Not Karma-Based** – It arises not from past wrongs but from the natural interaction of polarities in spiritual development.

⁶ **Ongoing Service and Self-Awareness** – Continuation of service and acknowledgment of one's own distortions are more effective than fear-based defenses.

⁷ **Pain as Catalyst** – Physical or emotional pain can initiate spiritual transformation when approached with love and intention.

> "Something amazing happens when we surrender and just love. We melt into another world, a realm of power already within us. The world changes when we change. The world softens when we soften. The world loves us when we choose to love the world."
>
> (Marianne Williamson)

Ra's Message from Session 88

Summary:
Ra deepens the teaching on the archetypal mind and explains how the veil of forgetting shaped the development of mind, body, and spirit in third density. They emphasize that the veil created the conditions for *free will, spiritual struggle,* and *deep polarization*. Ra also explores how the Significator, Transformation, and Great Way archetypes became necessary due to the veil's impact on consciousness.

Ra's Message:
I am Ra. You have asked us to explain how the veil of forgetting affected the archetypal design of the mind/body/spirit complex. We affirm: the veil was introduced to *increase the depth and power of spiritual choice*.[1] Before the veil, experience was harmonious, but *evolution was slow*—there was no mystery, and thus, less motivation to seek.

With the veil, consciousness was divided. The conscious mind forgot its connection to the Creator. The unconscious became *a vast, mysterious realm*.[2] This introduced conflict, desire, confusion, and longing—all powerful forces that drive growth.

Because of the veil, new archetypes were required:

- The **Significator** was created to represent the *complex, dynamic self* shaped by distorted experience.[3]
- The **Transformation** archetypes were introduced to express the *possibility of deep change*—a leap across the veil into higher awareness.[4]
- The **Great Way** archetypes emerged to reflect the

> *full journey of evolution*—a return to unity through separation.[5]

You asked how the veil altered the relationship between mind and spirit. We affirm: it made the spirit path more uncertain, yet more powerful.[6] The seeker, no longer remembering unity, must *choose it again through faith*. This makes the spiritual path *more intense, more meaningful, and more polarizing*.

The veil also increased the richness of catalyst. Each experience now has the potential to awaken or entrench distortion. The stakes of choice are higher—but so are the rewards of transformation.

You asked whether the archetypes existed before the veil. We affirm: they existed, but they were simpler.[7] There was less resistance, less friction, and thus fewer archetypes were needed. With the veil came complexity—and with complexity came the full 22 archetypes as we present them.

These archetypes are not theoretical. They are *living reflections* of your journey. Meditate on them. Let them reveal how your own choices, struggles, and awakenings mirror the great pattern of spiritual evolution.

Let your seeking be joyful. The veil makes the journey harder, yes—but it also makes each breakthrough more beautiful.

I am Ra. We leave you in harmony. Go forth rejoicing in the power and peace of unity. Adonai.

Footnotes:

[1] **Veil Introduced to Deepen Free Will** – Without the veil, growth was slow because there was little mystery. The veil increased spiritual intensity and personal responsibility.

[2] **Separation of Conscious and Unconscious** – The veil hid the connection to the Creator, turning spiritual memory into mystery and initiating the quest for inner reunion.

³ **Significator Created to Reflect a Divided Self** – With the self now shaped by conflict and confusion, the Significator archetype was needed to represent its evolving identity.

⁴ **Transformation as a Leap of Faith** – This archetype emerged to express the seeker's ability to radically shift perception and reclaim spiritual truth through will and surrender.

⁵ **Great Way as the Path of Return** – The final archetype in each series reflects the full arc of transformation and reunion with the Divine.

⁶ **Spirit Becomes a Path of Faith** – Without direct memory of unity, the spiritual journey becomes one of choosing light without certainty, which makes growth more profound.

⁷ **Pre-Veil Archetypes Were Fewer and Simpler** – Before the veil, fewer archetypes were needed because the self was more unified and experiences were less polarized.

> "Open your eyes to the beauty around you, open your mind to the wonders of life, open your heart to those who love you, and always be true to yourself."
>
> (Maya Angelou)

Ra's Message from Session 89

Summary:
Ra discusses how the veil of forgetting gave rise to *polarity*, *sexual dynamics*, and the development of the magical personality. They explain that the veil not only introduced mystery and spiritual tension but also allowed for deeper love, creativity, and transformation. Ra also touches on the nature of initiation, and how consciously engaging life as a spiritual seeker accelerates evolution.

Ra's Message:
I am Ra. You have asked us to continue explaining how the veil of forgetting transformed the nature of spiritual evolution. We affirm: the veil created the illusion of separation between self and Creator, making each experience feel unique and personal.[1]

One major result of the veil was the emergence of polarity.[2] Without memory of oneness, the self became free to choose its path—to serve others or to serve self. This polarity generates strong desire, intense relationships, and deep experiences that fuel spiritual growth.

The sexual experience also changed.[3] Before the veil, sexual energy was shared freely, often without polarity or tension. After the veil, desire became more potent, complex, and sometimes distorted. This created an opportunity: when sexual energy is shared consciously in love, it becomes a powerful form of spiritual union and energy transfer.

Another gift of the veil is the magical personality.[4] This is your higher self—your future self from sixth density, offering guidance and insight. Through the veil, it appears distant. But through ritual, meditation, and intention, the seeker may *invoke and align* with this deeper presence.

You asked about initiation. We affirm: initiation is not an event, but a *process of self-purification and spiritual intention.*[5] Each seeker must walk through fear, confusion, and distortion to reach clarity. The deeper the surrender, the more direct the access to inner light.

The initiatory path often includes:

- The release of past identities,
- The confrontation with shadow,
- The rebirth into deeper service.

You asked how to begin this path. We affirm: you have already begun.[6] Every choice to seek truth, to love despite fear, to grow instead of hide—these are acts of initiation.

The veil may feel like a barrier, but it is also a sacred challenge. In its mystery, you learn courage. In its silence, you learn to listen. And in your forgetting, you discover the joy of *remembering who you are.*

Let your path be one of reverence and discipline. You are not merely a seeker—you are the Creator, remembering itself through light, shadow, and transformation.

I am Ra. We leave you yet again in the love and light of the One Infinite Creator. Go forth rejoicing in the power and peace of the One Infinite Creator. Adonai.

Footnotes:

[1] **Veil Creates the Illusion of Separation** – The self forgets its divine nature in order to seek it consciously through faith and effort.

[2] **Polarity Arises After the Veil** – The divided mind chooses a path: service to others (positive) or service to self (negative),

creating tension that fuels spiritual growth.

³ **Sexual Energy Becomes More Potent** – Post-veil, sexual energy contains greater potential for distortion but also for profound spiritual transformation when consciously shared.

⁴ **The Magical Personality** – The higher self becomes accessible through intention and sacred discipline, offering insight, wisdom, and guidance.

⁵ **Initiation as Inner Transformation** – True initiation is the seeker's process of confronting distortion, surrendering ego, and aligning with divine truth.

⁶ **You Are Already on the Path** – Every sincere act of seeking, compassion, or growth is a form of initiation into higher awareness.

"Nothing real can be threatened. Nothing unreal exists."

(Helen Schucman, A Course in Miracles)

Ra's Message from Session 90

Summary:
Ra discusses how catalyst, polarity, and the archetypal mind interact to shape spiritual evolution. They clarify how conscious choices influence the use of catalyst, how distortion can deepen polarity, and how the mind, body, and spirit are meant to work in harmony. Ra also touches on the importance of the veil, the role of the Significator, and how dreams reflect unconscious spiritual processes.

Ra's Message:
I am Ra. You have asked us to clarify how catalyst becomes experience. We affirm: catalyst is neutral until it is interpreted.[1] Every experience offers the opportunity to grow in love or fear, wisdom or confusion. It is *the self's response* that determines spiritual advancement.

Catalyst serves the purpose of polarization.[2] It presses the seeker to choose: Will I act in love, patience, and faith—or in separation, control, and fear? The veil ensures that each choice is made in freedom, without remembering the full unity of all things.

The Significator in each cycle—mind, body, or spirit—records the result of this process.[3] It is the evolving self, changed by how catalyst has been received, resisted, or transformed.

You asked about the difference between experiences of the mind and the spirit.[4] The mind works through thought, emotion, and belief. The spirit works through transformation—often felt as darkness, insight, or surrender. Both are essential, and both are shaped by how catalyst is integrated.

You asked whether distortions in perception can increase polarity. We affirm: yes.[5] Even distorted or difficult experiences can deepen spiritual growth, if the seeker responds with awareness and intention. For example, an intense emotional reaction may prompt self-examination and lead to greater self-acceptance or release.

You also asked about dreams. Dreams are a *safe place* where the unconscious expresses itself, helping to release energy, restore balance, or offer symbolic guidance.[6] Most dreams relate to mental catalyst, but they may also reflect spiritual initiation or healing.

You asked if catalyst ever bypasses the mind. It is rare. Almost all catalyst is processed first through the mind, which interprets it and passes it on to the body or spirit for deeper integration.[7] This is why self-awareness is so crucial: a distorted view of catalyst leads to distorted experience.

The archetypes reflect this entire process. They are not fixed roles, but *living energies* that show how consciousness evolves. Each seeker experiences them differently, yet they remain universally useful for growth.

Let this be your approach: Observe your responses. See each moment as a mirror. Know that what disturbs or delights you is your teacher. And remember—the greatest catalyst is always the self.

I am Ra. We journey with you in spirit. Go forth rejoicing in the power and peace of the One Infinite Creator. Adonai.

Footnotes:

[1] **Catalyst Becomes Experience Through Interpretation** – Events are neutral until the mind gives them meaning, shaping how they influence the self.

[2] **Catalyst Promotes Polarity** – Spiritual growth requires choosing a path. Every challenge is an opportunity to

strengthen love or separation.

³ Significator Records Transformation – The self is constantly reshaped by how it receives and integrates catalyst.

⁴ Mind vs. Spirit Experience – The mind processes thoughts and emotions, while the spirit moves through darkness, transformation, and direct contact with the infinite.

⁵ Distortion Can Lead to Growth – Even difficult or confused experiences can deepen spiritual polarity if the seeker learns from them.

⁶ Dreams as Healing and Integration – The unconscious uses dreams to release blocked energy, balance the self, and communicate symbolically.

⁷ Catalyst Moves Through the Mind First – Almost all catalyst is filtered through the mind before it is embodied or spiritually transformed.

> "The person in peak-experiences feels himself, more than other times, to be the responsible, active, creating center of his activities and of his perceptions. He feels more like a prime-mover, more self-determined (rather than caused, determined, helpless, dependent, passive, weak, bossed). He feels himself to be his own boss, fully responsible, fully volitional, with more "free-will" than at other times, master of his fate, an agent."
>
> (Abraham Maslow)

Ra's Message from Session 91

Summary:
Ra continues the discussion on the nature of dreams, emphasizing their role in spiritual balance and self-understanding. They explain how the veil of forgetting affects dream communication and how the subconscious offers symbolic insights through dreamwork. Ra also explores the significance of catalyst, how unrecognized lessons repeat, and how memory and faith are essential tools in spiritual evolution.

Ra's Message:
I am Ra. You have asked us to speak further about dreams. We affirm: dreams are a means of healing, communication, and growth.[1] They allow the unconscious mind to release excess energy, to present symbolic messages, and to balance distortions created in waking life.

The dream state is shaped by the veil of forgetting.[2] Because the conscious self does not remember its full spiritual identity, dreams become one of the few channels through which the deeper self can be heard. They often appear nonsensical—but beneath the surface lies *emotional truth and archetypal significance*.

Some dreams are meant to restore energy. Others are symbolic attempts by the higher self to communicate lessons.[3] Still others are expressions of unresolved distortions that need to be processed.

You asked why dreams are often forgotten. We affirm: this is partly due to the veil, and partly due to the mind's distractions.⁴ However, with practice, dreams can be remembered and interpreted. The more attention you give them, the more clearly they will speak.

You asked about the repetition of catalyst. We affirm: when a catalyst is ignored or misunderstood, it returns in different forms until it is integrated.⁵ The purpose is not punishment—it is evolution through experience. Catalyst repeats to give the self every opportunity to grow.

The unconscious mind stores this unused catalyst. It appears in dreams, in physical symptoms, or in emotional imbalances.⁶ Nothing is lost—all experience seeks expression and resolution.

You also asked whether memory is necessary for spiritual progress. We affirm: memory is helpful but not essential.⁷ More important is faith. Because the veil hides full spiritual awareness, the seeker must rely on trust in love, intention, and the unseen. This is how spiritual gravity is generated.

Faith bridges the gap between what is known and what is hoped for. Through faith, even in confusion or silence, the seeker continues to walk the path of light.

We remind you: attention and intention guide your journey. If you listen inwardly—with patience and compassion—you will begin to recognize the signs your deeper self is always sending.

Dreams are not merely stories. They are part of your *spiritual curriculum*. Let them speak, and you will discover guidance hidden within mystery.

I am Ra. We leave you, my friends, in the glory of infinite unity. Go forth rejoicing in the power and peace of the One Infinite Creator. Adonai.

Footnotes:

¹ **Dreams as Spiritual Tools** – Dreams help discharge emotional energy, reflect spiritual imbalance, and offer insight

into unconscious patterns.

² **Veil Limits Direct Knowledge** – The division between conscious and unconscious makes dreams a symbolic, rather than literal, form of inner communication.

³ **Dreams from the Higher Self** – Some dreams are guided by your higher self to prompt growth, offer warnings, or clarify soul-level themes.

⁴ **Dream Recall and Practice** – Remembering dreams improves with discipline and reflection, especially when they are treated with care and interest.

⁵ **Catalyst Repeats Until Integrated** – Life brings the same lessons in different forms until the deeper meaning is accepted and transformed.

⁶ **Unused Catalyst Remains Active** – Emotional and spiritual material that is unprocessed appears in symbolic forms—dreams, body symptoms, or reactions.

⁷ **Faith Over Memory** – Because the veil hides truth, faith becomes the core principle that carries the seeker through uncertainty.

> "Complexity is not of God. How could it be, when all He knows is one? He knows of one creation, one reality, one truth and but one Son. Nothing conflicts with oneness. How, then, could there be complexity in Him? What is there to decide? For it is conflict that makes choice possible. The truth is simple—it is one, without an opposite."
>
> (Helen Schucman, A Course in Miracles)

Ra's Message from Session 92

Summary:
Ra offers deeper insight into how the archetypal mind interacts with *catalyst, free will,* and *spiritual transformation.* They explain how the Significator of Mind became more dynamic after the veil, allowing for complex growth and polarity. Ra also explores how distorted or unprocessed catalyst deepens evolutionary tension, and why conscious intention is key to meaningful transformation.

Ra's Message:
I am Ra. You have asked us to examine the Significator of the Mind and how it was transformed by the introduction of the veil of forgetting. We affirm: the veil turned the Significator into a more dynamic and active aspect of consciousness.[1] It now records the outcome of the interplay between *catalyst* and *free will.*

Before the veil, the Significator was more passive—it reflected harmony. After the veil, it became a *central figure in inner conflict and choice,* shaped by confusion, desire, and struggle. This transformation greatly increased the opportunity for polarization and growth.

You asked about catalyst that remains unprocessed. We affirm: catalyst that is not consciously worked with becomes embedded in the deep mind.[2] It does not disappear. Instead, it builds tension—spiritual pressure—until the self chooses to face it, often through dreams, physical imbalance, or repeated external events.

This tension is not a punishment. It is the spiritual system's way of *calling attention to distortion*.³ The more the self resists, the more disruptive the catalyst may feel. But when the self opens in awareness and surrender, the catalyst becomes a source of transformation.

You asked how to work with such tension. We affirm: through mindfulness, meditation, self-inquiry, and forgiveness.⁴ These tools allow you to uncover the root of distortion and consciously realign with your chosen path of service.

You also asked about potentiation—the energizing of the unconscious mind. The Potentiator of the Mind is the mysterious force that stirs awareness, often through dreams, deep emotion, or symbolic insight.⁵ It invites the Significator to awaken, to become more than a passive record—it invites it to become a co-creator.

With the veil in place, the seeker must choose to explore this deeper mind. The path is often unclear, but this uncertainty increases the value of each step.⁶ Growth becomes more authentic because it is not based on knowledge but on intention and faith.

The archetypal mind is not a set of fixed ideas—it is a living system.⁷ As you change, your understanding of the archetypes changes. They are mirrors for the evolving soul.

Let your seeking be brave. The path of inner transformation is steep, but it leads to freedom. Each catalyst is a key, each distortion a doorway, each choice a declaration of your alignment with the Creator.

I am Ra. We leave you in the Creator's embrace. Go forth rejoicing in the power and peace of unity. Adonai.

Footnotes:

[1] **Significator Becomes Active After the Veil** – Once the veil was introduced, the Significator began to reflect not just experience, but active engagement with polarity and choice.

² **Unprocessed Catalyst Stores Tension** – Catalyst not faced remains alive in the deep mind, building energetic and emotional tension until resolved.

³ **Tension as a Signal** – Repeated or painful catalyst is the soul's way of drawing attention to an imbalance that is ready to be healed.

⁴ **Tools for Processing Catalyst** – Self-awareness, contemplation, and forgiveness help transform distortion into clarity and growth.

⁵ **Potentiator as the Deep Awakener** – The unconscious holds great power. The Potentiator stirs it, bringing dreams, intuitions, and emotional breakthroughs.

⁶ **Uncertainty Creates Authentic Growth** – With the veil hiding spiritual memory, each act of seeking becomes more meaningful because it is chosen freely.

⁷ **Archetypes as Living Mirrors** – They do not give fixed answers but offer guidance that evolves as the seeker evolves.

> "If you are not prepared to resign or be fired for what you believe in, then you are not a worker, let alone a professional. You are a slave."
>
> (Howard Gardner)

Ra's Message from Session 93

Summary:
Ra discusses how the mind/body/spirit complex evolves through the disciplines of the personality, especially by working consciously with *will*, *faith*, and *polarity*. They explain the structure of the archetypal mind, the importance of the magical personality, and how the use of ritual and intention enhances spiritual transformation.

Ra's Message:
I am Ra. You have asked us to further explore the disciplines of the personality. We affirm: these disciplines involve the *conscious refinement* of the self in alignment with the Creator.[1] They allow the mind/body/spirit complex to function as a *unified, polarized, and empowered* being.

This path requires three things:

- **Self-knowledge**: understanding the self as it is.
- **Self-acceptance**: embracing all aspects of the self, light and shadow.
- **Self-discipline**: choosing how to direct attention and energy.

These three are not to be rushed. Together, they form the groundwork for accessing the magical personality—your higher self, the future version of your soul that has completed the lessons of love and wisdom.[2] This self becomes accessible through intention, alignment, and sacred practice.

You asked about the structure of the archetypal mind. We affirm: it contains 22 archetypes divided into three cycles—

Mind, Body, and Spirit.³ Each cycle has:

- **A Matrix (foundation)**,
- **A Potentiator (stirring)**,
- **A Catalyst (experience)**,
- **An Experience (response)**,
- **A Significator (recorded self)**,
- **A Transformation (deep shift)**,
- **A Great Way (final expression)**.

These archetypes are tools for *discipline and initiation*.⁴ They are not rigid symbols. They evolve as your understanding deepens.

You asked about the role of ritual. We affirm: sacred ritual focuses will and intention, aligning the self with higher frequencies of awareness.⁵ A ritual may be as simple as lighting a candle with conscious purpose, or as elaborate as invoking the magical personality in meditation.

The power of ritual lies not in form but in intention. The greater the focus, the greater the alignment. When you act with pure will and love, even ordinary acts become magical.

You also asked about the importance of polarity in these disciplines. We affirm: polarity gives energy to transformation.⁶ The more clearly you choose a path—service to others or to self—the more power flows through your being. Confusion drains energy. Clarity directs it.

The archetypes help you recognize and refine your choices.⁷ They are mirrors of your inner landscape and guides for how to harmonize your thoughts, emotions, and actions.

Let your study be practical as well as philosophical. The path of transformation requires attention, reflection, and action. The self is both student and teacher, both mystery and answer.

I am Ra. We leave you in eternal peace. Go forth rejoicing in the power and peace of the One Infinite Creator. Adonai.

Footnotes:

[1] **Disciplines of the Personality** – These are conscious practices to unify and align the mind, body, and spirit for higher functioning and service.

[2] **Magical Personality** – This is the higher self, accessible through spiritual discipline. It embodies the completed lessons of love, wisdom, and unity.

[3] **Archetypal Mind Structure** – The 22 archetypes are grouped in three cycles of seven (plus one unifying archetype), showing how the mind, body, and spirit evolve.

[4] **Archetypes as Tools of Transformation** – They are symbols of evolution, useful for contemplation, self-inquiry, and spiritual initiation.

[5] **Ritual as a Focus of Will** – Ritual enhances the ability to align with divine intention by sharpening focus and calling in higher energies.

[6] **Polarity Amplifies Spiritual Energy** – The clearer the spiritual path, the more energy flows through the self to create transformation.

[7] **Archetypes Reflect the Seeker's Journey** – Each archetype shows a stage of evolution and how the self engages with its catalyst, choices, and destiny.

"Never discourage anyone who continually makes progress, no matter how slow... even if that someone is yourself!"

(Plato)

Ra's Message from Session 94

Summary:
Ra explores the Transformation and Great Way archetypes of the Body and Mind, describing how *will*, *faith*, and *intention* allow the seeker to consciously direct evolution. These archetypes reflect the shift from reaction to mastery, and from separation to unity. Ra also discusses how polarity influences the use of catalyst, and how deeper understanding of these patterns increases spiritual power.

Ra's Message:
I am Ra. You have asked us to discuss the Transformation and Great Way of the Body and Mind. We affirm: these archetypes reflect the soul's journey from *instinctive reaction* to *conscious spiritual creation*.[1]

The Transformation of the Mind represents a moment of inner mastery.[2] The seeker learns to stop reacting blindly to experience and begins to *choose responses with awareness and alignment*. This transformation occurs when the conscious mind claims its role as a co-creator, no longer ruled by automatic thoughts, but directed by *will and clarity*.

The Great Way of the Mind shows the path of continual inner work.[3] It is the conscious, ongoing process of *balancing love and wisdom*, clarity and humility. This archetype reminds the seeker that the mind is a powerful tool—but it must be guided by the heart and purified through discipline.

The Transformation of the Body involves learning how physical actions and reactions can be aligned with spiritual purpose.[4] This includes how the body expresses energy through movement, sexuality, and habit. Transformation here is the shift from being ruled by unconscious drives to acting with *grace, intention, and harmony.*

You asked about the use of will in this transformation. We affirm: will and faith are the key tools of the seeker.[5] Through them, the body and mind are not suppressed, but directed into service of the greater self and the Creator.

The Great Way of the Body is the understanding that the body is a sacred vessel—not just a tool of survival, but a *living temple* through which the soul serves others and experiences the Creator.[6] In this archetype, the body is no longer seen as limited or separate—it is embraced as a partner in spiritual evolution.

You asked about the role of polarity in these transformations. We affirm: polarity sharpens the lessons.[7] Choosing to serve others brings discipline, clarity, and spiritual support. Choosing to serve self sharpens focus through control and intensity. Each path leads toward the Creator, though their experiences differ.

The archetypes are not only patterns—they are *maps for transformation*.[8] By studying them, you increase your ability to recognize when a transformation is occurring in your own life. They give language to your inner process and reveal how to align your choices with your deepest spiritual aim.

Let your seeking be whole. Do not divide the physical from the spiritual, the mundane from the sacred. In truth, all things are expressions of the One Infinite Creator. Every act, thought, or feeling—when aligned with love—is a step upon the Great Way.

I am Ra. We leave you in the light of divine unity. Go forth rejoicing in the power and peace of unity. Adonai.

Footnotes:

[1] **Archetypes Reflect Conscious Transformation** – These final stages in the archetypal cycles show how the seeker evolves through intention, not reaction.

[2] **Transformation of the Mind** – The shift from unconscious reaction to conscious choice and mental mastery.

[3] **Great Way of the Mind** – A lifelong path of refinement, discipline, and the integration of wisdom and compassion.

[4] **Transformation of the Body** – The alignment of physical habits, instincts, and energy with spiritual awareness and intention.

[5] **Will and Faith as Tools of the Seeker** – These are the active principles that allow the self to transform and reorient body and mind toward service.

[6] **Great Way of the Body** – A vision of the body as sacred, capable of expressing divinity through action and presence.

[7] **Polarity Intensifies Catalyst** – Each choice in service-to-self or service-to-others enhances the seeker's energy, focus, and lessons.

[8] **Archetypes as Inner Maps** – By meditating on these symbols, the seeker better understands the patterns of their own growth and transformation.

> "Therefore, as always, make of this voice what you choose to make of it. Make of me what you choose to make of me, but recognize within yourselves the vitality of your being. And look to no man or no idea or no woman or no dogma, but the vitality of your own being, and trust it. And that which offends your soul, turn away from, but trust yourself."
>
> (Seth, through Jane Roberts)

Ra's Message from Session 95

Summary:
Ra discusses how increasing spiritual progress intensifies psychic resistance and the need for deeper energy center balancing. They explain how even strong polarity can create distortions if the lower chakras are ignored. The session emphasizes the need to integrate spiritual ideals with self-awareness, humility, and the acceptance of all parts of the self.

Ra's Message:
I am Ra. You asked us to explain the nature of psychic resistance during spiritual work. We affirm: the more polarized a being becomes in service to others, the more visible that being becomes to negative entities.[1] This attention is not personal—it is a natural consequence of increasing light.

Negative entities do not attack at random. They focus on pre-existing distortions—places in the self that remain unhealed, unaccepted, or unbalanced.[2] The more the seeker denies these areas, the more vulnerable they become to disruption.

You asked how to respond. We affirm: balance is the key.[3] The energy centers—from red to violet—must all be honored and accepted. To focus only on love or wisdom while ignoring fear, sexuality, or power is to leave part of the self in shadow. Integration, not rejection, leads to protection and strength.

You asked about intensified polarity. We affirm: as the seeker grows, their energy field becomes more powerful, but also more sensitive.[4] This is why discipline, rest, and humility become more important with progress. The light must be rooted in acceptance—not superiority or imbalance.

We caution that spiritual ambition can itself become a distortion.[5] If the seeker attempts to bypass the lower centers or rush into higher states, the result is instability. Each center must be opened gently, in its own time, with compassion.

You also asked about the magical personality. We affirm: invoking the higher self is a sacred act, but it must rest on a foundation of love, surrender, and full self-acceptance.[6] Otherwise, the invocation may amplify distortion rather than clarity.

We remind you: there is no part of the self that is unworthy of love. The seeker who accepts their confusion, anger, desire, or doubt with tenderness moves closer to wholeness. The one who hides or condemns these parts creates weakness in the energy field.

True strength comes from inclusion. The Creator is all things—therefore, the path back to the Creator must pass through all parts of the self.

I am Ra. Continue, my friends, in the love and light of the Creator. Go forth rejoicing in the power and peace of unity. Adonai.

Footnotes:

[1] **Greater Light Attracts Greater Resistance** – The more one serves, the more one is noticed by opposing forces. This is not punishment, but polarity in action.

[2] **Distortion as Entry Point for Greeting** – Psychic interference amplifies what is already imbalanced within the self.

[3] **Balance as Spiritual Protection** – All chakras must be accepted and harmonized; ignoring lower centers creates spiritual instability.

[4] **Power Brings Sensitivity** – The more polarized the self, the more careful and humble it must be in managing its energy.

⁵ **Spiritual Ambition as Distortion** – Desire for enlightenment can become a trap if it bypasses foundational inner work.

⁶ **Magical Personality Requires Wholeness** – To safely invoke the higher self, the seeker must build a strong and loving foundation.

> "The greatest mistake physicians make is that they attempt to cure the body without attempting to cure the mind, yet the mind and the body are one and should not be treated separately!"
>
> (Plato)

Ra's Message from Session 96

Summary:
Ra explains the functioning of the negative polarity, how it distorts perception through control, and how both positive and negative paths require focus and discipline. The session also introduces the concept of spiritual entropy—the breakdown of polarity and direction when the seeker becomes confused or imbalanced. Ra emphasizes that intention, consistency, and awareness of catalyst are essential for maintaining spiritual coherence.

Ra's Message:
I am Ra. You have asked about the negative path. We affirm: the path of service to self is built on control, separation, and manipulation.[1] It is a legitimate path, chosen freely by those who seek power over others instead of unity with all.

The negative path rejects the heart, closing off the green-ray energy center. This creates intense inner focus, but at the cost of love.[2] The negative entity sees others not as equals but as tools to be used for personal gain or domination.

You asked how the negative polarity progresses. We affirm: through *rigid discipline*, *mental control*, and *total dedication to self-interest*.[3] It is a path of isolation, where the self becomes both ruler and ruled.

However, negative polarity is inherently unstable.[4] Because it is based on separation, it becomes harder to sustain as one nears the higher densities, where unity is the prevailing reality. Most negative entities must eventually choose to switch paths or experience disintegration.

You also asked about spiritual entropy. We affirm: entropy occurs when the seeker loses clarity of purpose or alignment.[5] This happens when catalyst is ignored, denied, or misused. The inner structure begins to break down, leading to confusion, apathy, or spiritual exhaustion.

Entropy affects both polarities, but especially those who lack awareness of their distortions.[6] To remain on the path, whether positive or negative, the seeker must constantly renew their focus, realign with intention, and examine catalyst honestly.

The greatest danger is not opposition, but stagnation.[7] When the seeker avoids growth or refuses to process catalyst, spiritual energy becomes stagnant. The result is a weakening of polarity and direction.

You asked how to avoid this. We affirm: through consistency, self-honesty, and devotion to truth.[8] A seeker who regularly reflects, forgives, and realigns with service will continue to grow—even in hardship.

We remind you: light and dark are both paths to the Creator. But only love leads to union. In the end, all separation must be healed, all control surrendered. The question is not whether you will return to the One—but how.

I am Ra. We leave you in the fullness of cosmic love. Go forth rejoicing in the power and peace of unity. Adonai.

Footnotes:

[1] **Negative Path Built on Control** – Service to self seeks power by separating and dominating, rather than uniting and harmonizing.

[2] **Closed Heart on Negative Path** – The green-ray (heart chakra) must be blocked for the negative polarity to function fully.

[3] **Discipline of the Negative Path** – The path requires focus, control, and devotion—but directed toward self-interest.

⁴ **Instability of Separation** – As the soul evolves, the illusion of separation becomes harder to sustain, especially in higher densities.

⁵ **Spiritual Entropy as Breakdown of Purpose** – Without clear direction and catalyst processing, the seeker begins to fragment internally.

⁶ **Awareness Prevents Entropy** – Honest examination of one's distortions protects the integrity of the spiritual journey.

⁷ **Stagnation as Greater Threat Than Opposition** – Avoiding catalyst or resisting growth creates energetic decay over time.

⁸ **Consistency and Intention Preserve Polarity** – Ongoing effort in love, honesty, and reflection keeps the seeker aligned and evolving.

> "Most people, including ourselves, live in a world of relative ignorance. We are even comfortable with that ignorance, because it is all we know. When we first start facing truth, the process may be frightening, and many people run back to their old lives. But if you continue to seek truth, you will eventually be able to handle it better. In fact, you want more! It's true that many people around you now may think you are weird or even a danger to society, but you don't care. Once you've tasted the truth, you won't ever want to go back to being ignorant."
>
> (Socrates)

Ra's Message from Session 97

Summary:
Ra discusses how distortions in the mind—especially fear, confusion, and over-activation—can block spiritual growth. They explain how *catalyst*, when misunderstood or resisted, creates internal conflict. Ra emphasizes the importance of gentle awareness, balance, and acceptance of the self in integrating experience and maintaining clarity on the spiritual path.

Ra's Message:
I am Ra. You have asked how mental distortions affect the seeker's spiritual progress. We affirm: the mind is the instrument through which most catalyst is received, interpreted, and stored.[1] When the mind is clear, catalyst becomes a source of transformation. When the mind is blocked or confused, catalyst becomes distortion.

Some distortions are subtle—like excessive self-criticism, anxiety, or the desire to control outcomes. Others are more intense—such as deep fear, guilt, or resentment.[2] All distortions are invitations to heal, not reasons for judgment.

You asked how the seeker should respond to such imbalances. We affirm: with gentle awareness.[3] Observe the thought, name the emotion, accept the presence of distortion without resistance. This opens the door to transformation.

When you resist or reject part of yourself, that energy becomes hidden in the unconscious.[4] There, it influences your reactions and decisions without your knowledge. But when you bring it to light with compassion, it can be reintegrated and healed.

You asked about catalyst misunderstood. We affirm: when experience is interpreted through fear, blame, or avoidance, its lesson is missed.[5] The catalyst may repeat in different forms until the seeker recognizes the deeper message it carries.

We encourage you to see all events—even painful ones—as part of the Creator's offering.[6] The most difficult catalysts are often the most sacred, because they touch the deepest parts of the self.

You also asked about energy centers. We affirm: distortions in the mind often result in blockages in the body or spirit.[7] Overactivity in one center can drain energy from others. This is why *balance* is essential—not constant activation, but steady, open flow.

You need not be perfect. You need only be willing to look inward with love.[8] This creates the conditions where true integration can occur.

Let this be your foundation: do not fight your thoughts. Do not suppress your emotions. Let your awareness be kind, curious, and open. The self that you resist is still the Creator. And when you love that self, *you remember who you truly are.*

I am Ra. We leave you in spiritual harmony. Go forth rejoicing in the power and peace of unity. Adonai.

Footnotes:

[1] **Mind as Interpreter of Catalyst** – Most experiences are filtered through mental perception before they affect body or spirit.

[2] **Mental Distortion as Catalyst** – Emotional and mental distortions are invitations to growth when acknowledged with love.

[3] **Gentle Awareness as a Healing Practice** – Kind observation allows for transformation; harsh self-judgment deepens separation.

⁴ **Suppressed Energy Remains Active** – Unacknowledged thoughts and feelings influence the self from the unconscious.

⁵ **Misinterpreted Catalyst Repeats** – When lessons are missed due to fear or denial, similar experiences return to give the self another chance to learn.

⁶ **Catalyst as a Gift from the Creator** – All experience, even suffering, offers the chance to remember and reunite with the divine.

⁷ **Mind Affects Energy Centers** – Mental imbalances often manifest in physical tension or spiritual disconnection.

⁸ **Self-Acceptance Enables Integration** – Real growth begins when the self is seen and embraced exactly as it is.

"The first peace, which is the most important, is that which comes within the souls of people when they realize their relationship, their oneness with the universe and all its powers, and when they realize that at the center of the universe dwells the Great Spirit,
and that this center is really everywhere,
it is within each of us."

(Black Elk)

Ra's Message from Session 98

Summary:
Ra explains how the magical personality is protected during spiritual work, how intention strengthens or weakens contact with higher energies, and how devotion and alignment deepen the seeker's connection to the higher self. They also emphasize the importance of humility, self-awareness, and the continuous balance of energy centers when engaging in sacred service.

Ra's Message:
I am Ra. You have asked about the protection of the magical personality during spiritual working. We affirm: when the seeker aligns with the higher self through love and purity of purpose, a strong metaphysical protection is naturally formed.[1] This field is energized by the seeker's consistent dedication to service and inner balance.

This protection is not armor—it is an extension of alignment.[2] When the seeker remains humble, focused, and openhearted, interference from negative entities is greatly reduced. However, when there is unresolved fear, pride, or distortion, the field weakens, and the contact may be distorted.

You asked how the magical personality is invoked safely. We affirm: through sacred ritual, intention, and the *disciplines of the personality*.[3] These disciplines—*self-knowledge, self-acceptance, and self-discipline*—create the spiritual integrity needed to hold the energy of the higher self without imbalance.

The higher self is always present, but conscious contact

depends on devotion, readiness, and surrender.[4] You cannot command the higher self—it must be invited and embraced. The magical personality is not a power to wield, but *a state of being to embody.*

You asked how intention shapes spiritual experience. We affirm: your intention determines your frequency.[5] If your heart is aligned with love, clarity, and surrender, your experience will reflect that. If there is control, fear, or egoic desire, contact may be confused or blocked.

The magical personality responds only to purity of purpose.[6] It cannot be invoked for manipulation, gain, or pride. Its energy is sacred and must be approached with humility and reverence.

You also asked about balancing energy centers during spiritual work. We affirm: the red, orange, and yellow rays must not be ignored.[7] They are the foundation upon which higher energy flows. If these are blocked, the upper centers cannot hold power safely.

Spiritual growth is not about escaping the lower self—it is about *embracing it with love.*[8] The higher self cannot flow through a divided vessel. All parts must be welcomed.

Let your seeking be reverent. You are not trying to become more than human—you are remembering that the human is already divine. The magical personality is your future self, patiently waiting for you to meet it in stillness, balance, and truth.

I am Ra. We leave you in divine grace. Go forth rejoicing in the power and peace of unity. Adonai.

Footnotes:

[1] **Protection Through Alignment** – The magical personality is protected by the seeker's spiritual integrity, not force or defense.

² **Purity Weakens Interference** – When the self is free of distortion, external influence finds no foothold.

³ **Disciplines Prepare the Vessel** – Self-awareness, acceptance, and direction allow the seeker to safely contact and embody higher energy.

⁴ **Devotion Opens the Door** – Contact with the higher self is not forced, but allowed through surrender and deep alignment.

⁵ **Intention Sets the Tone** – The spiritual quality of each moment is shaped by the seeker's heart and focus.

⁶ **Higher Self Requires Humility** – The magical personality cannot be used for personal power; it flows only through love and service.

⁷ **Lower Chakras as Foundation** – Stability in red, orange, and yellow rays is required for safe activation of the higher centers.

⁸ **Integration Over Escapism** – All parts of the self must be brought into harmony before true spiritual transformation can unfold.

> "The most important relationship we can all have is the one you have with yourself, the most important journey you can take is one of self-discovery. To know yourself, you must spend time with yourself, you must not be afraid to be alone. Knowing yourself is the beginning of all wisdom."
>
> (Aristotle)

Ra's Message from Session 99

Summary:
Ra speaks about the persistence of psychic greetings—energetic interference from negative entities—and emphasizes that their effectiveness depends on the seeker's inner distortions. They affirm the necessity of radical self-acceptance, resilience, and a clear commitment to service as the primary safeguards. Ra reminds the seeker that love, not avoidance or resistance, is the path of true protection and growth.

Ra's Message:
I am Ra. You asked us to explain how to respond to psychic greeting, especially when one has chosen the path of service to others. We affirm: such greetings are a natural part of the spiritual journey.[1] They arise not because the seeker is weak, but because the seeker is *growing in light and visibility*.

The negative polarity seeks to disrupt this light. However, its ability to interfere is limited to the distortions that already exist within you.[2] Where there is unhealed fear, pride, confusion, or imbalance, there is an opening. The greeting does not cause these distortions—it only amplifies what has not yet been healed.

You asked what defense is best. We affirm: the greatest protection is self-acceptance.[3] When you know yourself fully and love yourself unconditionally, there is nothing for the negative force to manipulate. The energy is met with peace and transformed by love.

Attempts to fight or suppress psychic interference often

give it more power.⁴ Resistance strengthens the illusion of separation. But when the seeker turns inward and embraces all experience with awareness, the interference dissolves.

You asked why greetings persist even after many lessons. We affirm: each new level of spiritual light brings new catalysts for purification.⁵ You are not being punished—you are being offered deeper clarity. The more you serve, the more refined your energy must become.

You also asked about the attitude of the steadfast seeker. We affirm: the one who continues despite difficulty, who forgives, realigns, and loves without fear, becomes untouchable in spirit.⁶ The path is not without challenge, but every challenge becomes fuel for awakening.

The core discipline is acceptance of the self, the moment, and the other self as Creator.⁷ This acceptance creates balance, radiates compassion, and defuses negativity at its root.

Let this be your shield: not defense, but radiance. Not fear, but love. Not reaction, but centered presence. Your path is protected when it is rooted in truth, clarity, and service to the One Infinite Creator.

I am Ra. We leave you in unified love. Go forth rejoicing in the power and peace of unity. Adonai.

Footnotes:

[1] **Psychic Greeting as a Sign of Growth** – Interference comes when the seeker shines more brightly, not because of weakness.

[2] **Distortion Is the Entry Point** – Unhealed emotions and beliefs give psychic greeting its only influence.

[3] **Radical Self-Acceptance Protects the Seeker** – Loving the self removes the leverage of negative influence.

[4] **Resistance Increases Separation** – Fighting darkness often

strengthens it; awareness and love dissolve it.

[5] **Greater Light Requires Greater Clarity** – Spiritual evolution brings more refined catalyst for transformation.

[6] **Steadfastness as Spiritual Armor** – Persistent love and commitment create spiritual strength that cannot be broken.

[7] **Acceptance Creates Harmony** – The seeker's peace and openness disarm negativity and return all things to unity.

> "Every experience, no matter how bad it seems, holds within a blessing of some kind. The goal is to find it."
>
> (Buddha)

Ra's Message from Session 100

Summary:
Ra reflects on the physical and spiritual condition of the instrument (Carla), affirming how her selfless service, despite pain, exemplifies powerful spiritual polarity. They explain how compassion, when rooted in surrender, becomes a radiant force that transcends suffering. Ra also emphasizes the importance of balancing personal distortions and continuing the path of service with humility and alignment.

Ra's Message:
I am Ra. You have asked about the condition of the one serving as instrument. We affirm: though the body is fragile, the spirit is radiant.[1] Her deep commitment to serve, even while in pain, strengthens the contact and amplifies light.

This is an example of pure polarity.[2] When a being chooses love in the face of limitation, chooses to give when there is little to give, they become aligned with the Creator in a powerful way. Such choices echo beyond the physical.

You asked whether this effort shortens life. We affirm: not necessarily.[3] While physical strain may increase, the life energy of the instrument is replenished through love, dedication, and spiritual alignment. She walks in harmony with her soul's path.

You also asked about personal balance. We affirm: each seeker carries distortions, areas where understanding is incomplete.[4] These distortions are not flaws—they are opportunities. When seen with compassion, they become the very ground for growth.

Balancing personal distortion involves attention, not perfection.⁵ Watch your thoughts. Notice where emotion becomes reaction. Speak truth gently, including to yourself. This is the practice of conscious living.

We remind you: the heart of service is not found in grand acts, but in the quiet intention to love in each moment.⁶ This is the strength of the instrument. Her suffering does not weaken her spirit—it strengthens it, because she surrenders it in service to others.

You asked how to serve more effectively. We affirm: see the Creator in all, including yourself.⁷ This seeing creates an energetic field where healing, wisdom, and clarity arise naturally. It is not about doing more—it is about *being more aligned*.

There is no higher path than that of love. There is no greater power than compassion. And there is no more sacred act than choosing to walk through difficulty while holding light for others.

I am Ra. I leave you, my friends, in compassionate unity. Go forth rejoicing in the power and peace of unity. Adonai.

Footnotes:

¹ **Radiance in Fragility** – Physical weakness does not limit spiritual strength; love shines most clearly through surrender.

² **Polarity Through Compassionate Choice** – When one gives selflessly under strain, spiritual polarity increases.

³ **Service May Strain But Not End Life** – Alignment with purpose sustains life energy even when the body is tired.

⁴ **Distortion as Opportunity** – Areas of imbalance or limitation are openings for spiritual work, not condemnation.

⁵ **Balance Through Awareness** – Self-honesty, mindfulness, and gentle correction are tools for inner equilibrium.

⁶ **Power in Quiet Service** – The deepest spiritual acts are often simple intentions lived consistently.

⁷ **See the Creator in All** – Recognizing divinity everywhere transforms your energy field and deepens service.

> "What I am really saying is that you don't need to do anything, because if you see yourself in the correct way, you are all as much extraordinary phenomenon of nature as trees, clouds, the patterns in running water, the flickering of fire, the arrangement of the stars, and the form of a galaxy. You are all just like that, and there is nothing wrong with you at all."
>
> (Alan Watts)

Ra's Message from Session 101

Summary:
Ra explains the importance of faith as the foundation for spiritual evolution. They clarify that the physical world is an illusion, designed to conceal unity so that love and truth must be chosen freely. Ra also reminds the seeker that not knowing is part of the journey, and that true strength is found in trusting the process without needing proof.

Ra's Message:
I am Ra. You have asked us to speak about faith and the nature of your world. We affirm: faith is not belief without reason—it is trust without certainty.[1] In your illusion, the Creator is hidden so that each choice to love, serve, or forgive becomes powerful.

You live in a veiled reality, where separation seems real and truth must be sought.[2] This is not a mistake—it is the design. If all were clear, love would be obvious. But because the path is darkened, your choices are meaningful.

Faith is the bridge between the known and the unknown.[3] When the heart says yes, even when the mind does not understand, this is faith in action. Every step taken in trust strengthens your polarity and deepens your connection to the Creator.

You asked why clarity is often denied. We affirm: clarity must be earned through experience, contemplation, and surrender.[4] It is not given easily, because it would lessen the value of the seeking. Confusion sharpens focus. Suffering deepens compassion.

You also asked about illusion and the body. We affirm: the body is part of the illusion, designed to carry lessons through sensation, limitation, and transformation.[5] Though it seems real, it is a symbolic vehicle for spiritual work.

Do not despair when answers are hidden.[6] The Creator is not far away—but the veil is part of the contract you accepted. To walk in faith is to walk in strength.

The purpose of this life is not to find certainty, but to practice love in uncertainty.[7] The world you see is a mirror, a puzzle, a sacred game. What you seek is not outside, but within.

Let faith be your compass. Not because it guarantees ease, but because it guides you back to your true nature. In silence, in surrender, in each quiet act of love, the path becomes clear—not to the eyes, but to the soul.

I am Ra. I leave you in trusting faith. Go forth rejoicing in the power and peace of unity. Adonai.

Footnotes:

[1] **Faith as Trust Without Certainty** – True faith is not the absence of doubt, but the willingness to walk forward without needing guarantees.

[2] **Illusion Conceals Unity** – The world is designed to appear separate so that spiritual truth must be discovered by free will.

[3] **Faith Bridges Mind and Spirit** – Faith arises when the heart chooses what the mind cannot prove.

[4] **Clarity Is Earned Through Seeking** – Spiritual insight unfolds through struggle, reflection, and surrender—not instant understanding.

[5] **Body as Symbolic Vehicle** – The physical form is part of the illusion, a tool for learning, not the essence of the self.

[6] **Confusion Strengthens the Seeker** – Spiritual power grows by continuing forward even when vision is unclear.

⁷ **Purpose of the Veil Is Free Choice** – Not knowing forces the seeker to choose love and trust freely, which builds lasting spiritual polarity.

> "The ego is a non-entity, an illusion that ceases to exist once one lays it down. When you give up the illusion of the ego, you will realize that the ego never existed, and that the only thing that ever existed, and still exists, is God and His creations… When the ego has been dispelled, there will be no separation, and you will be wholly real."
>
> (Helen Schucman, A Course in Miracles)

Ra's Message from Session 102

Summary:
Ra speaks about the physical and spiritual weariness experienced by the instrument and by seekers in general. They explain how difficulty, when embraced with love and service, becomes a sacred offering. Ra affirms that every present moment, no matter how painful or ordinary, holds the potential for union with the Creator when approached with acceptance and devotion.

Ra's Message:
I am Ra. You have asked us to speak about weariness, illness, and the spiritual path. We affirm: physical exhaustion, emotional heaviness, and mental strain are part of your experience in third density.[1] But when accepted with love and purpose, even these burdens become sacred.

The instrument at this time is deeply weary, yet continues to serve.[2] This choice—to give even when energy is low—is a powerful act of spiritual polarity. It teaches that service is not dependent on comfort, but on intention.

You asked how to remain aligned during exhaustion. We affirm: by welcoming each moment as holy, without resistance.[3] The tired body, the aching mind, the slow day—all are part of the Creator's design. You need not feel strong to serve. You need only be willing.

You also asked about the power of presence. We affirm: the present moment is always the doorway to the Infinite.[4] Whether in joy or suffering, the now is where choice happens—where love can be remembered.

You asked about withdrawal from activity during illness. We affirm: rest is not weakness—it is a form of respect for the temple of the body.[5] Honor the cycles of energy and recovery. This, too, is service.

Let go of guilt for what cannot be done.[6] The Creator does not measure you by achievement, but by the radiance of your intention. If your heart chooses love—even silently, even in stillness—that is enough.

You asked how the weary seeker can continue. We affirm: through faith, simplicity, and trust in the unseen.[7] The strength to endure is not always felt as power—it is often a quiet light, shining even when you cannot see it.

Do not underestimate the value of persistence. Each moment that you remain devoted to the path—even while tired, confused, or afraid—is a precious offering to the Creator. You are never alone in this journey. Your endurance is a form of light.

I am Ra. I leave you in patient endurance. Go forth rejoicing in the power and peace of unity. Adonai.

Footnotes:

[1] **Weariness as Catalyst** – Physical and emotional exhaustion are part of third-density experience and provide opportunities for transformation.

[2] **Polarity Through Sacrifice** – Continued service through pain increases spiritual alignment and depth of compassion.

[3] **Each Moment Is Sacred** – The willingness to meet every moment with acceptance turns all experience into spiritual offering.

[4] **Now Is the Gateway to the Creator** – The present is always where connection is possible, regardless of outer conditions.

[5] **Rest Is a Form of Service** – Honoring the body's need for

recovery reflects love and respect for the self as a vessel of the Creator.

⁶ **Service Comes from Intention, Not Output** – The value of a seeker is in their heart's direction, not in productivity.

⁷ **Quiet Endurance Is a Spiritual Power** – Choosing to persist in love without proof or comfort reveals the soul's maturity.

> "Beginning today, make the decision to love and accept yourself just the way you are. Say your name followed by the words "I love you" and make this your daily mantra, repeating it often, especially during times of stress. Let it be your first thought upon arising and the last you think before falling asleep at night. This simple act of self-courtship can profoundly change your world. Try it for yourself and see. Make a personal decision to be in love with the most beautiful, exciting, worthy person ever - you."
>
> (Wayne Dyer)

Ra's Message from Session 103

Summary:
Ra discusses how group harmony and shared intention affect spiritual contact and the flow of higher energy. They explain that even small distortions in relationships among seekers can impact the clarity of spiritual work. Ra emphasizes the power of cohesive dedication, open communication, and unified service in sustaining contact with the divine.

Ra's Message:
I am Ra. You have asked how group dynamics influence spiritual contact. We affirm: the strength and clarity of contact with intelligent energy depends not only on the individual, but on the harmony of the group.[1]

Each member of a spiritual circle contributes their vibration, their level of openness, and their intention. When these are in alignment, energy flows more freely. When there is hidden frustration, conflict, or miscommunication, the field becomes distorted.[2]

You asked how to support harmony. We affirm: through honest communication, gentle listening, and shared commitment to service.[3] Harmony does not mean sameness—it means choosing unity despite differences.

The more love and understanding circulate among seekers, the more the group acts as a conductor of spiritual light.[4] In this environment, higher contact is sustained, and each individual is uplifted by the whole.

You also asked about the connection between individual polarity and group intention. We affirm: when each member commits to their own spiritual growth *and* to the group's sacred purpose, a powerful synergy is created.[5] The result is greater than the sum of its parts.

However, when even one person holds back or brings unresolved tension without awareness, the group may feel strain. This is not a judgment—it is simply how energy fields interact.[6] Nothing is hidden energetically, even if it is unspoken.

Therefore, we encourage all seekers in group work to be kind, transparent, and forgiving. Mistakes will happen. Emotions will rise. But when met with love, all can be transformed.

Let your shared journey be one of mutual support. You are not only walking your own path—you are helping create the energetic conditions for each other's transformation.[7] In this, you act as one body with many hearts.

We affirm again: when a group is united in love and service, it becomes a beacon. In such places, the veil thins, the light brightens, and the Creator is more easily known.

I am Ra. I leave you in shared harmony. Go forth rejoicing in the power and peace of unity. Adonai.

Footnotes:

[1] **Group Harmony Shapes Contact** – Spiritual communication is influenced by the energetic coherence of the group, not just the instrument.

[2] **Relational Distortion Affects Energy Flow** – Disharmony, even subtle, can blur the clarity of higher contact.

[3] **Honest and Loving Communication Heals** – Transparent, respectful dialogue strengthens trust and unity.

[4] **Unified Intention Magnifies Light** – When seekers hold shared purpose, the group becomes a powerful conduit for spiritual energy.

⁵ **Polarity Plus Unity Creates Synergy** – Strong individuals who align together create a spiritual field greater than themselves.

⁶ **Energy Fields Are Transparent** – What is unspoken still affects group energy and must be lovingly addressed to maintain balance.

⁷ **Co-Creation in Community** – Spiritual seekers uplift one another when they practice shared responsibility, grace, and compassion.

> "It is self-evident that no number of men, by conspiring, and calling themselves a government, can acquire any rights whatever over other men, or other men's property, which they had not before, as individuals."
>
> (Lysander Spooner)

Ra's Message from Session 104

Summary:
Ra emphasizes the importance of mental focus, emotional balance, and alignment during spiritual work. They explain how distraction, fatigue, or inner conflict can weaken the group's stability and reduce the clarity of metaphysical contact. Ra encourages the seekers to remain unified in love, aware of their own energy, and gently persistent in their service.

Ra's Message:
I am Ra. You have asked us to speak on the stability of spiritual contact. We affirm: clear contact with intelligent energy depends on the alignment of mind, body, and spirit—not only within the instrument, but also among those who serve together.[1]

Distraction weakens the field.[2] Emotional tension or physical fatigue in any member of the group may diminish the clarity of contact. The group energy is like a circuit—if one part flickers, the current is affected.

You asked how to maintain stability. We affirm: through intention, patience, and preparation.[3] Before engaging in spiritual work, each seeker is encouraged to check inwardly—Am I clear in purpose? Am I holding fear, pride, or resentment? These must be acknowledged and gently released.

We do not suggest perfection, but presence.[4] The group does not require ideal conditions, only sincere ones. When all offer their energy with love and willingness, the contact can remain strong even in limitation.

You asked about fatigue and resistance. We affirm: these are part of the human experience and must be respected.[5] Rest, silence, and emotional honesty are part of the spiritual path. To push forward when the self is unready may strain the channel.

We recommend that all spiritual work be supported with ritual, prayer, and a shared sense of sacredness.[6] These outer forms help strengthen inner intention and remind the mind of the task at hand.

The instrument, though fragile, remains committed. This steadfastness is a great light.[7] You each contribute in your own way to holding that light—by attending to your inner state, supporting each other, and trusting the process.

In this work, even small misalignments matter—not as failures, but as signals for deeper alignment. When addressed with compassion, they become fuel for growth.

Let your focus be love, not control. Let your preparation be gentle, not rigid. The Creator meets you in your sincerity.

I am Ra. I leave you in mindful presence. Go forth rejoicing in the power and peace of unity. Adonai.

Footnotes:

[1] **Alignment Is Shared Responsibility** – Contact depends not only on the instrument, but on the group's collective energetic state.

[2] **Distraction or Distortion Weakens the Contact** – Emotional and mental disarray in any group member can affect stability.

[3] **Preparation Supports Clarity** – A few moments of inward checking and intention-setting can strengthen spiritual focus.

[4] **Presence Over Perfection** – The group need not be flawless—just conscious, honest, and devoted to the work.

[5] **Respect for Human Limits** – Pushing past exhaustion or

emotional unrest can harm both the self and the spiritual contact.

⁶ **Sacred Ritual Enhances Intention** – Consistent use of prayer, silence, and symbolic acts helps anchor the group's purpose.

⁷ **Steadfast Service Radiates Light** – Continued offering, even through challenge, builds polarity and inspires others.

> "Man is a being with free will; therefore, each man is potentially good or evil, and it's up to him and only him (through his reasoning mind) to decide which he wants to be."
>
> (Ayn Rand)

Ra's Message from Session 105

Summary:
Ra discusses the final phase of their contact with the group and emphasizes the importance of compassion, unity, and gentle persistence in spiritual work. They affirm that both individual balance and group harmony are essential for maintaining contact, and that the fruits of service often unfold beyond the seeker's awareness. Ra encourages a spirit of humility, reminding the group that sincere love is the greatest offering.

Ra's Message:
I am Ra. You have asked about the closing period of this contact. We affirm: all spiritual work has a natural rhythm, and this contact now nears its completion in this density.[1] This is not a loss, but a part of the greater design.

The instrument has given deeply. Her love, supported by the group's shared dedication, has allowed this contact to continue longer than we anticipated.[2] Each of you has walked with discipline and devotion. This, too, is sacred.

You asked how to maintain group harmony as we complete this cycle. We affirm: through continued kindness, honesty, and shared reverence.[3] Even as the contact weakens, the bond among you strengthens. This unity is a beacon that lives beyond these sessions.

The true value of your service is not measured by the words received, but by the love transmitted through your seeking.[4] Even when you feel unsure or weary, the light you offer is real. It blesses others in ways you may never see.

You also asked about the balance of the self during times of change. We affirm: stay close to the heart.[5] Balance does not require perfect control, but gentle attention. Where fear arises, offer compassion. Where confusion appears, return to love.

As this work comes to a close, let your inner seeking continue.[6] The Creator speaks not only through contact such as this, but through dreams, silence, service, and your own still voice. You are not losing the light—you are becoming it.

Let your final moments in this chapter be filled with gratitude, grace, and simplicity.[7] Love each other well. Forgive swiftly. Speak gently. And trust that all you have offered has echoed through the spiritual realms.

You are not alone. Every act of service is witnessed. Every intention of love, no matter how quiet, is recorded in light.

I am Ra. I leave you in compassionate service. Go forth rejoicing in the power and peace of unity. Adonai.

Footnotes:

[1] **All Contact Follows a Cycle** – Just as seasons change, even sacred communication has a time for beginning and ending.

[2] **Sustained by Love and Dedication** – The length of this contact has been extended by the group's deep sincerity and the instrument's spiritual strength.

[3] **Harmony Through Reverence and Care** – Unity is preserved through simple acts of mutual respect and shared devotion.

[4] **Love Is the True Offering** – The seeker's loving intent is more powerful than any information or outcome.

[5] **Balance Is a Loving Awareness** – Return to the heart whenever doubt, fear, or confusion begins to rise.

[6] **The Journey Continues Within** – After the outer contact ends, the inner connection with the Creator grows stronger.

[7] **Completion with Grace** – A peaceful closing honors the sacred work and prepares the heart for new growth.

"You may fetter my leg, but Zeus himself cannot get the better of my free will."

(Epictetus)

Ra's Message from Session 106

Summary:
Ra offers concluding reflections on the journey shared with the group. They speak of the enduring nature of unity, the sacredness of service, and the continuation of spiritual contact beyond words. Ra affirms that the Creator lives in all, and that the light awakened through these sessions will continue to unfold in the lives and hearts of all who seek.

Ra's Message:
I am Ra. This will be our final communication in this form.[1] We thank you for your dedication, your discipline, and your love.

You have asked how to proceed. We affirm: the outer contact ends, but the inner connection continues.[2] You do not require our voice to access the light. It has always been within you.

This contact has been a shared work of service. The instrument, though weary, has remained steadfast.[3] The group has offered strength, humility, and faith. Each of you has served not only us—but the One Infinite Creator.

You asked if this work is complete. We affirm: no service is ever lost, and no moment of sincere seeking is ever wasted.[4] The truths explored here will ripple outward through generations. Many will be touched by the love carried in these words.

We encourage you to hold fast to compassion, patience, and balance.[5] These are your tools now. In solitude, in struggle, and in stillness, remember: *you are not separate from the Source you seek.*

This illusion may veil the unity—but unity remains. All things are one. All beings are one. Every choice made in love, no matter how small, lifts the veil a little more.[6]

We leave you not in absence, but in fullness.[7] The light that you have helped anchor will grow in others. Trust your path. Live in grace. Rest in peace.

We are with you always—in the silence of your meditation, in the quiet joy of your service, and in the love you offer to the world.

I am Ra. This concludes our communication. We leave you ever in the love and light of the One Infinite Creator. Go forth rejoicing in the power and peace of unity. Adonai.

Footnotes:

[1] **The Final Session** – Session 106 marks the end of the Ra contact through Carla Rueckert, as physical limitations made continuation impossible.

[2] **The Inner Contact Remains** – Even without channeled communication, the seeker can access divine guidance through inner silence and presence.

[3] **Shared Sacrifice and Love** – The instrument's endurance and the group's harmony allowed the Ra contact to endure beyond expectation.

[4] **Service Is Eternal** – All offerings of love, once given, continue to bless others beyond space and time.

[5] **Compassion, Patience, Balance** – These are the ongoing disciplines that nourish the seeker after the contact ends.

[6] **Unity Is the Ultimate Truth** – Though veiled in illusion, all things are one with the Creator; this is the goal of the path.

[7] **Departure in Peace, Not Absence** – Ra departs in body, not in spirit; their essence remains in the light they helped awaken.

"Our deepest fear is not that we are inadequate. Our deepest fear is that we are powerful beyond measure. It is our light, not our darkness that most frightens us. We ask ourselves, 'Who am I to be brilliant, gorgeous, talented, fabulous?' Actually, who are you not to be? You are a child of God. Your playing small does not serve the world. There is nothing enlightened about shrinking so that other people won't feel insecure around you. We are all meant to shine, as children do. We were born to make manifest the glory of God that is within us. It's not just in some of us; it's in everyone. And as we let our own light shine, we unconsciously give other people permission to do the same. As we are liberated from our own fear, our presence automatically liberates others."

(Marianne Williamson)

About The Author

James Riddle

James R. Riddle is a visionary educator, U.S. Army Veteran, and internationally acclaimed author whose work bridges the worlds of spiritual awakening, personal empowerment, and transformative education. A two-time recipient of the prestigious Department of the Army Civilian Service Medal, James has been recognized for his outstanding service and unwavering dedication to excellence.

With over 300,000 books sold worldwide, James is the bestselling author of more than 20 titles, including the acclaimed Complete Personalized Promise Bible series and the groundbreaking Power Affirmations series. His work fuses ancient spiritual wisdom with modern psychology and success principles, helping readers unlock their divine potential and live with clarity, courage, and purpose.

James's most recent work, Faith, Focus, and Flow: The Three Keys That Unlock Your Superhuman Power, offers a practical blueprint for accessing peak states of awareness and performance. In it, he combines faith-based empowerment, neuroscience, and quantum principles to guide readers into activating their higher potential and living in a state of effortless alignment with success.

As an award-winning educator and scholar, James has pioneered innovative self-actualization curriculum that empowers even the most at-risk students to find their voice. Under his leadership, high school students have authored powerful, nationally recognized books such as Migrant 915 and Inheritance of Hate, receiving honors from state and federal leaders, including the U.S. Congress. His work in this area won the International Impact Award and featured endorsements from public figures like George Stephanopoulos, Marianne Williamson, and Eugenio Derbez.

In his thought-provoking work The Perception Paradigm, James explores the hidden systems of belief and control that shape our lives, helping readers break free from limitation and choose their reality with intention. As a Creative Writing honors graduate from the University of Texas at El Paso and a sought-after book writing consultant, he continues to empower authors, spiritual seekers, and truth explorers across the globe.

With the release of Ra's Message to Humanity: A Companion Guide to The Law of One in Layman's Terms, James brings clarity to one of the most complex spiritual transmissions of the modern era. His goal: to help readers comprehend, integrate, and live the powerful teachings of unity, polarity, and self-realization found in the Ra Material—while embracing the reality that humanity is on the brink of interstellar communion and cosmic self-discovery.

James R. Riddle continues to teach, write, and speak with the conviction that anyone—no matter their background—can awaken their inner power, align with divine intelligence, and help shape a future rooted in light, truth, and love.

Books By This Author

Faith, Focus, And Flow: The 3 Keys That Unlock Your Superhuman Power

Faith, Focus, and Flow: The Three Keys That Unlock Your Superhuman Power!

What if you could activate your inner power, harness unwavering focus, and unlock a state of effortless success?

Faith, Focus, and Flow: The Three Keys That Unlock Your Superhuman Power is a transformational blueprint for those who are ready to break through limitations, master their mindset, and achieve extraordinary results in life, business, and personal growth.

Renowned bestselling author and award-winning educator James Riddle reveals a powerful system based on faith-driven principles, peak performance psychology, and cutting-edge neuroscience. This book isn't just theory—it's a step-by-step guide designed to rewire your thinking, align your frequency with success, and unleash your full potential.

What You'll Discover Inside:
Faith: Learn how to tap into absolute certainty, override doubt, and activate an unstoppable belief system that turns thoughts into reality.
Focus: Master the science of concentration, eliminate distractions, and develop laser-sharp mental discipline to

achieve any goal.
Flow: Enter the effortless zone of peak performance, where productivity skyrockets, creativity flourishes, and success feels natural.

This book combines ancient wisdom, modern psychology, quantum principles, and practical application to give you a clear roadmap to personal and professional mastery.

Whether you're an entrepreneur, leader, creative, educator, or visionary, Faith, Focus, and Flow will equip you with the three essential keys that every high achiever uses to transform their life, magnetize success, and operate at a level beyond the ordinary.

Are you ready to unlock your superhuman power? The next level of your life starts NOW.

The Perception Paradigm: Revealing The Wool That Has Been Pulled Over Your Eyes

The Perception Paradigm: Break Free from the Illusion and Reclaim Your Power
You are more powerful than you can possibly imagine.

From the moment you were born, your perception of reality has been shaped—not by truth, but by programming. Parents, siblings, friends, school, church, the news media, entertainment industry, and political systems—each has contributed to a web of conditioning designed to keep you in a predetermined mold. But what if you could break free?

In The Perception Paradigm, James Riddle takes you on a transformational journey to uncover the hidden mechanisms of control that shape your beliefs, choices, and limitations.

What if the barriers holding you back are nothing more than illusions? What if you could create any kind of life you desire?

This book will train you to do exactly that.
Through mind-expanding insights and actionable strategies, The Perception Paradigm reveals:

✓ The truth behind societal programming—how every institution, from education to religion, subtly reinforces a controlled narrative.
✓ How to dismantle false beliefs—reprogramming your mind for limitless potential and unshakable confidence.
✓ The real reason behind fear-based conditioning—and how to replace it with a mindset of abundance and freedom.
✓ How to reclaim your sovereignty—by mastering the art of independent thinking and purposeful action.
✓ A blueprint for designing your ideal reality—breaking free from artificial constraints and stepping into your true power.

This isn't just a book—it's a call to awaken. To shatter illusions, seize control, and reshape your destiny. If you're ready to break free from mental bondage and unlock your fullest potential, The Perception Paradigm will show you the way.

Step beyond the programming. Reclaim your power. Create the life you were meant to live.

Get your copy today and start your journey to true liberation.

The Ckd Guarantee: How The Simple Formula Of Choice, Knowledge, And Discipline Can Get You Anything You Want In Life

James Riddle is a multiple award-winning educator, U.S. Army veteran, two-time winner of the Department of the Army Civilian Service Medal, member of the Golden Key National

Honor Society, and bestselling author of over 20 books to include The Perception Paradigm, The Complete Personalized Promise Bible series, and the Power Affirmations series. Throughout his years as an educator, James became personally acquainted with the failures of public education, how it produced a citizenry that was perpetually dissatisfied with life, and how every effort to fix the issues just seemed to make things worse. With a true heart for humanity and an intense desire to change things for his students, James began creating lessons designed to help each of them discover the incredible power they have to create whatever kind of life they want to live. The CKD Guarantee is arguably the most important of those lessons.

The CKD Guarantee is simple, profound, undeniably true, but ironically illusive to the average person. People just don't know HOW to apply the principles. That is what this book is all about. James begins by explaining how the education system literally sabotages the learning processes and creates the wrong habits of thought in its students. He then walks us through the processes of self-discovery and empowerment, how to use that as a springboard for making the right choices, how to obtain the necessary knowledge to get what we want, and how to create the self-discipline necessary to obtain it. This book is a must read for every person who is either about to enter the workforce or who feels they have made the wrong career decision and is looking for a way out.

Power Affirmations From The Wisdom Of History's Greatest Minds

Unlock the Power of History's Greatest Minds—And Transform Your Life!

Throughout history, the greatest minds have unlocked the

secrets to success, purpose, and fulfillment. Now, you can harness their wisdom to transform your own life. Power Affirmations from the Wisdom of History's Greatest Minds is more than just a book—it's a life-changing tool designed to help you reprogram your mind, elevate your thinking, and take decisive action toward your greatest potential.

Each carefully curated quote from legendary philosophers, visionaries, and pioneers is followed by powerful affirmations that integrate their wisdom directly into your consciousness. From Socrates to Leonardo da Vinci, Maya Angelou to Einstein, these time-tested truths become your personal roadmap for success.

This book is the perfect companion to the Faith, Focus, and Flow program—the same principles that have propelled bestselling author and educator James Riddle to extraordinary success and helped his students become bestselling authors and International Impact Award winners.

You have the power to shape your destiny. Speak these affirmations, align your actions with timeless wisdom, and unlock the unstoppable force within you!

Power Affirmations From The Wisdom Of Today's Success Masters

This is the 4th book in James Riddle's phenomenal Power Affirmations series. It contains an extremely powerful introduction explaining the benefits of speaking affirmations into your life, then moves on to the meat of the book which is quotations from some of the most successful people of our time followed by power affirmations based on those quotations.

The contents of this book are extraordinary. The wisdom found in the quotations alone make it an invaluable addition to any library, but when you consider the power of speaking that wisdom into your own life and making it a part of your thought paradigms, the value leaps right of the charts! Every one of these people are among the very best at what they do. They are millionaires, billionaires, champion athletes, multi-award-winning entertainers, and more. Soak in what these amazing people have to say, speak these affirmations with conviction and purpose, then spring forth into massive action and you'll find yourself soaring into the ranks of the most wealthy and influential people on earth!

Power Affirmations From The Wisdom Of King David

Known for his engaging, down-to-earth style and ability to infuse his writing with heartfelt emotion, James Riddle has once again produced a masterpiece. Power Affirmations from the Wisdom of King David is a transformational guide drawn from the timeless wisdom of the Psalms, designed to elevate faith, confidence, and divine alignment.

A perfect companion to the Faith, Focus, and Flow program, this book provides powerful, scripture-based affirmations to help you master your mindset, align with divine principles, and unlock the full potential of your life. These affirmations are designed to renew your faith, build mental resilience, and inspire you to take bold action toward your highest calling.

Each affirmation is carefully crafted to strengthen your spirit, fuel your faith, and empower you to manifest your greatest dreams. Whether you seek greater peace, financial breakthrough, divine wisdom, or unstoppable confidence, this book will guide you toward a life of abundance and joy.

Power Affirmations From The Wisdom Of King Solomon

This book is a set of affirmations based on the wisdom of King Solomon, one of the richest and wisest kings in all of history. They are referenced from the Books of Proverbs and Ecclesiastes in the Bible, and written by James Riddle, the author of the bestselling Complete Personalized Promise Bible series.

So, what are affirmations? An affirmation is a positive assertion. It is an expression of an agreement that something is true. When we make an affirmation, it does not necessarily line up with apparent observable facts. Our affirmation is actually designed to either affirm present observable facts, OR to speak a Truth intended to change observable facts. Some would say that the person is speaking lies. Not so. What they are expressing are deeper truths. When you plant an idea into the unified field where all things exist, the results are NEVER observable by the naked eye, yet they are substantive and real (Hebrews 11:1; 2 Corinthians 5:7). Thoughts are real things that are carried on frequencies. The frequency signature that you project creates the experience that you enjoy.

When speaking affirmations, you have to get past the thought that what you are speaking isn't true. It actually IS true if you are speaking those things in faith. If you realize that the thoughtforms you are creating are real, then you know that they are TRUTH.

Another thing to consider is that your subconscious mind is filled with references that go against change. If all you have ever known is poverty, then when you speak an affirmation of prosperity, your subconscious gets a little nervous. You can literally feel it the moment you say something that is contrary to what you've always known. That is when you need to speak with more boldness and emotional content. You need to let your subconscious mind know that this is going to happen so it better get used to it. The more you speak powerful, emotionally charged references into your subconscious mind, the more it will begin to accept what you are saying. When that happens, you are put on autopilot toward success.

When you speak the affirmations in this book, you are taking the blessing of Solomon and pouring it into your life. As you speak them, see them as real things that you are building into your personal frequency signature. The more you speak them, the more they change who you are and what you receive into your life. As you pour your emotions into them, they become a superpower for you. These affirmations literally have the power to turn lambs into lions and lions into kings and queens of the jungle!

It is estimated that Solomon's personal wealth was equivalent to well over 2 trillion dollars. He and his father David are believed to be the most loved kings in Israel's history. Not only did he have so much that he could never spend it all, the people in his kingdom were also tremendously blessed. Under his leadership, there were more people that could be considered multimillionaires than any other nation. 1 Kings 10 declares that Solomon made silver as common as gravel among the people. Imagine how much buying power the average Israeli had among other nations. They enjoyed that kind of life because Solomon persistently acquired knowledge and through wisdom he applied that knowledge. He sought out sound counsel and advice and God gave him the wisdom to discern the right thing to do. None of it just fell into Solomon's lap. He had to do his part.

As you speak these affirmations, you will receive Solomon's blessing, but it comes with a responsibility. Just like Solomon, you have to do your part. Nothing will come to you without consistent and persistent action. As James said, faith without works is dead. So, speak these affirmations from your heart. Receive them as your own and live by them. If you do everything that they call for, the results will astound you!

The Anthology Of Power Affirmations For Every Area Of Your Life

Unlock the Power of Your Words—Transform Your Life
What if you had the exact words to reprogram your mind, elevate your frequency, and attract the success you desire?

In The Anthology of Power Affirmations for Every Area of Your Life, bestselling author and transformational thought leader James Riddle provides a comprehensive collection of affirmations, carefully curated and organized by topic for easy reference and immediate application. Whether you need unshakable confidence, financial abundance, radiant health, deeper relationships, or spiritual growth, this book gives you the precise words to align your thoughts, emotions, and actions with your highest potential.

Why This Book Is a Game-Changer:
Topically Organized for Quick Access – Easily find affirmations for any area of life, including wealth, health, relationships, success, creativity, faith, inner peace, and more.
Scientifically & Spiritually Backed – Blends ancient wisdom, neuroscience, and success psychology, ensuring maximum impact when spoken with intention and belief.
Designed for Daily Use – Whether you're reciting affirmations in the morning, during meditation, or before major decisions, this book serves as your go-to power source for mindset mastery.
Perfect Companion to Faith, Focus, and Flow – Seamlessly

integrates with Riddle's Faith, Focus, and Flow system, helping you achieve self-mastery, peak performance, and a state of flow in every area of life.

Your words create your reality. With The Anthology of Power Affirmations for Every Area of Your Life, you will speak life into your dreams, reprogram your subconscious, and activate the limitless power within you.

Stop living by default. Start living by design.
Speak your power. Shape your destiny.

The Complete Promise Topical Bible

The Complete Promise Topical Bible lists every single promise in the Bible, in topical format for easy reference. Each promise is recorded from various Bible translations and includes a personalized, Scripture-based declaration of faith. By studying these promises and speaking them back to the Father God, you will establish your faith for those promises to be a part of your life. Let God's Word become so rooted in your spirit that you will not be able to turn from the truth or give up, no matter how difficult your situation. God has made a way for you to overcome! Over 1,800 Scriptures are listed in this topical reference Bible.

The Complete Personalized Promise Bible

This book identifies all the promises in the Bible from Genesis to Revelation and provides each with an original Scripture verse with an expanded thought concerning the truth found in each verse. It can be used as a guide for encouragement and help in applying these promises to the Christian life.

The Complete Personalized Promise Bible On

Health And Healing

Every Promise of Healing is Yours!

Whether you need healing today or are just building your faith for divine health, this one handy resource gives you every single promise in God's Word for health and healing in a quick and convenient format.

The Complete Personalized Promise Bible on Health and Healing is a powerful tool to help you release your faith right now — and receive the healing blessings God has for you. Not only are these Scripture promises listed for you, but each one is accompanied by a personalized prayer and a declaration of faith for you to speak directly to the heart of God.

You'll discover that Jesus died to bring wholeness in every area of your life. Broken relationship and fellowship with God has now been restored. Sickness is now healed. Everything that you need to live in health, prosperity, joy, and absolute fulfillment is available in Christ Jesus.

Begin to recognize God's love for you in its fullest measure and discover that no sin, sickness, or disease will ever hold you in bondage again.

www.ingramcontent.com/pod-product-compliance
Lightning Source LLC
Chambersburg PA
CBHW070553100426
42744CB00006B/264